Beyond Performance

Beyond Performance

How Great Organizations Build
Ultimate Competitive Advantage

SCOTT KELLER
COLIN PRICE

WILEY

John Wiley & Sons, Inc.

Published by John Wiley & Sons, Inc., Hoboken, New Jersey.
Published simultaneously in Canada.

For general information on our other products and services or for technical support, please contact our Customer Care Department within the United States at (800) 762-2974, outside the United States at (317) 572-3993 or fax (317) 572-4002.

Wiley also publishes its books in a variety of electronic formats. Some content that appears in print may not be available in electronic books. For more information about Wiley products, visit our web site at www.wiley.com.

Library of Congress Cataloging-in-Publication Data:

Keller, Scott, 1972-
  Beyond performance : how great organizations build ultimate competitive advantage / Scott Keller, Colin Price.
    p. cm.
  Includes index.
  ISBN 978-1-118-02462-1 (cloth); ISBN 978-1-118-09744-1 (ebk);
  ISBN 978-1-118-09745-8 (ebk); ISBN 978-1-118-09746-5 (ebk)
  1. Organizational behavior.   2. Corporate culture.   3. Performance.   I. Price, Colin.   II. Title.
  HD58.7.K437 2011
  658–dc22

                                                                    2011011002

Printed in the United States of America

10 9 8 7 6 5 4 3 2

Contents

matters most. Is there a recipe for success? In fact, there
are four. Discover what a lottery ticket has to do with
deciding which one is right for your organization.

Foreword

Perhaps the most important question facing leaders today is this: How do you build an organization that performs flawlessly *and* evolves rapidly, one that delivers sterling results today *and* changes fast enough to be relevant tomorrow? There can be no either/or here. We live in a world that offers no refuge for mediocrity; a world in which competitors quickly and mercilessly exploit any operational weakness. We also live in an era of wrenching change: a world in which the future is less and less an extrapolation of the past. Thus what matters is not just an organization's competitive advantage at a point in time, but its evolutionary advantage over time. Trouble is, most of us know a lot more about how to build an organization that can execute in the short run than we do about how to build one that has the health and vitality to thrive over the long term.

In most industries, it's the newcomers that have been creating the lion's share of new market value and new wealth. As the barriers that used to protect incumbents from the forces of creative destruction crumble and fall, once-great companies increasingly find themselves on the defensive. Turns out a lot of companies weren't quite as invincible as they thought they were—and were overly dependent on customer ignorance, distribution monopolies, knowledge asymmetries, and other fast-disappearing sources of economic friction.

In this hyper-dynamic, hyper-competitive environment, every organization is either going forwards or going backwards—there's no standing still. Getting better is no longer enough; today, a company must be capable of getting *different*—of proactively challenging and changing the fundamental assumptions that underlie its business model. Problem is, the legacy management processes found in most organizations do little to serve the cause of proactive change.

Building organizations that are deeply adaptable, that are innovative at their core, and that are engaging, exciting places to work—building *healthy* organizations—requires some deep rethinking about how we put our organizations together. In my book *The Future of Management*, I made the case for radical management innovation. Scott and Colin have now pushed this thinking further. In their incisive and thorough work, they set out to close the gap in our knowledge about building an organization that can perform in the short term *and* thrive in the long term. Combined, they have nearly four decades of professional experience helping organizations transform themselves in pursuit of better performance and health. They have worked with organizations of all kinds—public and private, large and small—across the globe. In writing this book, they have drawn on their experience, on that of dozens of colleagues from McKinsey, and on wide-ranging research.

The result, *Beyond Performance*, is far more than a guide to leading a successful change program. It's a manifesto for a new way of thinking about organizations. Scott and Colin identify the essential components of long-term organizational health and then go on to lay out a clear plan, which, if followed, will help any organization become more vigorous and dynamic—become, fundamentally, pro-change. As the authors point out, organizational success has never been more fragile. But in *Beyond Performance* you will find a wealth of ideas that can help you lower the odds that your organization ends up marooned by the rapidly shifting tides of change.

The strengths of this book are many. The conclusions contained herein aren't hunches; they're deep empirical truths. Scott and Colin *know* what makes a healthy company. First, they have the data to prove links between specific organizational capabilities and high performance. They've drawn on a unique database of survey results from hundreds of thousands of executives who've reported how they work. The survey has been developed over 10 years and is unprecedented in its scope and revolutionary in its conclusions. The answers to the survey, combined with data regarding each company's performance over time, have enabled Scott, Colin, and their colleagues to figure out which combinations of management practices enable organizations to excel over the long term.

Second, Scott and Colin's insights have been forged in the crucible of real-world practice. There are dozens of illuminating anecdotes that give shape and heft to the book's underlying conceptual framework. One of my favorites: how to use a "story-telling cascade" to build a shared and compelling narrative about the need for change. The authors go beyond conventional wisdom to offer new insights and practical prescriptions for creating and delivering a change story, such as tapping into "five levels of meaning"—from the intimately personal to the broadly societal—and letting

employees "write their own lottery ticket" to create a sense of shared ownership for bringing the story to life in their areas of influence (see Chapter 3
for more details). It's this ability to build on established practices and take
them to the next level of effectiveness that sets *Beyond Performance* firmly
in the tradition of management classics such as *In Search of Excellence* and
Built to Last.

Third, the most important insights from recent scholarship on organizational change and renewal are woven into the fabric of this book. Colin,
like me, has a parallel life as an academic, and is steeped in theory as much
as practice. Scott has long been a management innovator, drawing on the
latest research from disciplines as far afield as chaos theory and cognitive
psychology to develop new tools and techniques that enable leaders to
make change happen at scale in their organizations. With the support of
many colleagues, they have sifted through more than 900 books and articles
in the writing of *Beyond Performance*—so you don't have to. The scholarly
work that will be most helpful to you is already here, in an accessible and
digestible form.

And finally, while the arguments laid out in this book are clear and
concise, they are never simplistic. Changing things at scale is never easy:
the endeavor is always complex, perilous, and gut-wrenching. The authors
know this. In the time I've spent with them—be it facilitating large group
discussions in Amsterdam, conducting interviews together in London, or
debating the state of management across the kitchen table at my home in
California—they have always struck me as experienced, battle-tested change
masters. That's why you won't find any silver bullets in this book. What you
will find are ways to deal forthrightly and creatively with the challenges
of overcoming stasis and embracing change. Scott and Colin deliver game-
changing anecdotes, academic rigor, empirical research, hard facts, and
novel and creative ideas on what makes a company evolve and prosper
long term.

In their roles as leaders of McKinsey & Company's Organization Practice,
Scott and Colin are also deeply involved in the work of the Management
Innovation eXchange (www.managementexchange.com). The MIX is the
world's first open-innovation platform designed to spur fresh approaches to
management. So if this book sparks a new thought in your mind about how
to build a company that is truly fit for the future, take a moment and share
your idea with the MIX community—and help build on the great foundation
that Scott and Colin have laid.

I have long believed that as human beings we are limited not by our
resources but by our aspirations. The authors of *Beyond Performance* share

this belief. They know that at the heart of every successful transformation effort lies a stretching and soul-stirring sense of purpose. If your purpose is to build an organization that is truly fit for the future, I urge you to turn the page and get started.

Gary Hamel

May 2011

Gary Hamel was recently acclaimed by the Wall Street Journal *as the world's most influential business thinker. He is the author of the bestselling management books* Leading the Revolution, Competing for the Future, *and* The Future of Management, *and has contributed to many leading publications, including the* Wall Street Journal, Fortune, *and the* Financial Times. *He is a fellow of the World Economic Forum and visiting professor of strategic and international management at London Business School.*

Introduction

Excellence Found?

What is the greatest invention of all time? In our view, it isn't the wheel, it is organization: people working together toward a common goal. Organizations can achieve feats that go far beyond anything that individuals can accomplish alone. As each successive generation finds better and better ways of working together, it performs at levels that could barely have been imagined a few decades earlier. And when there are improvements in the effectiveness of our organizations—whether they be private enterprises, governments, public agencies, charities, community groups, political parties, or religious bodies—these gains translate into benefits for society as a whole. Innovations such as mass production, public transport, space travel, the internet, and the mapping of the human genome are all products of human organization.

Fittingly, the book you're now holding is itself the product of a collective feat of organization: many colleagues and friends have worked with us to advance the state of the art in management thinking. For Colin, this book marks the intellectual culmination of his leadership of McKinsey's global Organization Practice. For Scott, it represents a manifesto for an approach to management that he has long advocated and practiced, and at times staked his career on.

But *Beyond Performance* wasn't written for us; it was written for you. If you are a leader who wants to change things for the better, this book is for you. If you want to leave a profound and lasting legacy for your organization and its stakeholders, this book will help you do so. The concepts and approaches we describe apply broadly to anyone who leads people in an organization, whether you are the CEO of a company, the managing partner of a professional services firm, or the head of a public sector body, an activist group, a nongovernmental organization, or a social enterprise.

Much as we hope that every leader who reads the book will benefit from it, we would like its impact to ripple out still further. If we can help improve the way that people manage organizations, we hope that in some way we can also help advance the progress of society itself. It is our firm belief that the human race is capable of achieving far more by working together in the future than we are capable of achieving today.

Ultimate Competitive Advantage

This book explains, both conceptually and practically, what it means to achieve excellence in leading and managing organizations. Although a multitude of volumes have already been written on this topic, we believe no other work offers what we are trying to provide. Our approach combines two views. The first view is of a "stable equilibrium" state of organizational excellence in which high performance can be sustained; the second is of the dynamics of the transition required to reach that state. This effort is, perhaps, a kind of management equivalent to the attempt by modern-day physicists to combine classical Newtonian physics with subatomic physics in order to advance the field and develop a deeper understanding of the fundamental nature of reality. In much the same way, by combining static and dynamic views of organizations, we aim to arrive at a fuller understanding of their fundamental nature.

To that end, we aim to shift the "installed base" of management thinking. In what follows, you'll learn what management courses don't teach, at least not yet. Our central message is that focusing on organizational health—which we define as the ability of your organization to align, execute, and renew itself faster than your competitors can—is just as important as focusing on the traditional drivers of business performance. That's because, as Sir William Castell, chairman of the Wellcome Trust, puts it, "Healthy organizations get things done quicker, better, and with more impact than unhealthy ones."[1]

In this book, you learn how to set aspirations for performance and health that are unique to your organization. You learn how to assess how ready your organization is to change so that it can achieve those aspirations. You learn how to develop a powerful plan to move your organization from where it is today to where you want it to be. You master what it takes to implement this plan successfully. And you discover how to help your organization make a gradual transition to a self-sustaining state of continuous improvement in performance and health. In short, this book is a field guide to harnessing the full potential of your organization.

Unlike many business books, this book does *not* suggest that you study what other organizations do to succeed and then apply their recipe to your own situation. How many companies have analyzed how General Electric replicates its business model across multiple industries, or how Southwest Airlines delivers low-cost air travel, or how the Ritz-Carlton sets standards in customer service, or how Procter & Gamble manages its brands, without ever being able to replicate the success these companies have achieved? The answer must be "too many." Although there are always helpful things we can learn from others, the recipe for excellence in a particular organization is specific to its context: its history, the capabilities and passions of its people, its external environment, and its aspirations. Creating and sustaining your own recipe—one uniquely suited to these factors—delivers results in a way that your competitors simply can't copy (or copy at their peril). This, we believe, is where ultimate competitive advantage lies.

The forces that shape today's global economy have weakened or even wiped out our customary sources of competitive advantage. Consider the instant, often cost-free availability of information facilitated by the staggering growth (more than 20 percent per year) in the international use of internet bandwidth.[2] Such ready access to information undermines the advantage that companies have traditionally gained from smarter strategies and superior assets, which can now be copied with great speed and efficacy. The competitive advantage of the twenty-first century is increasingly derived from hard-to-copy intangible assets such as company culture and leadership effectiveness. Saad Al-Barrak, former CEO of Zain, a Kuwait-based telco, puts this well: "In the west, you can no longer create a competitive advantage with a new product or a new service, because everybody will follow suit. The level of development is so high and access to resources is so rich that cloning a product or a service takes no time. But to clone a community takes all the time in the world."[3]

Why It Matters for Business

The pace of change in business is increasing faster than ever. Consider how long an average company from the S&P 500 stays in the index. In 1955 it was estimated to be 45 years; in 1975, 26 years; and in 2009, 17 years.[4] At this rate, half of the companies that appeared in the 2010 S&P 500 Index are likely to have left it before 2020.

Moreover, in recent years many former household names have fallen not just out of a business index but out of existence: consider Enron, Digital Equipment Corporation, Lehman Brothers, Arthur Andersen, and

British Leyland. Which of today's household names will have ceased to exist in 10 or 20 years' time?

It's a question that's even harder to answer in times of rapid and far-reaching economic change. As we write, the world appears to be emerging from the most profound economic crisis since the Great Depression of the 1930s. No one knows how the situation will evolve, but there is broad consensus that the "new normal" will be characterized by increased volatility and unpredictability in capital markets, in consumer confidence, and in government policy. Charles Darwin's observation that "the fittest win out at the expense of their rivals because they succeed in adapting themselves best to their environment" may have become something of a cliché in the literature on change management, but it has never rung more true in the business world. The ability to manage an organization dynamically so that it can both shape its environment and rapidly adapt to it is becoming the most important source of competitive advantage in the twenty-first century.

Success is about winning not just in the marketplace for customers, but also in the marketplace for talented employees. The role of business in society is changing. As we work more and socialize less, the time we have left for traditional activities involving our family, our local community, and our religious institutions is declining. As a result, our sense of meaning and identity is increasingly derived from the workplace (our jobs) and the marketplace (the products and service we buy).

So work occupies a central place in our lives. But what do we expect from it? To answer this question, we surveyed more than 5,000 executives from the top 200 of their respective organizations, and asked what factors they saw as essential when deciding to join, stay with, or leave a company. Among the highest-rated factors were "freedom and autonomy" and "exciting challenges." These factors were chosen by more than half of the survey respondents, whereas less than a quarter chose "high total compensation." Among the lowest-rated factors were "high job security" (chosen by 8 percent) and "reasonable pace and low stress" (chosen by 1 percent).

The message is that talented employees are not content to be cogs in a machine geared to hitting quarterly performance numbers. They want to work in dynamic workplaces where they feel empowered to make meaningful, positive change happen. As Adam Crozier, former CEO of Royal Mail, notes, "People are looking for a sense of belonging, a sense of meaning. . . . Graduates are asking the questions, do I want to belong here? Do I see a future here? What kind of training do you give? What do you do for the community?"[5] Another CEO, Roberto Setubal of Brazil's Itaú Unibanco, concurs: "Talented people don't come here just to perform tasks. They want to offer their ideas, discuss freely, grow professionally, and contribute to the future of the company."[6]

So are we getting better at creating meaningful contexts for people to work in? Unfortunately not; in fact, we're getting worse. Take job satisfaction in the United States as an example. In 1987, 61 percent of employees reported they were satisfied with their jobs. By 2000, satisfaction was down to 51 percent. Fast-forward to 2009 and the share had dropped to 45 percent.[7] This trend holds true for all ages and income brackets.

Less satisfied is one thing, but are we at least more productive? No: between 1995 and 2009, the output of U.S. businesses increased more slowly than in any 15-year period since 1950.[8] The vast majority of developed-market economies exhibit similar trends.

As our economies emerge from recession, the ability to lead and manage organizations in a way that motivates employees and helps them be productive is more important than ever. An Ipsos Mori poll of 100 board-level directors from the 500 biggest companies in the UK reported that "attracting, motivating, and retaining the best employees" was the number-one priority for business, ahead of improving efficiency or having the right strategy.[9]

Why It Matters for Society

If we look beyond the marketplace for customers and talent to society at large, organizational excellence has never been more important. In the political process, for instance, leaders committed to change are attracting unprecedented levels of public engagement. This engagement is driven less by their personal charisma than by a growing acknowledgment that current approaches to health care, education, economic regulation, foreign relations, and other major issues simply aren't working.

In the United States, President Obama was elected on a promise of large-scale change across the whole political system. In France, President Sarkozy is driving the largest transformation project ever undertaken in the country's public sector. In the United Kingdom, leaders are pushing through a raft of reforms to change the way public institutions work, with new service agreements between ministries and central government, decentralized decision making, and broad-based efforts to improve skills.[10] In Malaysia, prime minister Dato' Sri Najib Tun Razak has introduced a program to make the government more effective and more accountable as part of the country's mission to become a fully developed nation by 2020. These are but a handful of many wholesale reforms happening at government level across the globe.

Outside politics, nongovernmental and not-for-profit organizations continue to tackle key cross-border challenges such as sustaining the environment and helping the developing world break the cycles of poverty, corruption, and inadequate education.

In the world as a whole, at least five factors are driving widespread change: the historic shift in economic growth from the developed to the developing world; the unprecedented imperative for mature economies to raise productivity to preserve living standards; the rise of new networks of hitherto unimaginable complexity for communication and trade; the increasingly urgent challenge to balance economic growth with environmental sustainability; and the expanding role of the state in regulating markets and influencing economic development. These factors are likely to continue to drive change for decades to come.

The way we respond to these challenges will have a profound effect on all our futures. Will our efforts be underpinned by organizational excellence? What are the odds of their being successful? And what will be the consequences if they aren't? What will be the social costs? And who will bear them?

Excellence Lost

Almost three decades ago, McKinsey's Tom Peters and Robert Waterman published what was to become one of the best-selling and most influential business books of all time, *In Search of Excellence: Lessons from America's Best-Run Companies.* Perhaps the book's most powerful legacy is its famous "7S framework." Having examined 43 of the Fortune 500 list of top-performing companies in the United States, Peters and Waterman identified seven factors involved in organizing a company in an effective and holistic way: strategy, structure, systems, staff, skills, style, and shared values.

Since *In Search of Excellence,* there has been a torrent of business titles providing accounts of organizational excellence and theories about what drives it. One of the best-known examples is Jim Collins and Jerry Porras's 1994 book *Built to Last,* which analyzed patterns among 18 successful companies.

Unfortunately, it seems that the recipes for excellence offered by these landmark publications provide no guarantee of staying power. It's revealing to look at what has become of the "excellent" companies lauded in the pages of *In Search of Excellence* and *Built to Last.* By 2006—well before the recent financial crisis—20 percent no longer existed, 46 percent were struggling, and only 33 percent remained high performers.[11] Why was this?

Not all of these changes in fortune can be attributed to the companies themselves, of course. Performance is partly driven by macroeconomic forces, industry attractiveness, and sheer luck. But it's also driven by the decisions leaders make, what they do and don't do, and the way they lead, which are things under every leader's control.

Our research, as we show in Chapter 1, suggests that many companies fall from grace because of an excessive bias toward a static view of managing performance. They synchronize their "7S" dials to deliver against quarterly and annual targets instead of taking a more dynamic view that encompasses not only their company's performance but also its health: its ability to align, execute, and renew itself faster than the competition.

So if organizations need to take a more dynamic view of excellence, how can they achieve it? This takes us to the question of how leaders make rapid, large-scale change happen, and how they develop cultures of continuous improvement.

In 1996, when John Kotter published *Leading Change*—widely considered to be the seminal work on change management—he reported that only 30 percent of all change programs succeed. Fifteen years later, we can choose from more than 25,000 books on organizational change, and hundreds of business courses on how to lead and manage it. In spite of this abundance of advice, all available research suggests that—you guessed it—still only one in three programs succeeds. The field of change management, it would seem, hasn't really changed a thing.

Only a third of excellent companies remain excellent over the long term. Even fewer change programs succeed. Why is this?

We don't claim to have all the answers, but at this point in our research efforts, we're confident that we do have insightful (beyond common sense) and pragmatic (readily applicable) advice that will help leaders beat these odds and achieve sustained organizational excellence. In fact, we've observed so many successes in so many industries and from so many different starting points using the approaches we describe that we regard successful transformation and sustained excellence as a real possibility for almost any organization.

The Science of Organization

The world of management is rife with opinion and conjecture. In writing this book, we have endeavored not only to draw on our own experience as management consultants, but to ensure that our arguments are as objective and fact-based as possible. Whereas *In Search of Excellence* was based on a study of 43 American companies and *Built to Last* on 18, this book draws on a much broader array of evidence. We have had the benefit of the results of surveys on the drivers of organizational performance and health from more than 600,000 respondents from more than 500 organizations across the globe, surveys on the experience of transformational change from more than 6,800 CEOs and senior executives, reviews of more than 900 books and articles from academic journals, one-on-one interviews with 30 CEOs and other senior executives who shared their personal experiences of leading change and driving performance, data and learning from more than 100 clients served by McKinsey on engagements specifically related to performance and health, and close working relationships with four eminent scholars who helped to challenge and augment our findings. In fact, we are confident that *Beyond Performance* represents the culmination of one of the most extensive research efforts ever undertaken in this area.

We realize that most of our readers will be more interested in the practical lessons we can draw from the research than in the research itself, so most of the book focuses on helping leaders get better results from their organizations. However, Chapter 2 provides details of our sources and methods for anyone who is interested in our fact base and technical approach. Other readers may want to skim through this section to understand the evidence base that underpins the assertions we make.

■ ■ ■

If this book helps more organizations to become and stay excellent, and more change programs to succeed, it will have done its job. If it also helps people make faster progress in tackling the major social and political issues of our time, it will have achieved everything we could have hoped for. But setting these grand aspirations aside, if you put this book down feeling that you are better equipped to make a positive difference in the world through the way you lead and manage your organization, we will feel that our work as authors has been accomplished.

PART I

Why Performance Is Not Enough

CHAPTER 1

The Big Idea

Performance and Health

In early 2004, the Coca-Cola Company was struggling. Since the death of CEO Roberto Goizueta in 1997, its fortunes had suffered a sharp decline. Over that seven-year period, Coke's total return to shareholders stood at minus 26 percent, while its great rival PepsiCo delivered a handsome 46 percent return. Two CEOs had come and gone. Both had overseen failed transformation attempts that left employees weary and cynical. A talent exodus was under way as leaders in key positions sought to join winning teams elsewhere.

At this less than auspicious moment, enter Neville Isdell. As vice chairman of Coca-Cola Hellenic Bottling Company, then the world's second-largest bottler, he had enjoyed a long and successful career in the industry. Since retiring from that role he had been living in Barbados, doing consultancy work and heading his own investment company. However, the opportunity to lead the transformation of one of the world's iconic companies was a powerful lure, and he was soon installed in the executive suite at headquarters in Atlanta.

Isdell had a clear sense of what needed to be done. The company had to capture the full potential of the trademark Coca-Cola brand, grow other core brands in the noncarbonated soft drinks market, develop wellness platforms, and create adjacent businesses. But how could he follow these paths to growth when his predecessors had failed?

Experience told him that focusing solely on improving performance wouldn't get Coke where it needed to be. There was another equally important dimension that wasn't about the performance of the organization, but its health. Morale was down, capabilities were lacking, partnerships with bottlers were strained, the company's vision was unclear, and its once-strong performance culture was flagging.

Just a hundred days into his new role, Isdell announced that Coke would fall short of its meager third- and fourth-quarter target of 3 percent earnings growth. "The last time I checked, there was no silver bullet. That's not the way this business works," Isdell told analysts.[1] Later that year, Coke announced that third-quarter earnings had fallen by 24 percent, one of the worst quarterly drops in its history.

Having acknowledged the shortfall in performance, Isdell ploughed onward, launching what he called Coke's "Manifesto for Growth." This outlined a path to growth showing not just where the company aimed to go, but what it would do to get there, and how people would work together along the way. Working teams were set up to tackle performance-related issues such as what the company's targets and objectives would be and what capabilities it would require to achieve them. Other teams tackled health-related issues: how to go back to "living our values," how to work better as a global team, and how to improve planning, metrics, rewards, and people development to enable peak performance. The whole effort was designed through a collaborative process. As Isdell explained, "The magic of the manifesto is that it was written in detail by the top 150 managers and had input from the top 400. Therefore, it was their program for implementation."[2]

It wasn't long before the benefit of addressing performance and health in an integrated way became apparent. Shareholder value jumped from a negative return to a 20 percent positive return in just two years. Volume growth in units sold increased from 19.8 billion in 2004 to 21.4 billion in 2006, roughly equivalent to sales of an extra 105 million bottles of Coke per day. By 2007, Coke had 13 billion-dollar brands, 30 percent more than Pepsi. Of the 16 market analysts following the company as of July 2007, 13 rated it as outperforming, and the other three as in line with expectations.

These impressive performance gains were matched by visible improvements on the health side. Staff turnover at U.S. operations fell by almost 25 percent. Employee engagement scores saw a jump that researchers at the external survey firm hailed as an "unprecedented improvement" compared with scores at similar organizations. Other measures showed equally compelling gains: employees' views of leadership improved by 10 percentage points to 64 percent, and communication and awareness of goals increased from 65 percent to 76 percent.

But the biggest change could be felt in the company's halls. In a 2007 interview, Isdell noted that "When I first arrived, about 80 percent of the people would cast their eyes to the ground. Now, I would say it's about 10 percent. Employees are engaged."[3] When he returned to retirement in July 2008, he was able to hand over a healthy company that was performing well.

The Health of Organizations

Neville Isdell's actions at Coca-Cola revealed his intuitive grasp of a great paradox of management. When it comes to achieving and sustaining excellence in performance, what separates winners from losers is, paradoxically, the very focus on performance itself. Performance-focused leaders invest heavily in those things that enable targets to be met quarter by quarter, year by year. What they tend to neglect, however, are investments in company health—investments in the organization that need to be made today in order to survive and thrive tomorrow.

Perhaps surprisingly, we have found that leaders of successful and enduring companies make substantial investments not just in near-term performance-related initiatives, but in things that have no clear immediate benefit, nor any cast-iron guarantee that they will pay off at a later date. At IT and consultancy services company Infosys Technologies, for instance, chairman and chief mentor N. R. Narayana Murthy talks of the need to "make people confident about the future of the organization" and "create organizational DNA for long-term success."[4]

So why is it that focusing on performance is not enough—and can even be counterproductive? To find out, let's first look at what we mean by performance and health.

Performance is what an enterprise delivers to its stakeholders in financial and operational terms, evaluated through such measures as net operating profit, return on capital employed, total returns to shareholders, net operating costs, and stock turn.

Health is the ability of an organization to align, execute, and renew itself faster than the competition so that it can sustain exceptional performance over time.

For companies to achieve sustainable excellence they must be healthy; this means they must actively manage both their *performance* and their *health*. Our 2010 survey of companies undergoing transformations revealed that organizations that focused on performance and health simultaneously were nearly twice as successful as those that focused on health alone, and nearly three times as successful as those that focused on performance alone.[5]

High performance is undoubtedly a requirement for success. No business can thrive without profits. No public sector organization can retain its mandate to operate if it doesn't deliver the services that people need. But health is critical, too. No enterprise that lacks robust health can thrive for 10, 20, or 50 years and beyond.

In fact, we would argue that strong financial performance can have a perverse effect: it sometimes breeds a degree of complacency that leads to health issues before long. In the months before the 2008 economic crash, the financials of most banks were at record highs. Similarly, oil at record prices of more than US$200 per barrel led the oil majors to declare record profits. As it turned out, this didn't mean that the banks and the oil companies were in the best of organizational health.

The importance of organizational health is firmly supported by the evidence. When we tested for correlations between performance and health on a broad range of business measures, we found a strong positive correlation in every case. For example, companies in the top quartile of organizational health are 2.2 times more likely than lower-quartile companies to have an above-median EBITDA (earnings before interest, taxes, depreciation, and amortization) margin, 2.0 times more likely to have above-median growth in enterprise value to book value, and 1.5 times more likely to have above-median growth in net income to sales (Exhibit 1.1). Across the board, correlation coefficients indicate that roughly 50 percent of performance variation between companies is accounted for by differences in organizational health.

The results from our large sample of companies are mirrored by the results within individual organizations. At a large multinational oil company, we analyzed correlations between performance and organizational health across 16 refineries. We found that organizational health accounted for 54 percent of the variation in performance (Exhibit 1.2).

So strong is this relationship between performance and health that we're confident it can't have come about by chance. We'd be the first to admit that correlations need to be treated with caution. Take an example: education and income are highly correlated, but that doesn't mean that one causes the other. It's just as logical to argue that a higher income creates opportunities for higher education as it is to argue that higher education creates opportunities for a higher income (and even if it does, we can't infer that everyone who gains more education will have a higher income).

Exhibit 1.1
Healthy Companies Perform Better

Likelihood that companies with strong health profile
have above-median financial performance, %

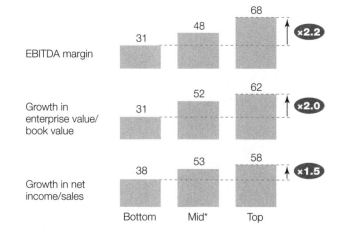

* Comprised of second and third quartiles

But our argument doesn't rely solely on correlations. On the strength of our research and analysis, we assert that the link between health and performance is more than a correlation, and is in fact causal. We argue that the numbers show that at least 50 percent of your organization's success in the long term is driven by its health, as we see in Chapter 2. And that's good news. Unlike many of the key factors that influence performance—changes in customer behavior, competitive moves, government actions—your organization's health is something that *you* can control. It's a bit like our personal lives. We may not be able to avoid being hit by a car speeding round a bend, but by eating properly and exercising regularly we are far more likely to live a longer, fuller life.

To shed more light on this causal link, here's an anecdote from our own experience. At McKinsey, we hold an internal competition called the Practice Olympics to develop new knowledge. A "practice" is a group of consultants dedicated to a specific industry (such as financial services) or function (such as strategy). In the Practice Olympics, teams of consultants

Exhibit 1.2
Impact of Health on Performance at Business-Unit Level

Example: Refineries at an oil company

US$ per unit produced

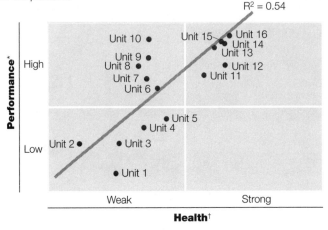

* Relative to industry average
† Relative to OHI database average

compete to develop new management ideas and present them to a panel of judges at local, regional, and organization-wide heats. In 2006, the topic of performance and health made it through to the last round.

A few days before their final presentation, the performance and health team decided to add in an extra ingredient. Rather than drawing conclusions from a retrospective view of performance and health at various organizations, they asked themselves, "If we look at the health of today's high-performing companies, what does it tell us about their prognosis for performance in the future?" After reviewing publicly available information about Toyota, the team concluded that it would face performance challenges within the next five years. What were the reasons for this seemingly unlikely verdict? The team noted that Toyota's strong focus on execution meant that its organizational health was partly driven by how well it developed talent in key positions—something that was likely to come under strain before long because of the way it was pursuing performance.

In 2005, Toyota had set itself the aspiration to overtake General Motors as the world's largest carmaker. Renowned for its manufacturing expertise, the company had developed unusually close collaborations with suppliers during decades of shared experience. But this new aspiration would force it to expand so rapidly that it was hard to see how its supply-chain management capability could keep up. The company would have to become increasingly dependent on new relationships with suppliers outside Japan, yet it didn't have enough senior engineers in place to monitor how these suppliers were fitting into the Toyota system. And those engineers it did have wouldn't be able to give new suppliers a thorough grounding in how to do things the Toyota way in the limited time available.

In front of the judges at the finals of the 2006 Practice Olympics, the team put their stake into the ground. Toyota, with its proud reputation for building quality into its products at every step, was likely to have health issues that would affect its medium-term performance. Having sat through a day of novel ideas, the panel of judges reacted with outright disbelief. Toyota had just posted a 39 percent increase in net profit largely driven by U.S. sales, and appeared to be on a roll. One of the judges remarked that the team's prediction was "provocative, but completely ridiculous."

Fast forward to 2010, and Toyota was in the throes of recalling a number of models on safety grounds. So serious was the situation that its president Akio Toyoda was called before the U.S. Congress to offer an explanation and an apology for the defects. The general consensus on the reasons for the breakdown in quality was in line with the turn of events that the team had foreseen four years earlier.

That organizational health matters is repeatedly borne out by leaders' testimonies. Larry Bossidy, former chairman and CEO of Honeywell and Allied Signal, comments that, "The soft stuff—people's beliefs and behaviors—is at least as important as the hard stuff. Making changes in strategy or structure by itself takes a company only so far."[6] Don Argus, retired chairman of BHP Billiton, suggests the key to long-term success is to "mobilize and develop our people to unleash their competencies, creativity, and commitment to get things moving forward."[7] We could fill a chapter with similar quotes from virtually every successful leader we have spoken to.

The notion that organizational health matters as much as performance makes intuitive sense when we consider that ultimately it isn't organizations that change; it's people. Take people away and the life-blood of the organization is gone, leaving only the skeleton of infrastructure: buildings, systems, inventory.

Because getting and staying healthy involves tending to the people-oriented aspects of leading an organization, it may sound "fluffy" to hard-nosed executives raised on managing by the numbers. But make no mistake: cultivating health is far from a soft option. As the co-founder of *Fast Company*, William C. Taylor, observed in his book *Practically Radical*: "The truth is, the work of making deep-seated change in long-established organizations is the hardest work there is."[8] Nor should health be confused with other people-related management concepts such as employee satisfaction or employee engagement. Organizational health is much more profound and far-reaching. It is about the extent to which your organization is able to adapt to the present and shape the future faster and better than your competitors can. In that sense, health encompasses all the human elements required to achieve sustainable success.

The Perils of Performance

Ask almost any business leader about a company's goals and you are likely to hear some variation on the performance mantra: "We want to outperform our peers." "We aspire to lead the market in performance." A laser-sharp focus on performance—on doing better according to metrics such as profits and share price—pervades modern business. Of course, there's nothing wrong with focusing on performance, or profits, or a rising share price—unless, that is, a fixation on short-term results debilitates the organization and jeopardizes its future, leaving it incapable of achieving more than a brief moment of glory.

Here the history of Atari provides a cautionary tale. The company was founded in 1972 to exploit what was then no more than a figment of a designer's imagination: the electronic game. In 1973, Atari sold US$40 million worth of these games (remember Pong?) and earned US$3 million in profits. Not long after, it was bought by deep-pocketed owners who invested heavily in R&D. In 1980, it was on top of the world, posting record revenues of US$415 million and being hailed as the fastest-growing company in U.S. history. Two years later, it was saluted by Thomas Peters and Robert Waterman in their book *In Search of Excellence*.

But even as the book's readers were discovering how Atari excelled, the company was crumbling. Teamwork began to decline, communication broke down, a culture of risk avoidance set in, investment in R&D was cut, and product quality was sacrificed to the cause of faster time-to-market.

The result was some of the biggest duds in video-gaming history. The shoddy visuals and poor playing characteristics of the games console versions of Pac-Man and ET alienated hitherto devoted customers. Fed-up engineers left in droves, many to set up or join rival companies whose innovative products would soon woo away Atari's fan base. By 1983, the rot had set in. The company lost US$536 million and resorted to massive layoffs.

Atari never recovered the glory of its heyday. The shell of the company, by then little more than a brand name, was sold in 1998 for a paltry US$5 million. Although Atari may have been consigned to history, the gaming market to which it belonged has gone from strength to strength. Worth US$25 billion globally, it is still growing at a tremendous pace.

Two questions arise from this sorry story. Where did Atari go wrong? And how did Peters and Waterman miss it?

A single answer will suffice. Both the company and its chroniclers were so intently focused on performance that they were oblivious to the symptoms of deteriorating organizational health: declining teamwork, reduced investment in R&D, and the other factors that we noted above.

By way of contrast, consider the case of Pixar. The CGI animation studio had earned 24 Academy Awards, six Golden Globes, and three Grammys at the last count—all the more impressive given that its president, Ed Catmull, had no business experience before he co-founded the company. In a talk about Pixar's creative process, he noted that the company's development process differs from that at most Hollywood studios: "Our development team doesn't look for stories. Their job is to create teams of people that work well together."[9]

While an average Hollywood studio produces between six and 12 films in a year, Pixar produces just one, a risky bet given that an animated film costs approximately US$180 million to make. "We have realized that having lower standards for something is bad for your soul," Catmull explained. Pixar's internal culture, known for its alternative, lifestyle-oriented feel, focuses on avoiding "no, but..." responses to other people's ideas and suggestions. "What you need to create," states Andrew Stanton, the writer and director of *Finding Nemo*, "is the most trusting environment possible where people can screw up."[10] Taking the right risks and accepting that bold, innovative ideas require a tolerance for uncertainty are central to the whole culture. As Catmull says, "Talent is rare. Management's job is not to prevent risk but to build the capability to recover when failures occur."[11]

Another company from Peters and Waterman's research on excellence, General Motors, provides a further chastening example of the consequences of poor organizational health. In 2009, the company that once led America's "Big Three" automakers and dominated the world's car market filed for bankruptcy and received a government bailout of US$50 billion to resurrect itself. This was not a sudden fall from grace, but a calamity that had crept up on the company over time. In 2005, GM posted a loss of US$10.6 billion. By 2007, its losses for the year were US$38.7 billion. Sales for the following year dropped by a whopping 45 percent. By the fourth quarter of 2008, GM had reported it would run out of cash around the middle of the following year unless it was able to secure government funding, a merger, or a sale of assets.

Following an 18-month turnaround, GM made a return to the stock market in late 2010. Although the stock offering raised almost US$20 billion and helped to reduce the government's stake in the company from 61 percent to 33 percent, many would agree with an article that described GM as "a shadow of the company that once symbolized U.S. might" and saw it as still plagued by the repercussions of its short-term performance focus.[12] Mark Reuss, the head of North American operations, admitted that, "We have a lot of work to do. . . . There are a lot of people who do not understand who we are. We need to re-create the soul of the company."[13]

What had gone wrong? On the face of it, GM fell victim to its own strategic and operational choices. For instance, it had eight distinct brands while competitors such as Honda had just two. This drove up marketing spending, yet it still wasn't enough to saturate the target audiences, given that the investment had to be spread across such a broad portfolio. Innovation—or rather the lack of it—was another weak spot. As fuel prices soared and environmental concerns grew more urgent, competitors responded by investing in hybrid technologies, but GM stuck with its traditional focus on large vehicles with poor fuel efficiency. Product quality didn't keep pace with the competition either: for instance, in industry comparisons, every single Chrysler model was rated in the bottom quartile for quality.[14] At the same time, a fully funded pension plan negotiated with unions put GM at a strategic disadvantage in terms of its labor costs.

Scratch beneath the surface, though, and we can trace back the source of these strategic and operational failures to breakdowns in organizational health. GM had been aware of all these issues for 20 years. In the 1990s and early 2000s it had plenty of cash, but failed to use it. In discussing the company's downfall, the *New York Times* reported that "GM's core problem is its corporate and workplace culture—the . . . essential attitudes, mindsets and relationships that are passed down, year after year."[15] The article quotes from a "brave and prophetic" memo written by former GM executive Elmer Johnson as early as 1988: "We have vastly underestimated how deeply ingrained are the organizational and cultural rigidities that hamper our ability to execute." In the end, the company's undoing came down to decisions that overemphasized short-term performance and neglected factors contributing to long-term success.

Perhaps the starkest example of the perils of pursuing performance at the expense of health is the story of Albert J. Dunlap, famous for taking over struggling companies, ruthlessly downsizing them, and selling them at a profit. Dunlap's mantra was "If you're in business, it's for one thing—to make money." In 1996, he took over U.S. appliance maker Sunbeam Products and, true to his "Chainsaw Al" nickname, sold two-thirds of its plants and fired half of its 12,000 employees. Ironically, at this point Sunbeam's stock price proceeded to rise so high that it wrecked his plans to sell the company. Having compromised Sunbeam's health, Dunlap now found he needed to sustain its performance for the coming years. But the damage was too great. By 1998, Sunbeam was facing quarterly losses as high as US$60 million, and Dunlap was fired.

Compare Dunlap's tactics to those of Lou Gerstner when he took the helm at IBM in 1993. Despite pressure from Wall Street to engineer a rapid turnaround at the ailing technology giant, Gerstner decided not to focus exclusively on improving its performance, but to put considerable effort and resources into improving its health as well. Under Gerstner's stewardship, the company worked on collaborating as "one IBM" across businesses. It became more externally oriented, reduced bureaucracy, and moved from an arrogant to a continuous learning mindset. By the time Gerstner retired nine years later, the stock had increased in value by 800 percent, and IBM had regained its leadership in multiple areas of the computer, technology, and IT consulting industry.

In retrospect, it's easy to see that the period of economic history between the collapse of Enron in 2001 and that of Lehman Brothers in 2008 was characterized by an obsessive focus on short-term business performance. During this time wealth creation as measured by shareholder value rose dramatically, only to crash leaving shareholders with huge losses. Although the crisis can be blamed on a multitude of factors, including strategic errors and ineffective regulatory regimes, the failure of large companies to tend to their organizational health is clearly implicated.

Take Enron: part of the blame for its collapse has been attributed to dubious accounting practices that allowed the energy giant to keep its spiraling debt off its balance sheet. A bigger question, though, is why Enron had allowed itself to become so highly leveraged in the first place. The story goes that it had taken a number of hasty investment decisions in its desire to continue to show shareholders impressive growth in the face of mounting losses. At the time, a source close to top Enron executives neatly phrased this as "You make enough billion-dollar mistakes and they add up."[16]

In order to retain shareholder confidence, Enron's top management developed increasingly complex off-balance-sheet financing systems that were a mystery to most employees, outside observers, and even members of the company's own board. Enron's steadily rising stock price and investment grade shielded it from public scrutiny until the very end, when concerns about its accounting methods and complex financial arrangements came to the surface. Its subsequent declaration of losses in October 2001 led its stock price to tumble, triggering arrangements with investors that required loans to be paid back immediately. Unable to generate further leverage thanks to its nose-diving stock price, Enron eventually filed for Chapter 11 bankruptcy—another sobering example of the possible consequences of an excessive focus on performance.

The Enron collapse prompted a number of financial and accounting reforms designed to prevent similar situations from arising in the future. Yet these reforms did little to curb the appetite for quick returns and consequent performance focus that led to a number of equally spectacular collapses during the 2008 financial crisis. Lehman Brothers, a 158-year-old Wall Street bank that had financed corporate giants such as Macy's and 20th Century Fox, stands out as one of the sorriest cases.

At the beginning of the financial crisis in 2006, Lehman was no more or less entrenched in the housing market than other banks. However, it was one of the few that had made direct investments in commercial real-estate deals. In 2007, when even U.S. treasury secretary Henry Paulson was encouraging securities houses to scale back their balance sheets, Lehman continued to invest, doubling its real-estate commitments from US$20 billion to US$40 billion in the space of just one month.[17] Betting against the market had paid handsome dividends for the bank during previous crises such as the Russian ruble devaluation of 1998.

Ignoring warnings of an imminent collapse, Lehman continued on its downward path, bolstering its market position by overvaluing its deadly mortgage assets and announcing record profits in 2007. Once again, the desire to continue to deliver short-term performance overshadowed the need to conduct an honest assessment of the firm's position and take corrective measures. Eventually the bank had to revise its valuation of its mortgage assets, which led it to declare losses in late 2008. The market reacted almost immediately, sending Lehman's stock price into free fall. The bank made a number of internal changes in the hope of bolstering the market, but it was too little, too late. Lehman Brothers eventually filed for the largest corporate bankruptcy in U.S. history.

A more recent and equally sobering account is that of energy giant BP and its 2010 Deepwater Horizon disaster, the largest marine oil spill ever experienced in the petroleum industry. After an explosion in a drilling rig that killed 11 men and injured 17 others, a seafloor gusher proceeded to leak more than 200 million gallons of crude oil into the Gulf of Mexico. According to White House energy adviser Carol Browner, the spill was the worst environmental disaster the United States had ever faced.[18]

How did such a devastating turn of events come to happen at BP, once voted Europe's most admired company, and an organization with a long and impressive heritage? Press reports have pointed to cost pressures and tight deadlines as possible causes of the difficulty BP had in handling the disaster. Similar causes had been cited before for smaller-scale crises at the company. Inquiries into an incident at the Texas City refinery in 2005, for example, cited BP's "short-term focus" as a key factor. Bob Dudley, the recently appointed CEO, has conceded that BP must "look at risk management of safety in a different way."[19]

The tendency to emphasize performance at the expense of health is not confined to the private sector. The National Health Service in England harnesses the talents of 1.4 million people to pursue the noble purpose of providing universal health care that is free at the point of service. Yet even the best-intentioned institutions are not immune to unhealthy subcultures. A recent inquiry into "shocking" systematic failures of hospital care at the Mid Staffordshire NHS Foundation Trust revealed that patients were left, as one newspaper reports, "routinely neglected, humiliated and in pain as the trust focused on cutting costs and hitting government targets."[20]

The inquiry concluded that the failures of care, which led to between 400 and 1,200 more deaths than at other hospital trusts between 2005 and 2008 (after correction for patient numbers and pathology), was driven by a host of factors. These included short-term target-driven priorities, disengagement of clinicians from management, low staff morale, lack of openness, acceptance of poor standards of conduct, and denial of criticisms. In other words, the Mid Staffordshire NHS Foundation Trust was suffering from a breakdown in organizational health.

In a bid to maintain its Foundation Trust status,[21] the hospital had undertaken crippling cost-cutting measures that had left it with too few clinical staff and nurses, inadequate training, and problems with the availability and functioning of vital equipment. The accident and emergency (A&E) department, one of the hospital's worst offenders, would often rely on unqualified receptionists to triage patients, and then simply leave the patients in a nearby ward to ensure that the national four-hour target for A&E waiting time was met. Overburdened clinical staff raised concerns, but were mostly ignored. Things got so bad that the majority of staff didn't want to be treated by their own hospital if they became ill.[22]

The chairman of the independent inquiry into the case, Robert Francis QC, observed that "Such a culture does not develop overnight but is a symptom of a long-standing lack of positive and effective direction at all levels. This is not something that it is possible to change overnight either, but will require determined and inspirational leadership over a sustained period of time from within the Trust."[23]

The Genius of "And"

The Mid Staffordshire case is a sharp reminder that poor organizational health doesn't just hit shareholders, but also hurts employees, customers, and communities. A McKinsey survey of more than 2,000 senior executives carried out in 2010 reveals that transformations that ignore health and focus only on performance are 1.5 times more likely to fail in the long run.[24] Leaders could hardly have a stronger rallying call to give equal weight to health and performance. The good news here is that research and experience both tell us that performance and health are not in conflict, but are complementary. In fact, the most important word in "performance and health" is the "and."

To see why, consider a sports team that is focusing single-mindedly on its performance. If all it thinks about is winning games and titles this season, it will have a rude awakening in years to come. It will have failed to recruit new members, develop the bench, secure stakeholder support, obtain financial backing, build community relationships, and so on.

On the other hand, if the team takes steps to improve its health, it will improve its performance as well. Recruiting promising new members will help it perform better in the future. In turn, performing better will make it easier to recruit new members and secure financial backing. A team that performs well this year is a product of superior financing, recruitment, and training in the past. In this way, paying attention to performance *and* health creates a virtuous cycle of sustained excellence over time. An important aspect of the "and" concept is that both performance and health require action *today*, even though returns on investments in health may not materialize for many years.

Let's take another analogy from the sporting world. For athletes, the route to future performance comes from tending to underlying health right now, long before any signs of deterioration or illness set in. World-class athletes don't just perform, they also monitor their body fat, diet, fitness regime, and lifestyle in general, and curb bad habits such as smoking, drinking, and staying up late. They also monitor leading indicators of health such as blood pressure, cholesterol level, and heart rate. If today's performance was their only concern, they wouldn't worry about most of these measures. And if they waited for their performance to decline before doing anything about their health, it could be a long road back to the top. Worse yet, if they waited for alarming symptoms such as chest pains before acting, it might be too late for any corrective measures to make a difference.

As with our bodies, so too with our organizations. The evidence, as we'll see in Chapter 2, supports the conclusion that sustainable organizational excellence requires a focus on both performance and health. But health is not a word that you'll often encounter in companies' annual reports or in the business press. Do capital markets understand organizational health? Or will a company that chooses to invest in its health be punished before its investments begin to pay off by markets that would prefer to see it focus on enhancing performance in the short term?

There is undoubtedly a noisy segment of analysts and traders fixated on the next quarter's earnings. Contrary to conventional wisdom, however, markets *do* recognize that health is essential for turning a company's growth prospects, capabilities, relationships, and assets into future cash flows (which are what most investors are looking for). As a former managing director of McKinsey, Ian Davis, observes, "An examination of share prices demonstrates that expectations of future performance are the main driver of shareholder returns. In almost all industry sectors and almost all stock exchanges, up to 80 percent of a share's market value can be explained only by cash flow expectations beyond the next three years. These longer-term expectations are in turn driven by judgments on growth and—a lesson relearned after the dot-com bust—on long-term profitability."[25]

The Five Frames of Performance and Health

If achieving sustained excellence means paying close attention to performance *and* health, how can leaders bring about significant and mutually reinforcing improvements on both these fronts at the same time? The answer is to follow a structured process designed to transform performance and health in an integrated manner.

The mathematician and philosopher René Descartes advised us to "Divide each difficulty into as many parts as is feasible and necessary to resolve it." For a large corporation, achieving organizational excellence is an enormous undertaking that can involve tens if not hundreds of thousands of people. Various academics, commentators, and practitioners have recommended breaking down the change process in a multitude of different ways: you can identify, plan, adopt, maintain, evaluate; believe, decide, act, achieve, maintain; evaluate, vision, organize, link, vest, embed; prepare, connect, discover, activate, integrate; or define, discover, dream, design, destiny. However, the good news for leaders is that most of these people are saying much the same thing.

We've chosen to describe the process for achieving organizational excellence in terms of five basic questions that need to be answered in order to make change happen. Each question is summed up in a word beginning with the letter "A" to make it simple and memorable, and so the five stages in the process are collectively known as the "5As." Here they are:

- *Aspire:* Where do we want to go?
- *Assess:* How ready are we to go there?
- *Architect:* What do we need to do to get there?
- *Act:* How do we manage the journey?
- *Advance:* How do we keep moving forward?

In turn, each of the 5As translates into a specific challenge for performance and for health, and a particular approach for tackling it.

In performance, these challenges (and approaches) are:

- *Aspire:* How to develop a change vision and targets (the strategic objectives).
- *Assess:* How to identify and diagnose an organization's ability to achieve its vision and targets (the capability platform).
- *Architect:* How to develop a concrete, balanced set of initiatives to improve performance (the portfolio of initiatives).

- *Act:* How to determine and execute the right scaling-up approach for each initiative in the portfolio (the delivery model).
- *Advance:* How to make the transition from a transformation focused on a one-time step change to an era of ongoing improvement efforts (the continuous improvement infrastructure).

And in health, the challenges (and approaches) are:

- *Aspire:* How to determine what "healthy" looks like for an organization (the health essentials).
- *Assess:* How to uncover the root-cause mindsets that drive organizational health (the discovery process).
- *Architect:* How to reshape the work environment to influence healthy mindsets (the influence model).
- *Act:* How to ensure that energy for change is continually infused and unleashed (the change engine).
- *Advance:* How to lead transformation and sustain high performance from a core of self-mastery (centered leadership).

In Part II of this book we show you how you can successfully navigate through the five stages in a transformation (the 5As) by adopting the approaches listed above, which are summarized visually in Exhibit 1.3. Taken together, these approaches are known as "the five frames of performance and health." We use the word "frames" to acknowledge that change doesn't happen in a linear way in real life, even if it may sometimes be portrayed that way on paper. When an organization undergoes a transformation, it experiences a process that is dynamic and iterative, rather than a one-way sequence of separate steps.

For example, when a company looks at where it is today during the "assess" stage, it often uncovers information and insights that send it back to refine the change vision and targets it developed earlier during the "aspire" stage. In much the same way, a company may need to go back and forth between the performance and health frames within a particular stage. When it is working on health essentials during the "aspire" stage, for instance, it may uncover health constraints that lead it to tone down the strategic objectives it had initially planned to set for its performance.

We should also stress that the approach we propose in this book is designed not only to support an organization through a one-time cycle of major change, but to help it increase its capacity to change and keep changing over time. In effect, our aim is not to help organizations "learn

Exhibit 1.3
The Five Frames of Performance and Health

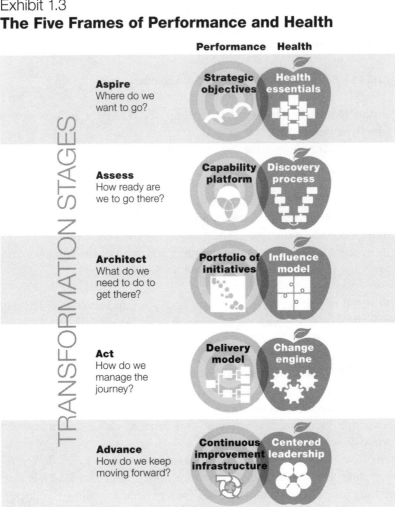

to adjust" to their current context, or to challenges that lie just ahead, but to help them "learn to learn" so that they will be able to respond flexibly to, and even shape, whatever the future may hold in store. The old adage applies: give a man a fish and he will eat today; teach a man to fish and he will eat every day. To extend the metaphor, teach a man to learn and he will be able to hunt and gather and farm as well as fish.

Organizations that learn are able to keep finding new sources of value and capturing them more quickly and effectively than their peers, creating the ultimate competitive advantage that we talked about in the Introduction.

To see how the five frames of performance and health work together, imagine that you *aspire* to become a marathon runner. You decide which marathon you'd like to compete in, find out when it takes place, work out how long you have to train for it, and set your performance targets accordingly. Perhaps you even have a finishing time in mind. Having decided on your performance aspiration, you can then work out your health aspiration: the level of fitness you'll need to run the marathon in your chosen time.

Next you need to *assess* your current capability as a runner. On the performance side of things, how fast can you run? How good is your technique? Do you have the right equipment? Can you get access to the facilities you need? On the health side, do you have the mental toughness to achieve your target fitness level? What dietary changes are you prepared to make to get into better shape? How much time are you willing to dedicate to training? If you have unhealthy habits like smoking or staying up too late, do you have the willpower to give them up?

Armed with this information, you can *architect* a training plan to improve your performance by alternating high- and low-intensity workouts and extending your range gradually over a few months. On the health side, you can plan a diet that will give you the energy you need. You may also want to make adjustments in other aspects of your life: letting go of commitments to free up time, telling your friends you won't be seeing them so often for a while, finding the money to pay for a trainer, and so on.

Then it's time to *act* on the plan. In terms of performance, you start out gradually and then ramp up your training. In terms of health, you change your diet and your life in general in the ways that you've planned, monitor and review your results, adjust your approaches as you go, and find ways to keep your energy levels and motivation high.

As you get closer to the date of the marathon, you consider how to make this more than a one-off event—how you can *advance* your running afterward. On the performance side, what will be your baseline training regime before you ramp up again for your next marathon? On the health side, how will you prepare yourself mentally to make marathon running a regular part of your life? What if you get injured? How will you keep a good balance between your training, your work, and your personal life?

It isn't hard to see how this way of thinking can be applied in a management context. We've found that the concept of tending to both the performance and the health of an organization makes intuitive sense to most experienced managers. Indeed, the case for promoting health is easy to make. The real challenge, however, is to adopt it as our "permanent residence," and not just a nice place to visit during episodes of discursive thinking. As Chris Argyris, a business theorist and expert on learning organizations, might say, it needs to become the "theory-in-use."

Apart from the next chapter, in which we describe our evidence base, research, and analytical methods, the rest of the book is devoted to exploring how leaders of organizations can approach the five frames of performance and health. Although both aspects are critical, we go into much more depth on health. Why? Because that's where the greatest need exists. Most companies already know how to keep a close eye on performance; it's their health that more often suffers from neglect. By way of example, when we asked more than 2,000 executives to nominate the areas where they wished they had better information to help them design and lead transformation programs, only 16 percent chose "determining what needs to be done to generate near-term performance." On the other hand, more than 65 percent chose "determining what needs to be done to strengthen the company's health for the longer term."[26]

This appetite for guidance on long-term health makes sense when we look at the data regarding why change programs fail. What we might think of as the usual suspects—inadequate resources, poor planning, bad ideas, unpredictable external events—turn out to account for less than a third of change program failures. In fact, more than 70 percent of failures are driven by what we would categorize as poor organizational health, as manifested in such symptoms as negative employee attitudes and unproductive management behavior (Exhibit 1.4).[27]

In the chapters that follow, we look at numerous examples of organizations that have grappled with such symptoms, traced their root causes, and brought themselves back to sound health—and have stayed that way. Their stories show that it can be done, but it is no easy task. As Roger Enrico, former chairman and CEO of PepsiCo, put it, "The soft stuff is always harder than the hard stuff."[28]

Of course, no two change programs are alike; any organization embarking on a transformation will need to devise its own journey in the light of its own internal and external context. Having said that, we believe that the five frames of performance and health contain all the key ingredients to deliver a successful organizationwide transformation in almost any circumstance. Is your performance under pressure from mounting shareholder expectations, rising consumer demands, increasing competition, a changing regulatory

Exhibit 1.4
Barriers to Organizational Change

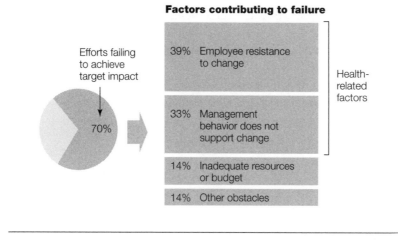

Factors contributing to failure

Efforts failing
to achieve
target impact

70%

39% Employee resistance
to change

33% Management
behavior does not
support change

14% Inadequate resources
or budget

14% Other obstacles

Health-
related
factors

environment, or inefficient operations? The five frames can help you find better ways to tackle any and all of these.

The same goes for health concerns. Whether the issue is slow decision making, poor morale, a weak performance ethic, a lack of talent, or confusion over roles and responsibilities, the five frames can be used to tackle the causes and restore good organizational health.

■ ■ ■

Achieving sustained organizational excellence by understanding and applying the five frames of performance and health is undoubtedly more complex an answer than some readers will be looking for. After all, it involves working through 10 separate frames, each with several steps of its own. Where are the rules of thumb that typically reside in management literature, you may wonder? Not here—for the simple reason that such principles are all too often, paradoxically, both common sense and yet astoundingly difficult to put into practice.

Louis Lavelle, in a book review in *Business Week,* puts this well: "To hear most authors of business books tell it, there is no management conundrum so great that it can't be solved by the deft application of seven or eight basic principles. The authors are almost always wrong: Big public companies have too many moving parts to conform to any set of simple precepts."[29]

We agree. Our aim is not to offer a simplistic checklist, but to provide thoughtful insights and guidance to help leaders achieve excellence in anything from the smallest start-up to the largest and most complex multinational organization. At the same time, we've tried not to introduce any complexity that doesn't add value. We've done our best to abide by Einstein's edict that everything should be made as simple as possible, but no simpler.

CHAPTER 2

The Science
Hard Facts behind the Soft Stuff

W hy do so many organizational change programs fail? And why are so many "excellent" organizations unable to stay that way? These questions have preoccupied us for some time, and have been the focus of much of our work as leaders of McKinsey & Company's Organization Practice. To answer them, we sought to amass as much evidence as possible by undertaking extensive research and assembling reliable data on the factors that enable and sustain positive change.

When we reviewed the classics of management literature, we found that most were based on relatively small samples of companies and executives. It dawned on us that the organization we both belong to, McKinsey & Company, has a much greater global reach than it did in the early 1980s, when our fellow firm members Tom Peters and Robert Waterman wrote and published *In Search of Excellence*. We wondered what we might be able to learn if our research efforts were able to tap into McKinsey's presence in 99 offices in 57 countries. By drawing on the firm's unrivaled access to senior leaders at some of the most important organizations in the world, we would be able to gather information and test hypotheses on a scale beyond anything ever attempted before.

The Quest Begins

With access to such a vast pool of high-quality data, the first challenge was to decide what to ask. How could we investigate what creates organizational excellence and sustains it over the long term in a way that would yield robust new insights? Finding out which companies had been successful and which had failed would be relatively easy. So would probing what had happened to them. But how should we investigate the central question of *why?*

We began by invoking Isaac Newton's notion of standing on the shoulders of giants. Before we started to gather data at scale, we wanted to consult three groups of giants in particular: our colleagues, a small group of senior executives, and a select group of leading thinkers from the academic world. If we could draw on the help of these three sources to develop an integrated view of what makes organizations successful over time, we could then use McKinsey's global reach to test and refine it at scale.

Our first group of giants was by far the hardest to tame. We began by interviewing colleagues who had deep experience in leading major change programs, and colleagues whose clients had sustained high performance over long periods. We then brought our sources together for a series of working sessions. Discussions about the real drivers of sustainable performance soon turned into heated debates. One camp contended that "The right incentives are 80 percent of the answer," while another countered with "The real secret is to engage hearts and minds." Yet another insisted that "You start with strategy, then get the structure right, then produce a strong implementation plan and you're there," only to be contradicted with "Top-down solutions don't work in large, complex global organizations—what you need is a vision and values, then you kick off change from the bottom up." These debates went on late into the night and were continued via e-mail for months after the formal sessions were over.

Our second group of giants—the senior executives—were better behaved, but equally diverse in their recipes for success.[1] We heard everything from "It's all about your vision" to "A vision was the last thing on my agenda." Or from "Make a clear plan and pursue it consistently" to "Adapt as you go, and pray for all the things you can't control." Or from "Trust and collaboration are the key" to "Individual accountability and incentives are what matter." Or from "The secret is continuous improvement: doing better every day, week, year" to "Innovation is where it's at: always being able to find the next big thing before your competitor does." To say that no clear consensus emerged would be putting it mildly.

The third group—the academic giants we spoke to, and those authorities whose work we reviewed—also offered a vast array of contrasting advice. Some suggested that long-term competitive advantage is determined largely by the nature of the industry a company competes in; others placed the emphasis on the top team and on decision-making patterns within the organization. Still others argued that luck plays as big a role as any other factor. We were struck too by the spectrum of communication styles on offer. They ranged from the technical (we learned much about "meta-analytic path analyses," "empirical tests of relative inertia," and "efficacy-performance spirals") to the playful (as found in *Who Moved My Cheese?*, *The Complete Idiot's Guide to Change Management*, and *Fish! A Remarkable Way to Boost Morale and Improve Results*, among others), with seemingly every other approach in between.

None of the groups converged on an answer—that would have been too easy—but when we stepped back to look for patterns across everything we had heard and read, we saw three themes emerging.

There was no doubt that long-term success required some sort of *internal alignment* on direction—a compelling vision and well-articulated strategy that are meaningful to individual employees and supported by the culture and climate of the organization.

A high *quality of execution* was also key: this meant having the right capabilities, effective management processes, and high motivation.

The final common thread was a *capacity for renewal:* an organization's ability to understand, interact with, shape, and adapt to changes in its situation and the external environment.

With these three themes in mind, we put together a first draft of a framework to describe the essential components of organizational excellence.

The Road Less Traveled

At this point, the only thing we could be certain of was that we didn't have an answer. All we had was a starting point and a route. We also knew that there would be many roadblocks, detours, and dead ends along the way. So we set off on the next phase of our work.

Our journey involved three stages: expanding and validating our research, testing our hypotheses in practice, and refining our models and approaches. First, we started to gather data from hundreds of organizations and thousands of senior leaders around the world, using both surveys and workshop-based approaches. Second, we tested our hypotheses in the field by applying them in large organizations and monitoring their impact over long periods of time—not weeks or months, but years. Third, we embarked on a deeper dive into the relevant literature to pressure-test our emerging model.

On the survey front, our first step was to create a tool to measure the themes of alignment, execution, and renewal that had emerged from our earlier work. In putting it together, we used our experience to judge what to include, what to leave out, and how to group the various elements. We had an initial version of the survey by the end of 2002. As we gathered more data, we continued to develop and refine it. Over the next few years, it evolved rapidly, and by 2005 it had become a robust tool for measuring organizational health, and was known as the organizational health index (OHI).

By that time, we had a sizeable database that we could mine to validate the link between health data and financial performance. That gave us confidence that we were on the right road to what promised to be an exciting destination. The OHI enabled us to identify and measure the characteristics that underpinned an organization's ability to sustain high performance over time—in other words, the elements that made up its health. However, it didn't give us much insight into what the organization could do to *improve* its health.

Imagine you go to a doctor with a bad cold, and the doctor tells you, "You have a cold. It means your nose is running, your head feels stuffed up, your eyes are watering, you sneeze and cough, your temperature is all over the place, and you probably aren't sleeping well. When I look at the data on others with your condition, I can say with a high degree of certainty that you won't be able to achieve much in this state." So you ask, "Okay, what can I do to get better?" The doctor replies, "Good question. I'm not really sure." Chances are that's not a doctor you'll be visiting again.

The next step in our journey was to gather data related to our emerging hypotheses about how organizations could become healthy and keep up a high standard of performance over time. We started with a simple three-step model that we referred to as the 3D approach: *diagnose* your current state, *design* an intervention program, and *deliver* against the plan. Over time we came to believe that the diagnostic step should have two elements: setting a performance aspiration and assessing the organization's readiness for change. We also found it was helpful to separate the delivery step into two: delivering against the plan and making the transition from a transformation program to a state where continuous improvement is part of the organization's whole way of life. As we learned these lessons, the 3D approach became the 5As (aspire, assess, architect, act, advance).

So as to understand what work needed to be done on performance and health at each stage of a transformation, we looked to the *McKinsey Quarterly* to help us with data gathering. The *Quarterly* is a business journal that offers new ways of thinking about the management of private, public, and nonprofit organizations. Its combined print and web audience is in excess of 2,300,000 readers. We enlisted a portion of these readers—in excess of 32,000 as of spring 2011—to act as a panel to respond to online surveys created by McKinsey's practice teams in conjunction with research and editorial experts. With its broad geographic reach and representatives from the full spectrum of industries, functions, and ownership models, the panel was an ideal sounding board for testing our approach as it developed.[2] To date, we have conducted three surveys with this panel—in 2006, 2008, and 2010.[3]

As well as conducting surveys, we also gathered input through a series of workshops that we call the Change Leaders Forum. This is a regular peer-learning event involving executives from a cross-section of leading organizations throughout the world. Since 2005, we have held 18 forums in a variety of locations including the United States, the United Kingdom, France, Dubai, and South Africa. As participants share best practices at these events, we take the opportunity to refine our thinking about organizational health and its relationship to performance during what can often be heated debates. We also draw insights from a network of more than 1,000 past participants from these sessions, as well as gathering feedback from them on what works in the field and what doesn't.

Although surveys and focus groups give us huge amounts of data to work with, they ultimately rely on perceptions: we ask people a set of questions, and they report back what they think. We wanted to go further and test our emerging hypotheses in the crucible of real organizations that are trying to improve the way they work. To do that, we set out to compare experimental and control groups over a period of 18 months to two years. One group would embark on making change happen in a fairly traditional fashion, and the other would use the new approach we were starting to develop—an approach that gave equal weight to performance and health and employed our embryonic "five frames." By viewing performance over a relatively long period, we sought to remove any distortions that might derive from the Hawthorne effect, whereby subjects alter their behavior simply because they are being studied, not because of the interventions being tested.

At one large financial services institution, we selected an experimental group and a control group that were comparable and representative of the wider organization in terms of their performance across a range of criteria. These included net profit before taxes (in terms of overall growth and average over the longest coherent period of data available), customer economics (average income per customer in retail banking; industry composition in business banking), and branch staff characteristics (performance rating and

Exhibit 2.1

Testing the Power of Performance and Health Interventions

Comparison of traditional and experimental change efforts
over an 18- to 24-month period

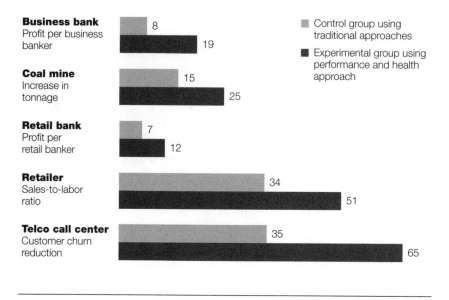

tenure). The two groups then pursued a sales stimulation program over an 18-month period, and we compared the results. We took care to minimize any distortions during the trial—operational restructuring, changes in leadership, significant staff turnover, or other corporate initiatives—that might have a disproportionate effect on one group.

The results of the study were compelling. In business banking, the traditional approach yielded improvements in value of 8 percent, whereas adopting our new "performance and health" approach delivered improvements of 19 percent. In retail banking, the traditional approach delivered a 7 percent improvement, compared with 12 percent for our new approach. Similar studies in other industries yielded similar results, as shown in Exhibit 2.1.

As well as gathering data through surveys and workshops and testing our hypotheses in the field, we also set out to explore in some depth the

academic literature available to leaders. In particular, we wanted to understand the state of the science that underpinned current thinking on organizational effectiveness and change management. To ensure that we were
reviewing the most thorough and credible material, we applied strict screening criteria. Studies needed to have applied tests of statistical significance
at 95 percent certainty levels; the impact reported had to include "hard"
financial, economic, commercial, technical, or social metrics; and articles
had to have been published in top-tier peer-reviewed journals.[4]

We are confident that the body of research we conducted is more
exhaustive than anything previously undertaken in the field. In combination,
it consists of:

- Responses to OHI surveys on the drivers of organizational performance
  from more than 600,000 employees at more than 500 organizations.
- *McKinsey Quarterly* survey panels asking more than 6,800 senior executives about their experience of transformational change.
- Data from more than 100 clients served by McKinsey on specific "performance and health" engagements.
- Reviews of more than 900 books and academic articles.
- In-depth personal interviews with 30 CEOs and other senior leaders
  who shared their personal experiences of leading change and driving
  performance.
- Close working relationships with four eminent scholars who helped to
  challenge and extend our findings.

But that certainly doesn't mean we feel we've reached our journey's
end. On the contrary, we've reached only the first staging post. We're convinced that many more new and valuable insights will emerge as our sample
continues to grow from 500 today to—who knows?—maybe 5,000 organizations one day.

Organizational Health Defined

So much for the journey to define organizational health and how it can be
achieved. What about the destination?

You'll remember that we identified three key attributes of good health:
internal alignment, quality of execution, and capacity for renewal. Working
from these attributes, we developed a definition of organizational health
that consists of nine elements that combine in different ways to support and
sustain them, as shown in Exhibit 2.2.

Exhibit 2.2
Nine Elements of Organizational Health

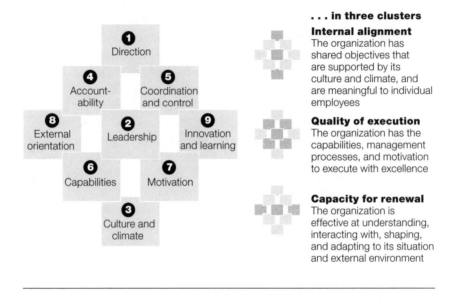

. . . in three clusters

Internal alignment
The organization has shared objectives that are supported by its culture and climate, and are meaningful to individual employees

Quality of execution
The organization has the capabilities, management processes, and motivation to execute with excellence

Capacity for renewal
The organization is effective at understanding, interacting with, shaping, and adapting to its situation and external environment

Let's take a quick look at each of these nine elements.

1. **Direction** is a clear sense of where the organization is heading and how it will get there that is meaningful to all employees.
2. **Leadership** is the extent to which leaders inspire actions by others.
3. **Culture and climate** is the shared beliefs and quality of interactions within and across organizational units.
4. **Accountability** is the extent to which individuals understand what is expected of them, have sufficient authority to carry it out, and take responsibility for delivering results.
5. **Coordination and control** is the ability to evaluate organizational performance and risk, and to address issues and opportunities when they arise.
6. **Capabilities** is the presence of the institutional skills and talent required to execute strategy and create competitive advantage.
7. **Motivation** is the presence of enthusiasm that drives employees to put in extraordinary effort to deliver results.

8. **External orientation** is the quality of engagement with customers, suppliers, partners, and other external stakeholders to drive value.
9. **Innovation and learning** is the quality and flow of new ideas and the organization's ability to adapt and shape itself as needed.

Each of these nine elements can be further broken down into a set of *practices* that go to make it up. For instance, one of the practices related to "direction" is "Articulating a clear direction and strategy for winning, and translating it into specific goals and targets." What these practices do is to take the high-level elements of health and make them tangible, observable, and above all actionable—not qualities that are always associated with models of organizational effectiveness. Exhibit 2.3 lists the 37 management practices that make up the nine elements of organizational health.

A New Management Accounting?

These nine elements of organizational health and their related 37 practices are at the heart of the OHI survey, a tool for measuring health in a rigorous and comprehensive manner.

We are sometimes asked how the OHI differs from other surveys, and in particular those used to assess employee satisfaction and engagement. These surveys, which many organizations run annually, generally focus on how employees experience the people-related dimensions of their working environment. Typical questions ask how far individuals agree or disagree with statements such as "I get good coaching," "I am satisfied with my job," and "I am rewarded for what I do." What's different about the OHI is that it generates insights not only into these outcomes—employees' perceptions of the quality of coaching, job satisfaction, and rewards, in this case—but also into the specific management practices that help to produce them. This makes the OHI far more actionable than other surveys because it identifies precisely what you need to change in order to achieve the results you desire.

Another key difference between the OHI and other surveys is its scope. Surveys of employee satisfaction and engagement rightfully claim that these factors correlate positively with business performance. However, there are other areas of organizational effectiveness that are equally correlated to performance—such as coordination and control, innovation and learning, external orientation, and capabilities—which are not covered in these other surveys, but are addressed in the OHI, as core elements of organizational health. When we've compared the OHI with other commonly used

Exhibit 2.3
The Practices Underpinning Organizational Health

Element	Practice	Description
Direction	1 Shared vision	Setting the direction by creating and communicating a compelling, vivid image of what the future will look like
	2 Strategic clarity	Articulating a clear direction and strategy for winning and translating it into specific goals and targets
	3 Employee involvement	Engaging employees in dialogue on the direction of the organization and discussing their part in making it happen
Leadership	4 Authoritative leadership	Emphasizing hierarchy and managerial pressure to get things done
	5 Consultative leadership	Involving and empowering employees through communication, consultation, and delegation
	6 Supportive leadership	Building a positive environment characterized by team harmony, support, and care for employees' welfare
	7 Challenging leadership	Encouraging employees to take on tough challenges and do more than they thought possible
Culture and climate	8 Open and trusting	Encouraging honesty, transparency, and open dialogue
	9 Internally competitive	Emphasizing results and achievement, with a healthy sense of internal competition to drive performance
	10 Operationally disciplined	Fostering clear behavioral and performance standards with close monitoring of adherence to those standards
	11 Creative and entrepreneurial	Supporting innovation, creativity, and initiative taking
Accountability	12 Role clarity	Accountability driven by clear structure, roles, and responsibilities
	13 Performance contracts	Accountability driven by clear objectives and formal, explicit performance targets
	14 Consequence management	Accountability driven by linking rewards and consequences to individual performance
	15 Personal ownership	Accountability driven by a strong sense of individual ownership and personal responsibility
Coordination and control	16 People performance review	Using formal performance assessments, feedback, and tracking to coordinate and control flows of talent
	17 Operational management	Focusing on operational KPIs, metrics, and targets to monitor and manage business performance
	18 Financial management	Focusing on financial KPIs and the effective allocation and control of financial resources to monitor and manage performance

Exhibit 2.3 *continued*
The Practices Underpinning Organizational Health

Element	Practice	Description
Coordination and control *(continued)*	19 Professional standards	Using clear standards, policies, and rules to set behavioral expectations and enforce compliance
	20 Risk management	Identifying and mitigating anticipated risks, and responding rapidly to unexpected problems as they arise
Capabilities	21 Talent acquisition	Hiring the right talent
	22 Talent development	Developing employees' knowledge and skills
	23 Process-based capabilities	Embedding capabilities and know-how through codified methods and procedures (e.g., training manuals, SOPs)
	24 Outsourced expertise	Using external resources to fill capability gaps (e.g., vendors, business partners, consultants)
Motivation	25 Meaningful values	Appealing to compelling and personally meaningful values to motivate employees
	26 Inspirational leaders	Inspiring employees through encouragement, guidance, and recognition
	27 Career opportunities	Providing career and development opportunities to motivate employees
	28 Financial incentives	Using performance-related financial rewards to motivate employees
	29 Rewards and recognition	Providing nonfinancial rewards and recognition to encourage high performance
External orientation	30 Customer focus	Understanding customers and responding to their needs
	31 Competitive insights	Acquiring and using information about competitors to inform business decisions
	32 Business partnerships	Building and maintaining a network of external business partners
	33 Government and community relations	Developing strong relationships with the public, local communities, government, and regulatory agencies
Innovation and learning	34 Top-down innovation	Driving innovation and learning through high-priority initiatives sponsored by senior leaders
	35 Bottom-up innovation	Encouraging and rewarding employee participation in the development of new ideas and improvement initiatives
	36 Knowledge sharing	Enabling collaboration and knowledge sharing across the organization
	37 Capturing external ideas	Importing ideas and best practices from outside the organization

Exhibit 2.4
Scale Reliabilities

	α		α
Direction	**0.910**	**Capabilities**	**0.922**
Shared vision	0.798	Talent acquisition	0.830
Strategic clarity	0.858	Talent development	0.794
Employee involvement	0.821	Process-based capabilities	0.810
Leadership	**0.952**	Outsourced expertise	0.791
Authoritative	0.720	**Motivation**	**0.869**
Consultative	0.837	Meaningful values	0.850
Supportive	0.892	Inspirational leaders	0.861
Challenging	0.885	Career opportunities	0.840
Culture and climate	**0.878**	Financial incentives	0.841
Open and trusting	0.816	Rewards and recognition	0.900
Internally competitive	0.695	**External orientation**	**0.915**
Operationally disciplined	0.763	Customer focus	0.827
Creative and entrepreneurial	0.769	Competitive insights	0.872
Accountability	**0.872**	Business partnerships	0.884
Role clarity	0.854	Government and community	0.796
Performance contracts	0.795	relations	
Consequence management	0.745	**Innovation and learning**	**0.904**
Personal ownership	0.809	Top-down innovation	0.889
Coordination and control	**0.900**	Bottom-up innovation	0.848
People performance review	0.875	Knowledge sharing	0.881
Operational management	0.849	Capturing external ideas	0.828
Financial management	0.818		
Professional standards	0.772		
Risk management	0.900		

employee surveys, we've found that on average only about 30 percent of its questions are similar to those included in other surveys, while the remaining 70 percent of the content is unique to the OHI.

The OHI establishes a powerful quantitative baseline against which organizations can check their progress toward their aspirations. It also enables them to benchmark their position against a huge and growing database of large companies. What's more, the OHI has been rigorously tested for reliability and validity, and provides global benchmarks from most major industry sectors. That makes it far more than just another organizational survey.

Let's start with the reliability and validity of the survey tool. For those interested in the specifics of the data, internal reliability (Cronbach's alpha) showed extremely high reliability (alpha scores above 0.85) in most cases, and acceptable levels of reliability in all cases (Exhibit 2.4). We observed no significant biases based on language, country, region, or industry.

Exhibit 2.5
Industries Represented in the OHI Sample

Sector		Percent of sample
1	Aerospace and defense	1
2	Automotive	1
3	Banking and insurance	29
4	Beverages	6
5	Building materials	1
6	Chemicals	4
7	Commercial services	3
8	Computer related	4
9	Electric utility	4
10	Food	5
11	Forest products and paper	3
12	Gas utility	1
13	Home building	1
14	Iron and steel	2
15	Machinery manufacture	2
16	Mining	4
17	Packaging and container	3
18	Petroleum	10
19	Pharmaceutical	2
20	Retail	5
21	Telecommunications	8
22	Transportation	1

In terms of benchmarking, our database spans all major industries in a ratio similar to that of the Datastream global index. Twenty-two industry sectors are represented, in the proportions shown in Exhibit 2.5.

In developing the OHI as such a comprehensive and robust tool, our aspiration was to do for organizational health what the accountancy profession has long done for financial health: to establish a consistent method of measurement that allows "apples to apples" comparisons to be made both within and between organizations. We were convinced that if organizations had at their disposal a reliable evidence-based tool for measuring organizational health, the results it reported would be just as important as this

quarter's profits or last year's operating performance as far as shareholders, customers, employees, regulators, governments, and other stakeholders
were concerned.

Whether the OHI fulfills this aspiration is not for us to judge. Our guess
would be, though, that if you're deciding whether to expand internationally,
you would find it extremely helpful to have not only economic, socio-
demographic, and market data at your fingertips, but also information on
the general heath of management practices in your target country. If you're
contemplating a merger, having a window into how well (or badly) your
management practices will dovetail with the other company's could give
you a head start. If you're making strategic decisions, knowing how healthy
your industry is compared with others could have a bearing on your future
direction. And if you're voting for elected officials, imagine the difference
it would make if you could understand the health of the institutions your
taxes pay for, and see the direct results of any changes as they happen
over time.

More on Our Methodology

By this point, we hope we've persuaded you that we've done our home-
work, and that the advice and guidance you'll find throughout this book
have a solid foundation in evidence. But we suspect there may be a few
statisticians or skeptics out there who'd like to know more about our survey methods or the analysis that underpins our definition of organizational
health. If you're one of these, please continue reading. If you aren't, we suggest you skip to the end of the chapter, unless you happen to be reading
in bed and need help going off to sleep. You have been warned!

What Research Underpins the Nine Elements
of Organizational Health?

Here is a brief summary of the primary and secondary research that contributed to our identification of the nine elements of organizational health.

1. **Direction.** Our analysis of the data gathered in our OHI survey shows
   that the EBITDA (earnings before interest, taxes, depreciation, and
   amortization) margin is 1.9 times more likely to be above the median
   when people feel clear about and excited by where their organization

is heading. External research by Bart and Baetz working with data from 83 of the largest organizations in the United States also found there was a strong correlation between a clear direction (where the company mission is aligned with performance management systems), employee behavior (0.59), and return on assets (0.37).[5] Research by Collins and Porras drawing on a survey of 1,000 CEOs confirms that visionary companies outperform their peers financially.[6]

2. **Leadership.** In 2005, Schneider, Ehrhart, Mayer, Saltz, and Niles-Jolly showed a clear linkage ($p = 0.40$) between leadership behavior, service climate, employee engagement, customer satisfaction, and sales.[7] McKinsey research provides confirmation: companies with top-quartile scores in leadership have a 59 percent likelihood of having above-median EBITDA. As long ago as 1972, Lieberson and O'Conner reported similar findings: in their review of data for 167 companies over 20 years, they found that performance is correlated with leadership across all industries (between 14 percent and 68.7 percent of the variance in company profit margin performance could be explained by a proxy for leadership).[8] Further analysis of the data set by Thomas in 1988 showed that senior leaders' influence on net income and sales was on average 62.8 percent and 71.5 percent respectively.[9]

3. **Culture and climate.** An analysis of the OHI data reveals that companies that are top quartile in their culture and climate are 1.8 times more likely to have above-median EBITDA. A landmark 1992 study by Kotter and Heskett that tracked 207 large U.S. companies in 22 different industries over an 11-year period yielded similar results.[10] Companies with strong cultures had a cumulative annual growth rate that far outpaced that of companies with weak cultures: 21 percent compared with 9 percent in revenue, 23 percent compared with 5 percent in stock price, and 22 percent compared with 0 percent in net income. Also in 1992, Gordon and DiTomaso found a strong correlation (0.78, $p < 0.01$) between culture strength and income growth when testing across management levels within the insurance industry.[11]

4. **Accountability.** Our research shows that the likelihood of demonstrating an above-median EBITDA margin for companies with an accountability score in the top quartile was 65 percent, 1.9 times more likely than for companies with a bottom-quartile score. A 2003 study by Wagner, Parker, and Christiansen demonstrated that employees who feel psychological ownership work harder at making their company more profitable because they feel ownership of the organizational outcomes.[12] The study showed a strong relationship between psychological

ownership beliefs and ownership behaviors (0.79, $p < 0.01$) and financial performance (0.35, $p < 0.01$). In 2009, Avey, Avolio, Crossley, and Luthans confirmed that psychological ownership is positively related to several performance-enhancing behaviors such as offering improvement ideas (0.57, $p < 0.01$).[13] Conversely, such ownership was inversely related to undesired work deviance (-0.36, $p < 0.01$).

5. **Coordination and control.** Our data shows that this is among the most critical of the nine elements of health: a high score on coordination and control gives an organization a 73 percent chance of an above-average EBITDA. We also know that balancing five measures of performance (financial, operational, people, professional, and risk) produces significant benefits. A study by Davis and Albright in 2004 showed that banks that introduce balanced scorecard systems outperform those that implement only financial metrics for at least 18 months after introduction in terms of noninterest income, percentage loan yield, and nonincome deposit volume.[14] Another study by Gittell in 2002 in a hospital setting showed that "relational" coordination (work routines, cross-functional liaisons, and team meetings) improves organizational performance by facilitating interaction among employees in the work process, and is positively associated with quality of care (0.26) and reduced length of stay (-0.46).[15]

6. **Capabilities.** The likelihood that a company with top-quartile capabilities has above-median EBITDA margin is 67 percent, suggesting it is a key contributor to financial performance. A study by McGahan and Porter (1997) indicated that 36 percent of the difference in performance between specific businesses can be attributed to institutional capabilities residing in organizations, with variations by industry ranging from 27 percent in agriculture and mining to 46 percent in retail.[16] Similar results were reported by McKinsey's John Stuckey in 2005, who found that 35 percent of business-unit profitability across all industries was explained by company-specific capabilities.[17] A further study by Takeuchi (2005) indicated a strong correlation (0.20, $p < 0.01$) between human capital (defined as the acquired knowledge, skills, and capabilities that enable individuals to act in new ways) and innovation and growth.[18]

7. **Motivation.** The likelihood of a company with top-quartile motivation also having above-median EBITDA margin was found to be 73 percent: 1.8 times the likelihood for comparable bottom-quartile companies. Companies showed a 42 percent chance of beating the

median no matter whether they were bottom-quartile scorers or in the middle half, indicating that only truly distinctive motivation provides real financial benefit. Research by Gallup in 2005 confirms the importance of employee motivation, indicating that unhappy, demotivated, and disengaged employees cost the U.S. economy up to US$350 billion a year in lost productivity from absence, illness, and other problems.[19] In 2006 Harrison, Newman, and Roth found a strong correlation (0.56, $p < 0.01$) between motivation and individual effectiveness based on correlations derived from 21 previously published meta-analyses.[20]

8. **External orientation.** Our research shows that the likelihood that a company with top-quartile external orientation has above-median EBITDA margin is 59 percent, and that the additional benefit gained from being in the top rather than middle quartiles is limited. This means most companies need not be concerned with excelling on this measure, although they should take care not to lag behind. Harrison-Walker's 2001 study of 137 business units to assess the impact of different aspects of market orientation on 12 key business performance indicators including customer retention, sales, and ROI found that customer orientation was positively linked to her compound performance measure (0.30, $p < 0.001$).[21] In a 2004 meta-analytic review of 58 studies conducted in 23 countries spanning five continents, Cano, Carrillat, and Jaramillo determined that market orientation is strongly correlated to business performance (0.35, $p < 0.05$) and is even more salient to service providers than manufacturers.[22]

9. **Innovation and learning.** Our research shows that the likelihood that a company with top-quartile innovation has an above-median EBITDA margin is 66 percent, suggesting that it is a key contributor to performance. Further, we found that the relationship between innovation and performance was relatively linear, with improvements in innovation showing roughly commensurate improvements in financial outcomes. A 1994 study by Zahra and Covin showed that product innovation was positively linked to net profit margin (0.31, $p < 0.001$), sales growth (0.29, $p < 0.01$), and return on sales (0.27, $p < 0.01$).[23] In 2007 Paladino sampled 249 senior executives from top-performing companies in a range of industries and found a correlation (0.2, $p < 0.01$) between innovation and product quality, itself an important driver of performance.[24]

This summary is not exhaustive, given the extent of our primary and secondary research as noted above, but it is representative, and indicative of why we feel confident in the robustness of our model of organizational health.

How Is the OHI Survey Organized?

Completing the survey involves answering a number of questions about health outcomes and management practices within each of the nine elements of organizational health.

OUTCOMES   In the "outcomes" part of the survey, we make statements describing a positive, healthy attribute of an organization and ask respondents to what extent the statement applies to their company or organization.

For instance, under the outcomes relating to the health element of "direction," we include the following statement: "The vision for the company's future is widely understood by its employees," and ask respondents the extent to which they agree. The possible responses are: 1 Strongly disagree; 2 Disagree; 3 Neutral; 4 Agree; 5 Strongly agree.

Each respondent is asked five outcome questions on each of the nine elements. We combine the answers to these five questions to determine an overall score for each element. This is reported in two ways: as an average between 1 and 5, and as an overall "agreement" score (defined as the percentage of respondents who answer 4 or 5). We typically report the latter, since many people find it easier to understand. The results of statistical analyses have been roughly the same for both measures.

PRACTICES   In the "practices" part of the survey, we make statements describing healthy, constructive actions that an organization and its leaders might take to drive the associated outcome, and ask respondents how often these practices are demonstrated at their organization.

For instance, in the section on the practice of "shared vision" under "direction," we include the statement "Management articulates a vision for the future of the company that resonates with my personal values." Respondents are asked the extent to which it is true of their organization. The possible responses are: 1 Never; 2 Seldom; 3 Sometimes; 4 Often; 5 Always.

Each respondent is asked three questions on each of the 37 practices. As with the questions on outcomes, the responses to all questions on a given practice are combined to arrive at an overall score for that practice.

For a list of the 37 practices covered in the survey, see Exhibit 2.3.

What Data Is Used in Analyzing the Correlation between Health and Financial Performance?

The data gathered during the OHI survey is culled in accordance with strict criteria. For inclusion in the analysis, surveys have to be completed in full, not in short or customized versions; they have to come from a broad cross-section of the organization in question, not just top-team members; and a large enough group must be involved to be representative of the organization concerned.

Surveys also have to meet one further requirement: that robust, publicly available data on financial results is available either for the organization concerned or for the broader corporation to which it belongs. Nonprofits, government entities, and private companies are excluded for analytical purposes if financial performance data is unavailable or inadequate.

The data from our survey is assumed to reflect the state of the organization's health at the time the survey is administered and for a period of roughly six months prior to that. Separate surveys for the same company are aggregated and matched to financial data for the appropriate fiscal year. In the analysis of the external data on financial results, scores are again aggregated at the company level.

We use Bloomberg and Compustat as sources for raw data on metrics such as sales, pretax income, EBITDA, net income, employee numbers, book value, shareholder equity, and net debt. We convert this data into ratios (such as return on sales and EBITDA to sales) and percentages (such as sales growth).

We normalize our data on financial results by constructing industry benchmarks for each of the sectors represented in the OHI. We select at least 100 publicly traded global companies for each sector and create percentile benchmarks for selected ratios and growth numbers. We then allocate each company in the survey a percentile ranking for each financial metric on the basis of benchmarks for the year in which the survey was conducted or the year after. Companies are categorized as to whether they were performing at, above, or below the industry median on the metric in question. We use this as the critical criterion or dependent variable for further analysis. The companies surveyed have shown a wide range of performance relative to industry peers, suggesting that our sample is robust and representative.

■ ■ ■

Albert Einstein had a poster in his office that declared "Not everything that counts can be counted, and not everything than can be counted counts." In the exhaustive research underpinning our definition of organizational health and the OHI measurement tool that we've developed, we believe we've been able to get closer than ever before to "counting what counts" in making organizations effective.

For those of you who have made it right through this chapter—however few!—we hope that the evidence underpinning our approach to improving performance and health will give you the confidence to put our recommendations into practice in your organization, and influence others to do so as well.

PART II

The Five Frames

CHAPTER 3

Aspire

Where Do We Want to Go?

In the summer of 2006, Mexico's largest national insurance company, Grupo Nacional Provincial (GNP), was facing challenges on many fronts. Founded in 1901, it had a proud heritage as the nation's first life insurance company. In 1969 it became a universal insurer, and in 1972 it was purchased by the family-owned Grupo Bal, one of the largest entrepreneurial conglomerates in the country. The company prospered for many years, enjoying a privileged position as the largest Mexican-owned insurer in a regulatory environment that favored domestic players.

But as the twenty-first century dawned, the industry began to experience a dramatic increase in competitive intensity. In the wake of sweeping government reforms, a host of new players piled into the market: multinational insurers, mono-line attackers specializing in particular products, and global banks looking to extend their reach into insurance. With them came a push toward doing business through direct channels, along with a number of product offerings that were not natural strengths for GNP.

At this point, enter new CEO, Alejandro Baillères, the son of the chairman of Grupo Bal, Don Alberto Baillères. The company he was inheriting was not in the best of shape. Prior to his appointment, GNP had lost money for two years running. Its market share was eroding fast, its cost structure was high for the industry, and employee satisfaction was on a downward trajectory. It was Alejandro's responsibility to restore GNP to its former glory and then take it to the next level of performance and health.

The first step for the company was to face the facts. That meant doing work to obtain management data that would paint a clear picture of performance. Traditional analytics focused on market share were augmented with new ones focused on profitability. Cost structures were compared not just to those from previous years but to those of competitors as well. And organizational health was measured using the OHI. The results told some hard truths about what had become a complacent culture, with low- to mid-quartile scores on most health elements.

Having gathered the data, the company's leaders rolled up their sleeves and got to work. In a series of sessions involving as many as 300 leaders at a time, GNP developed and agreed on a set of performance aspirations. Its broad goals were to restore profitability within 18 months; to give its parent company the confidence to invest in its proposed growth initiatives within 36 months; and to regain industry leadership within five years in four key areas (profitability, client service, operating efficiency, and attraction and retention of talent). GNP also set aspirations for its health, with a view to moving from complacency to a strong focus on execution and continuous improvement.

Equipped with a clear sense of its goals and readiness for change, GNP formally kicked off its transformation program in 2007. It committed to pursuing a raft of performance initiatives that included creating new product offerings for target segments, upgrading its risk-assessment capabilities, redesigning its claims-management processes, reducing its overhead costs, and improving its statistical controls. These performance initiatives were implemented in ways that would enable GNP to improve its organizational health as well as achieve its performance goals.

In addition, the company defined a short list of broad-based health initiatives. These included crafting a compelling transformation story and cascading it interactively through to the front line, creating a new leadership standard and development programs to build much-needed skills, developing individual performance contracts for all leaders with clear accountabilities for specific key performance indicators (KPIs), and overhauling the talent review process so that it would reflect and reward behaviors as well as performance. The new process introduced a committee structure for evaluation to eliminate favoritism, and a forced ranking system to foster a degree of internal competition and upgrade the talent pool.

By 2010, victory had been declared in the turnaround phase of the transformation. Return on invested capital had gone from a high single-digit negative return to a strong double-digit positive return. Similarly, the company's technical result (profits generated by the underwriting of insurance contracts, including financial revenues and capital gains related to these contracts) had gone from a loss to a profit of hundreds of millions. GNP had also achieved a reduction of more than 10 percent in its overall cost base.

There had been big improvements in the company's health, too. The number of employees who felt that their personal goals were in alignment with GNP's vision had risen from 33 percent to 86 percent, the number who felt that their behavior was guided by strategy had risen from 46 percent to 72 percent, and the motivation of the workforce had risen from a rating of 32 percent to 73 percent. In terms of its overall health, the company had shifted from the bottom to the top quartile.

As we write, GNP's transformation still has several more years left to run. This is a journey with many different facets, but it all started with setting the right aspirations. As Alejandro Baillères explains, "Our 'vision 2012' is our compass: it specifies what we are trying to achieve and by when. Our strategies follow from it in successive multiyear waves. Our annual performance contracts then link to how well we are delivering against our strategies. And our performance management system links to how well people deliver against those contracts and live our GNP leadership standard. The whole approach starts with a shared aspiration and makes it personal. The result is that as a company we are executing well, our confidence is building, and we're making a bigger difference than ever for our customers, our employees, our shareholders, and our country."[1]

As the work done by GNP's senior leadership team illustrates, any transformation program needs to start by figuring out what targets to set and how to go about setting them. This much is hardly news: management literature is virtually unanimous in extolling the virtue of setting clear aspirations. Yet when a recent McKinsey survey of almost 3,000 executives asked, "If your company undertook the transformation again, what, if anything, would you do differently?" nearly half (48 percent) picked "set clearer targets" as their top choice from a set of 16 responses.[2]

Clearly, there's still a gap between what senior managers *should* do (and probably *know* they should do) and what they *actually* do. To help leaders get it right from the start, we now offer our best guidance on how to go about setting performance and health aspirations for your organization.

Performance: Strategic Objectives

The aspirations your organization chooses will depend to a great extent on your starting point. They will also depend on your industry or sector: a bank's performance aspirations will be quite different from those of a mining company, or a hospital, or a government department. All the same, there are three lessons that almost any organization can apply when setting its performance targets: focus on your medium-term future, balance facts and intuition, and set tough but achievable goals.

Focus on Your Medium-Term Future

When it comes to setting aspirations, some companies opt for bold long-term visions. Jack Welch's famous call for GE to be "number 1 or 2 in every business we are in" is a prime example. Others are Stanford University's 1940s vision to become the "Harvard of the west" and Sony's 1950s drive to overturn the reputation of Japanese electronic goods for poor quality.

When Sir Terry Leahy announced in 2010 that he was stepping down from the CEO's job at Tesco, the U.K.-based supermarket chain, he was clear about the vision that had guided his leadership: "When I became chief executive I had a plan to build Tesco around its customers, to make it number 1 in the U.K., and to find new long-term growth in nonfood, in services, and in international expansion." During Leahy's 14 years in charge, Tesco quadrupled in size, to the point of taking £1 in every £7 that consumers spend in Britain. It also became the first British supermarket to transform itself into a global brand. Leahy notes: "It has taken all of those 14 years, but the strategy has become a firm reality."[3]

In practice, however, a bold long-term vision isn't the right approach for every company. Not long after Lou Gerstner took the helm at IBM, he shocked some observers by saying, "The last thing IBM needs right now is a vision."[4] It wasn't that he lacked a clear set of aspirations, just that he knew that his medium-term focus needed to be on fixing things that were clearly broken. Another incoming CEO, Procter & Gamble's Alan G. Lafley, argued that it is counterproductive to over-promise: "The first thing I did was to set lower, more realistic goals."[5]

With so many different approaches employed at successful companies— bold vision statements, no vision statements, high targets, low targets— where can leaders look for guidance? Our research and experience suggest that a feature common to the vast majority of successful change efforts is the clear definition of a medium-term future for each element of the transformation. Why is that? It's because having a sense of where you want to be two or three years from now is much nearer and clearer than having a long-term vision. It gives you the immediacy and tangibility you need to inspire stakeholders, set a rapid pace for change, break through resistance, and create an action-oriented attitude right through the whole organization to the front line.

When Ravi Kant became managing director of Tata Motors, an India-based vehicle manufacturer, the company was in crisis. After a decade of strong revenue and margin growth, it had been hit by the sudden collapse of demand for its trucks. At the same time, there were growing threats from overseas competitors, as well as cost pressures resulting from Tata's entry into the passenger car business and investment in complying with new emissions standards. In a turn of events that shocked the markets, Tata Motors reported a 5 billion rupee (US$110 million) loss for the fiscal year ending in 2001.

Under the circumstances, Tata might have been expected to devote all its energies to tackling the immediate problems that beset it. But that's not what happened. Instead, Kant worked closely with his senior leaders to create a bold vision for the company. They planned not merely to restore it to its former glory as India's leading truck manufacturer, but to turn it into a diversified automobile giant with global ambitions. Exciting though this vision was, Kant and his team knew that it wasn't enough. It would be unlikely to mobilize people's energies unless it was broken down into actionable pieces.

As Kant explains, "We decided on a recovery strategy that had three distinct phases, each of which was intended to last for around two years. Phase one was intended to stem the bleeding, since we just couldn't ignore the fact that our sales volumes were still falling with the shrinkage of the overall market. Costs had to be reduced in a big way, and that was going to be a huge challenge for a company that was not only the market leader but had been used to operating in a seller's market and employing a cost-plus approach to pricing. Phase two was to be about consolidating our position in India, and phase three was to involve going outside India and expanding our operations internationally."[6]

The plan proved remarkably successful. Having slashed 8 billion rupees (US$176 million) from its cost base in the first phase, Tata then made a successful entry into passenger cars in the compact, midsize, and sports utility vehicle markets. It was able to capture opportunities presented by favorable social and economic trends such as the new affluence and desire for mobility among young Indians and the government's substantial road-building program. By 2010, the company had become India's largest carmaker, and the winner of the coveted title of India's most valuable brand.[7]

Outside its home market, Tata built a significant presence both through its sales efforts in markets such as the former Soviet republics, Turkey, South Africa, and countries in the Middle East and South Asia, and through its acquisitions in the United Kingdom, South Korea, Thailand, and Spain. By 2010, it was the world's fourth-largest truck manufacturer and second-largest bus manufacturer, and it employed 24,000 workers.

Would Tata have been able to achieve its aspirations without breaking down its long-term vision into a series of medium-term objectives? It's hard to say, but there is little doubt that the immediacy of medium-term goals makes them more actionable. When managers are planning two or three years ahead, that period is close enough in time to allow them to choose relevant goals and identify specific initiatives to reach them.

On the other hand, what if Tata had simply set objectives in the form of year-on-year targets, without having a longer-term view? Again, we have no way of knowing, but certainly there are advantages in having objectives distant enough to reduce any temptation to rob tomorrow to pay for today—a constant battle for public companies under pressure to achieve quarterly results.

For a wider view, let's take a look at a couple of the companies we mentioned above to see how they went about setting their aspirations.

Shortly after taking the reins at GE in 1982, Jack Welch had announced his long-term vision. It was to transform the lumbering giant of a company he'd inherited into a leading player that would, as we saw earlier, be "number 1 or 2 in every business we are in." A bold vision indeed, but how was it to be realized? Again, by breaking down the effort into three phases. The first was about "fix, close, or sell"—a phase of massive portfolio restructuring in which Welch sold 125 businesses in the space of four years, including consumer brands that had long been core to GE's identity. It was then that Welch earned the less than flattering nickname of Neutron Jack, in an allusion to the way a neutron bomb eliminates people while leaving buildings intact.[8]

The second phase was about growing GE's services and high-technology businesses. In this phase, the company made several important purchases, including its largest to date, the acquisition of Radio Corporation of America (RCA), the owner of leading U.S. television network NBC, for US$6.4 billion. Another major purchase was financial services provider Employers Reinsurance Corporation, acquired from Texaco for US$1.1 billion. By 1988, 80 percent of GE's earnings came from services and high-tech businesses, up from 50 percent six years earlier.

In the third phase of the transformation, Welch emphasized the "software" of his organization, pumping money into the revitalization of Crotonville, a facility in New York that trained 10,000 employees a year. He also oversaw the creation of the "Workout" program, a town hall–style meeting where 30 to 100 employees would discuss common problems over the course of a few days. Bosses were not allowed to attend until the final hours, when they were obliged to make on-the-spot yes or no decisions on a list of action points that the group had compiled. In a five-year period, more than 200,000 employees—85 percent of GE's workforce—took part in a Workout session.

So what were the results? By 1993, every business in GE's portfolio had reached one of the top two rungs in its market, fulfilling Welch's vision. During his tenure as CEO, GE's stock consistently outpaced the market, and by the time he left its market value had increased by US$60 billion.

At IBM, Lou Gerstner may have had his doubts about the value of a long-term vision to a company in crisis, but that didn't stop him setting medium-term goals. When he became CEO in 1993, the company had just posted what was then the biggest annual loss in U.S. corporate history. So like the leaders of Tata, GE, and indeed most companies in need of a turnaround, Gerstner made cost cutting his first priority.

Having inherited an active plan to disaggregate the company, the new CEO also chose to set a medium-term strategic aspiration that would take it in the opposite direction. He pledged that in three years' time it would still be together as one organization, and would be positioning itself to become a broad-based technology integrator. In another seemingly contrarian move, he disregarded the prevailing wisdom that IBM's mainframe operation was headed for the scrapheap, and chose instead to put it at the core of the business.

The second set of medium-term aspirations that Gerstner and his team developed related to growing IT services and PC businesses. The third and final set was about enabling companies to move into a brave new networked world by providing guidance on their technology strategies, helping them build and run their systems, and acting as the architect and repository for their corporate computing.

The results of the program spoke for themselves. IBM's share price increased eightfold and its income more than doubled, from US$3 billion to US$7.7 billion.

In our view, the idea of defining your desired medium-term future gets less attention than it deserves in management literature. Accounts of successful transformations tend to overlook the vital distinction between long-term vision and medium-term future. When senior leaders look back on their success, they often define their long-term vision in retrospect, while creating the impression that they had it right from the start. Our experience with organizations undergoing transformations indicates that many leaders actually embark on their journey with a medium-term future in mind, and fill in the detail of their long-term vision along the way.

We don't mean to suggest that a long-term vision isn't helpful, just that it isn't enough. Even if your long-term vision is clear, it must still be rolled back to a desired medium-term future that is granular and actionable, but also ambitious about the scale and pace of change. And if on the other hand your long-term vision *isn't* clear at the outset, that's no reason not to embark on the journey. If your organization is constantly working toward the next stage in its medium-term future, your long-term vision is more than likely to emerge as you go along.

Balance Fact and Intuition

When an organization's performance aspiration is not strategically sound, the rest of the change process matters little. Consider the notorious remark made in 1977 by Ken Olsen, the CEO of Digital Equipment Corporation, at a meeting of the World Future Society. Olsen said that he saw "no reason for any individual to have a computer in his home." The company's subsequent pursuit of a strategy narrowly focused on the scientific and engineering community led to its eventual downfall and purchase by Compaq: a cautionary tale indeed.

So how can leaders minimize their chances of going in the wrong direction and maximize the likelihood of going in the right one? Clearly, hard facts have a part to play in determining your aspirations. Our research shows that those transformations where "considerable effort was made to create a robust fact base" are 2.4 times more likely to succeed than those "based largely on perception and gut feel."[9]

To obtain a robust fact base, companies need to ask themselves questions. What competitive pressures and opportunities do we face? What do our customers demand? What do our shareholders expect? How does our performance stack up against benchmarks? What would happen if we got better at sharing internal best practices? What if we pushed our processes and systems to their technical limits?

As part of the fact-gathering process, organizations can test scenarios in order to ensure that goals are set against the right measures and don't cause unintended consequences. A key factor in Enron's implosion was its system of sales goals and incentives. These were based solely on the revenues that salespeople generated, with no regard for the soundness and profitability or otherwise of the underlying trades.

Consider, too, the U.S. federal education program No Child Left Behind, enacted in 2001. It linked government aid to highly specific student performance targets based on standardized test scores. Critics argued that the program led teachers to focus on teaching the narrow skill sets required for the tests rather than on promoting wider values such as cooperation, innovation, thoughtfulness, and ethical standards.

However, relying on data alone is not enough. The brain is not an all-powerful computer capable of imagining countless future scenarios and calculating exactly how likely they are to come to pass. In real life, our thinking is hampered by biases, such as giving more weight to evidence that supports our argument than to evidence that contradicts it. We are also loss-averse: experiments have shown that our perceptions of probability change dramatically when we are asked to think in terms of losses rather than gains, even if the outcomes are identical. Does your organization's risk management process track only bad outcomes, or positive ones, too? We suspect the answer is the former.

So we need to guard against relying too heavily on the kind of fact-based logic that leads us to conclude that no individual has any need of a computer in the house. We agree with T. Gary Rogers, former chairman and CEO of Dreyer's Grand Ice Cream, when he says that "Successful leaders should follow their intuition—if it doesn't feel right in your gut, don't do it."[10]

Intuition involves knowing or sensing something without the use of rational processes, and generally comes from a combination of experience and self-awareness. At a time when information is so freely available, it might seem that intuition has had its day—but we think its role in decision making will only increase. As John Naisbitt, author of *Megatrends* and (with Patricia Aburdene) *Re-inventing the Corporation,* puts it, "Intuition becomes increasingly valuable in the new information society precisely because there is so much data."

Consider the experience of John Akehurst as CEO of Woodside Petroleum, an Australian petroleum exploration and production company partly owned by Royal Dutch Shell. During the construction of the Laminaria oilfield development facility, which represented the company's most promising growth investment, the project suffered a US$250 million cost overrun, and a delay of six months. These mishaps took Akehurst and his team completely by surprise. Why? Because the people working on the project had gone to great lengths to avoid giving their leaders any bad news along the way, always hoping they'd somehow find a way to catch up. The result was a major embarrassment in front of the board and a big disappointment for shareholders, many of whom felt they'd been misled.

Once the market had been informed and remedial actions had been taken (including dismissing some of the senior leaders on the project), the leadership team did a postmortem to work out how they'd failed to pick up that something was going seriously wrong. A number of team members admitted that they'd had a feeling in their gut that things were not going well, but didn't have any real evidence, so said nothing. The team agreed that if they ever had such intuitions again—no matter how unsubstantiated—they would share them.

One evening a few months later, after a day of reviewing data on development prospects, three of Akehurst's team entered his office looking sheepish. They indicated that while they had no hard evidence, something didn't feel right. This was a moment of truth for Akehurst. As he explains, "As an analytical person, I would previously have thrown them out, telling them to come back when they had something worth talking about. Or, more likely, they would never have raised their concerns with me for fear of being thrown out. This time, in line with our new appreciation of the value of intuition, we all sat down and shared how we felt."[11]

The discussion centered on the team's hunch that Shell, then a 34 percent shareholder, was preparing to make a hostile takeover bid. Even though there was nothing concrete to back this up, Akehurst and the team took steps to prepare themselves to defend a takeover should their intuition prove correct. Sure enough, a few months later it did, and Shell launched what turned out, thanks to the team's foresight, to be an unsuccessful bid.

More proof of the power of intuition comes from the example of Net-a-Porter, an online retailer of upmarket women's fashion. When Natalie Massenet set up the business in June 2000, the dot-com bubble was bursting and the world was awash with failing internet startups. "There were a lot of unimaginative private-equity people who said that women would never shop online. . . . I'm sure their wives are having Net-a-Porter bags delivered to their homes every day," she wryly remarks.[12] Jo Elvin, editor of *Glamour* magazine, observes that "The main thing Natalie did right was trust her gut. I admire her strength in sticking to her guns when everyone told her Net-a-Porter would never catch on—such was the perceived wisdom 10 years ago."[13]

Intuition continues to play a dominant role in the way Massenet runs her business: "If we come up with an idea and someone says it's never been done before, that's when we get going."[14] Employees are also encouraged to act on their gut instinct, and the company has a policy of not hiring experts. This novel approach to business has paid off: Net-a-Porter was sold to the Richemont luxury goods group in early 2010 for a reported £350 million (US$533 million).[15] Not bad for a business started with £800,000 (US$1.4 million) in funding.

Of course, intuition—and common sense—has its drawbacks, too. It tells us that the coin that has just come up heads four times in a row is going to come up tails next time, and that heavy objects fall faster than light ones. Fortunately, we can correct our intuitive response in these cases by using mathematics and logic.

Similarly, when leaders use instinct to make business decisions, they need to bring data and analysis into play too so that they don't get led astray. Economist and Nobel laureate Daniel Kahneman sounds a warning over the image of the CEO as the person with the "golden gut": "My general view [is] that you should not take your intuitions at face value. Overconfidence is a powerful source of illusions."[16]

The key is to balance intuition with fact and not allow either to have sole sway.

Set Tough But Achievable Goals

A survey of some 2,500 senior executives conducted by McKinsey in January 2010 indicates that programs that set tough but achievable goals are 1.2 times more likely to be considered a success than those whose targets are incremental and easy to reach, and 1.6 times more likely to be successful than those whose targets are considered to be impossible to reach.[17]

In our experience, targets are too often incremental, cautious, or tailored to existing capabilities. They fail to create momentum or pressure for an organization to push the limits of what is possible, and they seldom lead to breakthroughs. Naturally, if people see goals as beyond reach, they will become disillusioned and give up. But most organizations, whether strugglers or top performers, have more headroom than they think before goals truly do become unattainable.

In the financial services sector, for example, a bank that is in the lowest performance quartile of its industry could manage a sixfold increase in its ratio of operating profits to total revenue if it were able to move to the top quartile. Even a top-quartile bank could boost its performance by 50 percent if it combined the sector's peak level for income per employee with top-tier labor-cost efficiency. Our advice? Aim high.

That said, unrealistic or ill-conceived goals can create unintended consequences. In the early 1990s, U.S. retailer Sears set its auto-repair staff new billing targets of US$147 per hour. Unable to meet the goal in the normal course of their work, the mechanics started performing unnecessary repairs and overcharging their clients, triggering a major customer relations crisis.

Ford fell foul of the same trap. Its 1969 aspiration to design a new model that weighed less than 2,000 pounds, sold for less than US$2,000, and would be in showrooms within two years may have been catchy, but it backfired badly. The Ford Pinto was rushed out so fast that commonsense safety checks were skipped. So close was its fuel tank to its rear axle that rear-end crashes sent it up in flames, causing 53 deaths and numerous injuries, not to mention a string of lawsuits.[18]

By way of contrast, a powerful example of aspirations that are ambitious, granular, and clearly defined for the medium-term future comes from Poste Italiane. Under the leadership of new CEO Corrado Passera, it decided that within two and a half years, its post offices would have better-functioning layouts and processes than bank branches do, at 30 percent of the cost; that waiting times for 80 percent of customers would fall below 7.5 minutes; and that growth would rise from minus 2 percent to 5 percent a year. These goals were set against the backdrop of a broader vision to become a regional leader in financial services.

The results didn't just meet the goals, but exceeded aspirations. Customers opened 2 million checking accounts, and in just two years Poste Italiane rose to third place among the country's insurance providers. Productivity rose by 30 percent; revenues by 20 percent. The *Financial Times* reported that the reinvigorated organization had "begun to establish itself as a serious competitor to Italy's commercial banks,"[19] and the prime minister observed that citizens had one less topic to talk about: no more long lines at the post office.

Health: Essentials

When an organization sets aspirations for its health that are as clear and explicit as those for its performance, it significantly increases its chance of achieving a successful transformation. The McKinsey survey of senior executives mentioned above revealed that change programs with clearly defined aspirations for both performance *and* health are 4.4 times more likely to be extremely successful than those with clear aspirations for performance alone.

Let's start by taking another look at our definition of organizational health, and then focus on how to set the right health aspiration for your organization, including the important question of who should be involved in the process.

Checking Your Health

First, a quick recap. In Chapter 1 we introduced the idea of organizational health, defining it as an organization's ability to align, execute, and renew itself faster than the competition so that it can sustain exceptional performance over time. In Chapter 2 we identified the nine elements of organizational health, namely direction, leadership, culture and climate, accountability, coordination and control, capabilities, motivation, external orientation, and innovation and learning. We also broke down these nine elements into the 37 management practices that feed into them, and described how our survey-based tool, the organizational health index (OHI), can provide organizations with a comprehensive and rigorous understanding of their health.

For the purposes of this chapter, we've developed a high-level overview of the OHI to remind readers of what organizational health involves. This is illustrated in Exhibit 3.1. You can use it to conduct a rough assessment of how healthy your organization is. Think about where it belongs in each element: is it ailing, able, or elite? What elements are most important to you in achieving your medium-term performance aspirations? Where do you need to be on each element in two or three years' time? (If you'd like to make a deeper assessment of your organization's health without doing a full OHI survey, you can visit our website at www.mckinsey.com/beyondperformance, where you'll find tools and resources to help you set the right health aspirations to meet your organization's specific situation and needs.)

To get a full picture of organizational health, the OHI should be augmented with fact-based analyses where possible in order to confirm that perceptions are based on reality. If they prove not to be, the solution may lie in improving transparency and communication rather than changing practices. The types of analysis that are often helpful at this stage include customer loyalty scores (customer focus), hiring rates from target talent pools (talent acquisition), compensation systems (financial incentives), breakdowns of how executives spend their time (various of the leadership practices), and scorecards (strategic clarity).

One financial services organization discovered that its staff didn't find monetary incentives motivating because they perceived that pay didn't vary with performance. Analysis showed, however, that this was a

Exhibit 3.1
Assessing Organizational Health

	Ailing	Able	Elite
Direction	Creates a strategy that fails to resolve the tough issues	Crafts and communicates a compelling strategy, reinforced by systems and processes . . .	. . . and provides purpose, engaging people around the vision
Leadership	Provides excessively detailed instructions and monitoring (high control)	Shows care toward subordinates and sensitivity to their needs (high support) . . .	. . . and sets stretch goals and inspires employees to work at their full potential (high challenge)
Culture and climate	Lacks a coherent sense of shared values	Creates a baseline of trust within and across organizational units . . .	. . . and creates a strong, adaptable organization-wide performance culture
Accountability	Creates excessive complexity and ambiguous roles	Creates clear roles and responsibilities; links performance and consequences . . .	. . . and encourages an ownership mindset at all levels
Coordination and control	Establishes conflicting and unclear control systems and processes	Aligns goals, targets, and metrics managed through efficient and effective processes . . .	. . . and measures and captures the value from working collaboratively across organizational boundaries
Capabilities	Fails to manage talent pipeline or deal with poor performers	Builds institutional skills required to execute strategy . . .	. . . and builds distinctive capabilities that create long-term competitive advantage
Motivation	Accepts low engagement as the norm	Motivates through incentives, opportunities, and values	. . . and taps into employees' sense of meaning and identity to harness extraordinary effort
External orientation	Directs the energy of the organization inward	Makes creating value for customers the primary objective . . .	. . . and focuses on creating value for all stakeholders
Innovation and learning	Lacks structured approaches to harness employees' ideas	Able to capture ideas and convert them into value incrementally and through special initiatives . . .	. . . and able to leverage internal and external networks to maintain a leadership position

misapprehension. Instead of recommending a revamp of the compensation system, the firm quickly concluded that what was needed was a communications program to make the link between pay and performance clearer.

In our experience, though, employee perceptions are accurate in most cases, making the OHI a powerful and comprehensive management tool in and of itself.

Setting a Health Aspiration

Measuring health is one thing, but what is the right health aspiration for your organization? Our research indicates that organizations need to achieve a threshold level of health across all nine elements of organizational health. More specifically, they need to be above the bottom quartile on each of the 37 practices that drive the outcomes on these nine elements.

This makes sense when we think of the practices as simply those things a leader needs to do in order to align an organization on a common direction and enable it to execute and continuously improve. After all, leaders can't simply neglect to ensure that targets are set, strategies are developed, budgets are allocated, people are hired, performance is monitored, and so on.

Yet while all of these things must be done, not all of them necessarily require the same emphasis. To revisit the analogy with human health, what it means for individuals to be healthy, beyond the basics, will depend to some extent on their performance aspirations—what they want to do with their lives. A healthy weight for a body-builder is different from that of a jockey; a pilot requires a higher standard of eyesight than an academic; a ballet dancer needs more flexible joints than a lawyer.

Our research has shown that the same is true of organizations: they don't need to excel in every aspect of health. When we dug more deeply into the 37 practices, we found that a company that is in the top quartile for six or more of them has an 80 percent likelihood of being in the top quartile for *overall* health, which in turn drives superior business performance (Exhibit 3.2).

This means that beyond achieving an "able" standard (above the bottom quartile) on all practices, organizations need choose only six to 10 practices to be distinctive at. That's good news for leaders, since no organization can hope to achieve elite status on every aspect of health.

So how should you determine which practices your organization should drive to distinction? There are three questions to ask yourself. First, which practices are most likely to enable me to reach my performance aspirations?

Exhibit 3.2
Six Is the Magic Number

**Likelihood that an organization's overall health
will be in the top quartile if the stated number of
practices are in the top quartile,** %

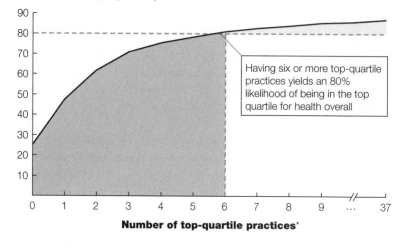

Having six or more top-quartile
practices yields an 80%
likelihood of being in the top
quartile for health overall

Number of top-quartile practices*

---

*All remaining practices are assumed to be above the bottom quartile

Second, where do my existing strengths lie? (It's much easier to build on strengths you already have than to develop them from scratch.) Third, which practices will complement one another?

The concept of complementarity is defined by John Roberts in his book *The Modern Firm*: "Two choice variables are complements when *doing (more of) one of them increases the returns to doing (more of) the other.*"[20] To see how this works, let's look at the example illustrated in Exhibit 3.3. If a company wants to increase motivation, it has various management practices at its disposal. If it decides to offer incentives to its staff, it has a 48 percent probability of increasing its motivation to the top-quartile level (perhaps surprisingly, the lowest probability for any motivation practice). However, if the company offers incentives *and* modifies its culture and climate to create a competitive internal environment, the probability goes up to 95 percent. Adopting two complementary management practices instead of relying on

Exhibit 3.3

Management Practices Work in Combination

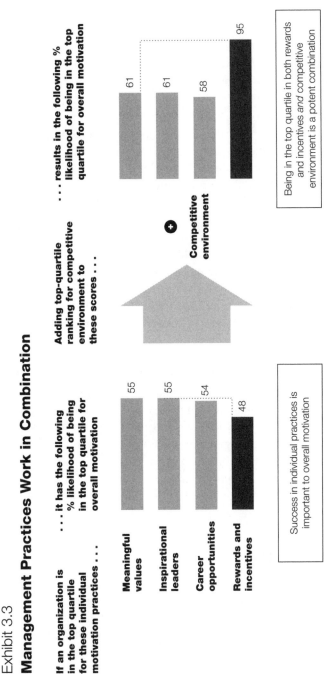

If an organization is in the top quartile for these individual motivation practices . . .

. . . it has the following % likelihood of being in the top quartile for overall motivation

Meaningful values — 55
Inspirational leaders — 55
Career opportunities — 54
Rewards and incentives — 48

Success in individual practices is important to overall motivation

Adding top-quartile ranking for competitive environment to these scores . . .

Competitive environment

. . . results in the following % likelihood of being in the top quartile for overall motivation

61
61
58
95

Being in the top quartile in both rewards and incentives *and* competitive environment is a potent combination just one greatly increases the chance of success—almost doubling it, in this case.

The concept of complementarity is easier to grasp if we think about cookery. Flour, yeast, and water are hardly exciting ingredients by themselves, but when they are used in the right proportions and prepared in the right way, they can turn into fresh, hot bread that tastes sensational. Or take peanut butter and jelly: combined in a sandwich, they have a salty-sweet taste that many people far prefer to either filling alone.

The food analogy also illuminates that complementarity has a flipside, as one of our colleagues can confirm. While he was in a client meeting late one night, his team decided to order dinner for everyone. They knew that his favorite dishes were pizza and seafood. Lo and behold, the menu offered a seafood pizza. What could be better, they thought? To this day, our colleague claims it was the worst meal he's ever eaten.

So adding one good thing to another doesn't necessarily create something better; it can create something worse. Let's see how this applies to combinations of management practices. If an organization wants to increase its innovation and learning, it has various practices at its disposal. If it decides to use top-down innovation as a lever, it has a 58 percent probability of increasing its innovation and learning to the top-quartile level. However, if it emphasizes incentives, internal competition, and talent-acquisition practices *in addition to* top-down innovation, the likelihood of achieving a top-quartile innovation and learning level drops to 44 percent. Why?

It turns out that large-scale innovation is by nature a collaborative effort. This particular combination of ingredients overemphasizes human capital (people's intellectual contributions and functional skills) at the expense of social capital (networking, collaboration, and information sharing). A far better recipe would combine top-down innovation with a shared vision, knowledge sharing, and customer focus, which yields a 78 percent likelihood of achieving a top-quartile level of innovation and learning.

The Four Archetypes

So far, we've established that to be healthy, an organization must be above the threshold level of health on all 37 of the management practices defined in the OHI. We've also established that an organization has a much higher likelihood of being in the top quartile of health overall (which is highly correlated with superior business performance, as we saw in Chapter 1) if it's in the top quartile for six or more of these practices. Finally, we've established that when certain management practices are carried out at distinctive levels, they can combine with others to deliver a "1 + 1 = 3" level of impact.

So the billion-dollar question is this: How do we find the six practices that we should excel at to achieve excellent organizational health?

The answer is that there is no one recipe. In fact, when we analyzed the complementarities among the practices underpinning organizational health, we found there are *four* recipes that can be used as a foundation on which to build. For simplicity, we've labeled each recipe as an "archetype" of a healthy organization. The four archetypes are leadership driven, execution edge, market focus, and knowledge core.[21]

Exhibit 3.4 shows the ingredients of each recipe—the distinctive management practices that contribute to the archetype—in rank order. Let's take a closer look at each archetype in turn.

LEADERSHIP DRIVEN   Companies that fit this archetype believe that leaders are the catalysts for performance, setting high expectations and supporting the organization in achieving them. So why aren't leadership practices at the top of the first list in Exhibit 3.4? It's because the highest priority for leaders in this archetype is to build a pipeline of future leaders, and the way they do that is by creating career opportunities, which *is* at the top of the list. In this archetype, leadership is learned by doing. Like riding a bike, it can't be learned simply through observation.

Leaders in this archetype are highly empowered, which explains why open and trusting management practices come second in the list. If empowered individuals are to channel their efforts in the right direction, accountabilities must be clear. The ingredients related to performance contracts and reviews, operational management and discipline, and consequence management all ensure that the right level of accountability and transparency is in place.

Beverages and convenience foods giant PepsiCo is a good example of a company that embodies the leadership-driven archetype. It's renowned for offering its employees excellent opportunities for early responsibility and a culture that encourages initiative, risk taking, and access to decision makers. Employees are given the freedom to pursue their goals without the burden of excessive structures.

Less well known is the rigor of PepsiCo's performance contracts, which tie each individual's objectives to the goals of the business. Performance evaluations are based on delivery against these objectives and on an assessment of 11 leadership competencies. They are also monitored centrally to ensure that an individual's evaluation aligns with the overall success of

Exhibit 3.4

The Four Archetypes and the Practices That Drive Them

Top 10 management practices for each archetype

	Leadership driven	Execution edge	Market focus	Knowledge core
1	Career opportunities	Knowledge sharing	Business partnerships	Talent acquisition
2	Open and trusting	Creative and entrepreneurial	Customer focus	Role clarity
3	Performance contracts	Employee involvement	Competitive insights	Consequence management
4	Inspirational leaders	Talent development	Government and community relations	Rewards and incentives
5	Strategic clarity	Internally competitive	Financial management	Personal ownership
6	People performance review	Personal ownership	Capturing external ideas	People performance review
7	Operational management	Bottom-up innovation	Process-based capabilities	Career opportunities
8	Operationally disciplined	Top-down innovation	Shared vision	Performance contracts
9	Consultative leadership	Meaningful values	Outsourced expertise	Professional standards
10	Consequence management	Consequence management	Strategic clarity	Financial management

their business unit. If a business unit is doing badly, for instance, its leaders can expect to have poorer performance reviews than they would if it were doing well. (Though this might sound like plain common sense, some organizations give their managers positive individual evaluations even as their business fails—not a healthy state of affairs.)

EXECUTION EDGE   Companies that fit this archetype believe that discipline, sound execution, and continuous improvement are the foundation for great performance. At the top of the list of ingredients for this recipe comes knowledge sharing: it's essential for getting things done in the best possible way and for creating an environment that supports continuous improvement. When something works, it gets shared, others pick up on it, and everyone wins. There's enough internal competition to drive adoption of best practices, yet the stakes aren't so high that they stop people sharing.

This also explains why practices such as operational discipline aren't in the top 10 ingredients. At first sight, that might seem surprising. How can a company achieve excellence in execution without a strong emphasis on standardization, for instance? In fact, companies that embody the execution-edge archetype do achieve a remarkable level of standardization, but not in the way we might expect. Standardization isn't driven by mandates from on high, but by the various parts of the organization *wanting* to adopt best practices. In other words, it's not a matter of enforced compliance and audits against rules and procedures, but a flexible approach to standardization that rests on a shared direction and shared set of values. Companies that fit this archetype are constantly looking for ways to do things better and taking steps to involve employees at all levels.

Walmart is an example of a company embodying this archetype. Its culture of driving out costs and working in partnership across the supply chain means that routine decisions are pushed down to the lowest level of the organization. This enables inventories to move flexibly across the system, and their status is tracked visually so that any problems can quickly be addressed. The entire system is adjusted in real time as numbers are updated from the point of sale, and sales and merchandise inventories in every store are tracked globally via satellite. This data-rich environment enables leaders to know what's working well and what isn't, facilitating best-practice sharing across the organization. Management processes such as these are complemented with Walmart's "grass-roots process"—a way to give every associate a voice in improving the company. The effect is to ensure that all ideas for improvement are captured on a regular basis.

MARKET FOCUS Companies that fit this archetype believe that shaping market trends and building a portfolio of strong and innovative brands keep them ahead of the pack. Not surprisingly, the hallmark of this archetype is a strong external orientation with emphasis on customers, competitive insight, and business partners.

This intense external orientation is channeled into a single direction through a shared vision that creates the space for new and exciting innovations that delight the customer. At Apple, Steve Jobs' rallying cry to "put romance into computing" gave rise to the sleek and stylish product designs that make customers clamor to get their hands on the latest offerings.[22] For P&G, as former CEO Alan G. Lafley explains, the heart of its vision is to be the globe's most connected company: "We are touching lives and improving life for consumers around the world."[23]

Why do business partnerships top the list? Because most organizations that excel at the market-focus archetype need partners to help them develop their products and get them to market with the right levels of quality and service. P&G established more than 500 business partnerships in the quest to source half its innovation from outside the company. But perhaps the most striking example of the role of business partnerships in the market-focus archetype is that of Apple.

When Steve Jobs returned to Apple as CEO in 1996 with a mandate to turn it around, he observed, "Apple lives in an ecosystem, and it needs help from other partners."[24] He went on to join forces with Microsoft's Bill Gates in announcing the launch of an Apple-compatible version of the ubiquitous Microsoft Office. In 2006–2007 alone, more than 200,000 companies from software houses to carmakers to newspapers signed up to partnerships with Apple.[25]

The company has also revolutionized the development of apps—third-party software programs—for its products, and hosts more than 300,000 of them on its website. It similarly forms partnerships with manufacturers to produce its products rather than making them itself. Apple's success in pursuing a strategy of innovation via a market-focus archetype can be judged from its nomination as *Fortune* magazine's most admired company in the world for three years running.

At first sight, one ingredient of this archetype—number five in the list—might seem puzzling. What does financial management have to do with market focus? On reflection, though, it makes perfect sense. The factor that differentiates successful from unsuccessful exponents of this archetype is the extent to which they are able to delight customers and beat the competition in the marketplace while earning a *profit*. P&G's Alan G. Lafley puts it succinctly: "Generating ideas is important, but it's pointless unless there is a repeatable process in place to turn inspiration into financial performance."[26]

KNOWLEDGE CORE Companies that fit this archetype believe that their pool of talent and knowledge represents their most important asset, and that their success depends on developing it effectively. As with managing a successful sports team, they need to get the right players (talent acquisition), put them in the right positions (role clarity), give them the right incentives (rewards and consequences), keep them focused (personal ownership), study how they've played in recent games (performance review), and so on.

One example of this archetype is our own organization. At McKinsey, we closely monitor our ability to attract, develop, and retain the best talent, and keep our value proposition for potential recruits under constant review. Our core HR resources are small; it's our partners who are responsible for providing feedback, coaching, and mentoring for junior colleagues. A small number of well-defined roles helps to create clear career paths, and a merit-based "up or out" model ensures that the talent pool is constantly refreshed and that high performers are able to develop at a rapid pace, opening up career opportunities both inside and outside the firm. Compensation at each level is strategically pitched to reward performance without being at the top of the market, ensuring that people are attracted not just by money but by McKinsey's values and development opportunities. A strong culture of collaboration and a state-of-the-art knowledge-sharing system ensure that consultants are continually learning from others and are able to bring the organization's full institutional knowledge to bear on their work for clients.

Another exponent of this archetype is investment bank Goldman Sachs. To ensure that it hires only top talent, it puts would-be recruits through more than 40 interviews before making an offer.[27] Such is its focus on acquiring and developing the right people that in 2010 a senior human resources manager was elected as partner, a privilege usually reserved for top-performing investment bankers. Employees who fail to meet Goldman's high standards are regularly moved out, even if they are elected partners.[28] With just five layers in the organizational hierarchy, employees are clear on what's expected of them and how to progress within the firm. This competitive environment gels well with Goldman's focus on rewards and incentives: employees receive generous bonuses and benefits, but tend to value the prestige of working for the bank above all else.

CHOOSING AN ARCHETYPE It's important to note that these four recipes are not a mere analytical construct, but a deeply ingrained fact of organizational life. We saw this recently when a company we were working with asked us how "real" the four archetypes are. By way of response, we asked a few questions. One of the executives had joined the company just two months earlier, so we asked him, "When was the first time you had any contact with customers?" His answer: on day one as part of his orientation, and again later that week during dinner with his sponsor (another executive charged with helping him in his transition).

We pointed out that this isn't the case in most organizations we encounter, and then asked, "When did your boss first give you feedback on your performance?" He was mystified. "What do you mean? I've only been on the job for two months. I haven't had any feedback yet." We then turned to one of our colleagues and asked, "When did you receive your first feedback at McKinsey?" The answer: "Day one, and virtually every day since."

The difference between the client's market-focus archetype and our knowledge-core archetype couldn't have been sharper. The message is that the practices at the top of the list for each archetype translate directly into the everyday realities of organizational life.

The four archetypes shed light on one of the reasons why management literature has largely been unsuccessful in helping leaders create sustainably excellent organizations. The vast majority of the books and articles we surveyed during our research turned out to have been written from the vantage point of promoting one particular archetype as the answer to all situations.

Pick up *Leadership without Easy Answers* by Ronald Heifetz, *John P. Kotter on What Leaders Really Do*, or *The Power of Servant Leadership* by Robert Greenleaf, and you'll notice that the recommendations they make rely on the leadership-driven archetype. Read *Built to Last* by Jim Collins and Jerry Porras, *Doing What Matters* by James M. Kilts, or *Execution* by Larry Bossidy and Ram Charan, and you'll find that the execution-edge archetype is the implicit model. Should you choose *Delivering Happiness: A Path to Profits, Passion, and Purpose* by Tony Hsieh, *The New Market Leaders* by Fred Wiersema, or *The Innovator's Dilemma* by Clayton Christensen, you'll discover that the discussion hinges on the market-focus archetype. Or study *Mobilizing Minds* by Lowell Bryan and Claudia Joyce, *Now, Discover Your Strengths* by Marcus Buckingham and Donald Clifton, or *The War for Talent* by Ed Michaels, Helen Handfield-Jones, and Beth Axelrod, and you'll see that the knowledge-core archetype is at the heart of the thinking. It's not that any of these books is unhelpful or misguided—just that their recommendations presuppose a desired archetype that may or may not be right for your organization.

So what *is* the right archetype for your organization? As we mentioned, it will be the one that plays to your greatest strengths and best supports your performance aspirations. And do you have to stick to just one? Not all healthy companies fit neatly into a single archetype, but most—around four-fifths—do.

Further guidance on your choice may come from the industry you are in: some industries lend themselves more to certain archetypes than others. For example, consumer packaged goods companies like P&G tend to be most successful with a market-focus archetype, whereas professional services firms like McKinsey do best with a knowledge-core archetype. But this isn't cast in stone: our data indicates that each archetype, if done well, can lead to success in *any* industry.

Another finding from our research that's helpful to bear in mind is that it's harder for an organization to change its archetype than to go from unhealthy to healthy *within* its archetype. As a neat way to see why this is so, fold your arms. Now try to fold them the opposite way (if you can even figure out how). Difficult, isn't it? What if we asked you to do this not once, but every time you fold your arms from now on? It's not likely the new behavior would last long, regardless of the aspiration. The same is true for management practices—the habitual ways we get things done in our organizations.

That said, this is a rule of thumb, not a law. There are exceptions. Some companies do make a successful move from one archetype to another. In fact, one of them is Grupo Nacional Provincial, the insurer whose story appeared at the beginning of this chapter. GNP started out with the defining characteristics of the market-focus archetype, yet chose to aspire to an execution-edge archetype, and has succeeded in making it a reality.

If you've worked through all these considerations and still not found a leading contender for your choice of archetype, don't despair: there is good news. At this point, it's simply a matter of choosing any of the archetypes that fit your organization, and doing it well. Once an effective archetype is chosen and put into place, it is exceedingly difficult to imitate because of the complementarities at work—which takes us back to why organizational health is such a powerful source of competitive advantage.

We end with a warning. Don't be tempted to look at the list of archetypes and say "We need to be great at all of these." Keep in mind that being leadership driven doesn't mean that an organization isn't market focused, can't execute, and has no knowledge core. In the same way, being execution focused doesn't mean neglecting leadership, the market, and knowledge. Healthy companies are good at all 37 management practices;

as we saw earlier, that means they are above the bottom quartile for performance across the board. What makes them great, though, is choosing the right complementary few practices—between six and 10—to be the best at.

Involving a Broad Coalition in the Process

Now we know what organizational health is, how to measure it, and how to set aspirations for it by referring to the four archetypes. But who should be involved in this process: the CEO? The top team? A project team?

We've found that the best approach is to get a broad coalition of leaders personally involved in setting the aspirations. That's true for performance aspirations, too, but even more so for health because of the emphasis on complementarity. To get the full mutually reinforcing impact from tackling multiple management practices simultaneously, it's essential that units across the organization synchronize their efforts.

Our research shows that transformations designed through a large-scale organization-wide collaborative effort are 1.5 times more likely to succeed.[29] Why? Because such a process builds buy-in from the outset. That makes it far more effective in creating energy and commitment for execution. Later in the transformation, there's no delay while the organization waits for communications programs or process changes to kick in. People who have been involved in designing the program are already primed to help make it a reality.

To understand why collaboration is so powerful, consider a famous experiment where researchers ran a lottery with a twist. Half the participants were randomly assigned a numbered lottery ticket. The remaining half were given a blank ticket and a pen, and asked to choose their own lottery number. Just before drawing the winning number, the researchers offered to buy back all the tickets. They wanted to find out how much they would have to pay people who write their own number compared with people who are handed a number at random.

The rational expectation would be that there should be no difference, since a lottery is pure chance. Every number, whether chosen or assigned, should have the same value. A more savvy answer would be that you should pay people *less* if they write their own number, because of the possibility that numbers will be duplicated.

Neither of these turned out to be the right answer. Regardless of nationality or demographic group, people who wrote their own number always demanded at least *five times more* for their ticket.

This reveals an important truth about human nature. When we're personally involved in "authoring" an outcome, we are far more committed to it because we feel we own it. The underlying psychology relates to our need for control, which is a deep-rooted survival instinct.

Consider another experiment that examined the importance of a sense of control among elderly people in a nursing home.[30] Some of the residents were given the opportunity to decide how their rooms should be set out, and asked to choose a plant to look after. The others had no say in the layout of their rooms, and had a plant chosen and tended for them. After 18 months, the survival rate among residents who had control was 85 percent, but among those who had no control it was just 70 percent. It appears that our desire for control is strong enough to keep us alive.

How does this apply to setting aspirations in large organizations? Consider some examples. In 2003, when CEO Sam Palmisano spearheaded an effort to move toward a values-based management system at IBM, more than 50,000 employees were given an opportunity to "write their own lottery ticket" by taking part in a three-day online discussion forum (dubbed ValuesJam) to rewrite the company's century-old values. Out of this effort came a new set of values to guide decision making and behavior throughout the organization. Following the exercise, more than 200,000 employees—nearly 70 percent of the workforce—downloaded the "values manifesto" that emerged out of the discussion.

A similarly collaborative approach to problem solving was adopted by Neville Isdell when he took charge at Coca-Cola in 2004. Once a month for three months, he brought together his top 150 people in two-day "real work" sessions so that they could create a change story together.[31] The story was then rolled out across the organization via one- or two-day sessions in which small working groups explored the implications for their particular parts of the business.

If we go back to the Tata Motors case we featured earlier in the chapter, it's interesting to see how managing director Ravi Kant went about getting widespread ownership for the company's new aspirations. He was aware that seasoned managers who had achieved career success under more favorable market conditions might well be resistant to the kind of changes the company would have to make to weather the difficulties it faced. He discovered that the best approach was "not to give orders but to 'sell' new ideas internally." He comments, "The trick was how to expose people to the outside world to allow them to see what is happening there rather than drilling change into them through speeches and letters."[32]

Tata got its people to listen to customers talking about problems and suggesting product improvements, and took competitors' products apart to see how they compared to its own. As Kant admits, "This process took longer, of course, but unless you convince people about what you are asking them to do, they are not going to make it happen." As it turned out, slow was fast. In less than three years, the company had successfully reduced its break-even from nearly two-thirds of capacity to around a third.

Admittedly, not all transformations allow much time for pursuing co-creative approaches like these, especially when companies need to turn around their performance. When Idris Jala became CEO of the ailing Malaysian Airlines in 2005, "We had three and a half months to fix the problem, and if we didn't fix it by then we'd be bankrupt—we'd have no money for salaries, no money for fuel."[33] Yet despite the burning platform, Jala still managed to adopt a collaborative approach. After spending time with the P&L to understand where transformation was most needed (in costs, yield, and network efficiency), Jala assembled groups of 10 to 15 people from various functions and backgrounds—"all people who had a direct stake in a given activity"—and made them accountable for "big results fast."

Executives who adopt the "write your own lottery ticket" approach to aspiration setting are often surprised not only by the sense of ownership and drive for implementation that it creates, but by the quality of the answers that emerge. That doesn't necessarily make it easy to do, however, especially for decisive leaders who are used to coming up with their own solutions.

John Chambers, chairman and CEO of networking specialist Cisco Systems, observes that "It was hard for me at first to learn to be collaborative. The minute I'd get into a meeting, I'd listen for about 10 minutes while the team discussed a problem. I knew what the answer was, and eventually I'd say, 'All right, here's what we're going to do.' But when I learned to let go and give the team the time to come to the right conclusion, I found they made just as good decisions, or even better—and just as important, they were even more invested in the decision and thus executed with greater speed and commitment."[34]

■ ■ ■

At the end of the "aspire" stage of transformation you'll have answered the question "Where do we want to go?" for your organization. You'll have used your intuition as well as hard facts to arrive at concrete medium-term goals for health as well as performance—and you'll have made sure that these goals will stretch your organization without creating unintended consequences. You'll also have discovered what you need to do to reach your aspirations: namely, to bring all your management practices to a threshold level of health and excel at certain practices that reinforce one another and support your aspirations for performance. And you'll have gathered together a broad coalition of leaders to set these aspirations so that you ensure broad ownership from the start. That way, you'll unleash the energy your organization needs to achieve its goals.

People who have been through this process know how powerful it can be. We began the chapter with GNP, so let's hear what CEO Alejandro Baillères has to say about his experience: "Setting the aspiration was challenging, but also exhilarating. From there the journey only becomes more intense, taking those same two emotions and magnifying them tenfold."

As this suggests, completing all the steps in the aspire phase gives leaders a great feeling. It's a bit like the one you might get after poring over a stack of tourist brochures for that once-in-a-lifetime vacation and agreeing with your holiday companions on your dream destination. But before you pick up the phone and make the booking, do a quick reality check. Will you be able to pay for it? Can you find the time to get away? Are your flights and hotels available? Are you willing to put up with the inevitable hassles of a long journey?

Questions like these take us to the next phase: looking at where we want to go and assessing "How ready are we to go there?"

CHAPTER 4

Assess

How Ready Are We to Go There?

When Pierre Beaudoin took over the aerospace division at Bombardier in 2001, he knew he was in for a bumpy ride. Heading up the third-largest civil aircraft manufacturer in the world put him in a good position, but times were hard: 9/11 had sent shockwaves through the industry, and demand had taken a sharp downturn.

Decisive action was needed, so Beaudoin quickly put new performance objectives in place. Foremost among these was the lifting of the aerospace division's EBIT (earnings before interest and taxes) margin from 2 percent or 3 percent to 8 percent, an improvement that would deliver C$500 million to the bottom line. On the health side, the objectives were equally ambitious. Aware that its culture was focused on engineering (sometimes for its own sake) and that there were deep divisions between different functions, the aerospace division sought to improve its health within its existing execution-edge archetype so as to deliver continuous improvement for the benefit of the customer.

After assessing its capabilities, the division concluded that developing lean manufacturing skills would be the key to achieving its aspirations. But Beaudoin knew that a successful transformation would require more than skill building—it called for a deeper shift in mindsets as well. Instead of letting the engineers get straight to work on improving the hardware and systems, he insisted that the organization should take the time to understand what was happening below the surface. Bombardier was a leader in the business and regional aircraft segments, yet its customers didn't seem all that happy. What was missing?

As Beaudoin admits, probing cultural issues wasn't an approach that came naturally to an organization that prided itself on its technical exper-tise. "It was a challenge for me and for my leadership team to explain why we were spending so much time on the soft stuff when we could be fixing factories, hardware, airplanes. We had lots of conversations explaining that, if we did the soft stuff right, our employees, with our help, would be more able to do what they're supposed to do, like make our factories efficient and work on engineering problems. For Bombardier, that's a hard change."[1]

The inquiry into the soft stuff revealed some uncomfortable truths about how things got done at Bombardier. How come managers recognized there was a problem, but everyone insisted it wasn't in their department? Why was it that if someone brought up an issue, someone else would reply, "You don't understand this properly. Actually, we're really good"? Why were employees unable to say what their organization's goals and values were?

The results of the assessment revealed a shortlist of limiting beliefs that affected the value placed on individuals, the role of teamwork, the efforts for continuous improvement, and the drive for results. One area where change was urgently needed was in attitudes to handling problems. As Beaudoin explains, "Suppose I come to a meeting and hear about four problems, and I slam my fists on the table and say, 'I don't want to hear about problems any more; you guys are there to fix them.' Well, guess what—I'm not going to hear about problems. And that's how you get yourself in deep trouble." Airplanes are complex products, so there will be problems every day. "To get it right, the team has to work together, share the problems, fix them, [and] make our engineers comfortable bringing an issue to the table so we can give them the tools to fix it."

So did the efforts to dig below the surface prove worthwhile? In fact, they paid dividends. Not only did the division reach all its performance goals, but surveys showed that engagement among its 30,000 employees climbed more than 15 percent between 2004 and 2010. Both performance and health held firm during the deepest recession the industry has ever seen, demonstrating the organization's resilience to external shocks. Moreover, a survey of consumers carried out in 2010 rated Bombardier as one of the three most admired and trusted brands in Canada, and ranked its workplace as the second most admired.[2]

For Beaudoin, though, the biggest prize is his company's eagerness to keep improving: "What I like most . . . is that we now have an organization that wants to get better." So what difference has that made to life at Bombardier? "We used to make excuses for why our performance was good enough. Today we say, 'What will it take to get to world class?' That is what has changed."

For most leaders, once they've set their performance and health goals, it's tempting to move straight into action. In our experience, this is seldom wise, and often counterproductive. Organizations that succeed in their change efforts take the extra time to assess how ready they are for change. That means working out whether they have the capabilities and mindsets to fulfill their performance and health aspirations. In our 2010 survey, we found that organizations that rigorously assess their change readiness as part of their transformation effort are 2.4 times more likely to be successful than companies that skip this stage.[3] Here's further evidence that slow means fast when you're laying the groundwork for a successful transformation.

Let's now take a quick look at how to assess whether your organization has the capabilities it needs to achieve your performance aspirations. We'll then take a deeper dive into how to assess your organization's mindsets to see how far they support your health aspirations. Broadly speaking, it can be helpful to think of capabilities as your organization's "skill" and mindsets as its "will," although as we'll see, our approach to both these elements is wider than these terms might suggest.

Performance: Capability Platform

Assessing the capability platform of your organization takes place in a two-step process: determining the capabilities that matter most in terms of your performance aspirations, and then evaluating the state of these capabilities in your organization today. This is a vital part of the transformation process: our survey indicates that organizations that explicitly assess their current capabilities against those required to fulfill their performance aspirations are 6.6 times more likely to succeed in their transformation.

Determining the Capabilities that Matter

What capabilities does your organization need to fulfill its performance aspirations? This is a valuable question to ask and answer. Consider an organization that needs to do something to stop its margins being squeezed. Its natural response will be to cut costs. But what capabilities will it need to implement this strategy? The answer will depend on where it intends to achieve the savings. Will it look to lean manufacturing? Better procurement? Supply-chain redesign? A review of overhead costs? Having targeted one or more areas, it faces another question: How good does it need to be at these areas to capture the savings? And looking further ahead, which of them is worth investing in strategically? In other words, which might yield competitive advantage in the future?

Answering questions like these will give you a clear view of the institutional capabilities you'll need. For some capabilities, bringing them up to industry parity will be enough. For others, those that are truly strategic, you'll need to make a much bigger investment to build distinctiveness. Determining which capabilities are genuinely strategic is difficult, but crucial.

Our research and experience suggest that there are three tests for strategic capabilities: they are scarce within the industry, superior to substitutes, and difficult to imitate. Capabilities that satisfy all these tests are generally few in number; an organization seldom has more than three. Successful companies take the time to understand which strategic capabilities are important for achieving their performance aspirations. When P&G underwent its transformation, for instance, it identified three strategic capabilities in which it needed to be distinctive: brand building, innovation, and leveraging scale.

At first sight, it might seem that most savvy organizations would have a good idea of where their strategic capabilities lie. But that's not necessarily the case. In practice, the truly strategic capabilities may not be the ones that first spring to mind.

Consider McDonald's. That supply-chain management and marketing are strategic capabilities for the world's largest fast-food chain will come as a surprise to no one, but the company's most strategic capability is neither of these things. So what is it? As founder Ray Kroc once remarked, McDonald's isn't in the restaurant business, it's in the real-estate business. In fact, it didn't start to turn a profit until Kroc set up a realty company to purchase prime tracts of land both for his own use and for renting out to other franchisees.[4] The care that McDonald's puts into selecting exactly the right locations for the properties in its vast portfolio—320,000 restaurants in more than 100 countries—enables it to maintain a clear edge over the competition, especially when establishing strong footholds in developing markets such as Russia well ahead of the pack.[5]

Rather more obvious examples of strategic capabilities include BHP Billiton's low-cost mining operations, IBM's consultative sales force, Coke's brand, GE's control processes and culture, and Google's ability to attract and retain talent.

So it's worth spending some time deciding which of your organization's capabilities are strategically important in achieving your aspirations. Which capabilities are scarce, superior to substitutes, and difficult to imitate? These are the areas where you'll need to focus your attention.

Once you've identified your strategic capabilities, it's time to assess the shape they are in.

Assessing Your Current State

Having decided which capabilities are strategically important for achieving your aspiration, you can then undertake a structured inquiry into the current state of these capabilities in your organization. Simple though this may sound, caution is needed. Even the best-laid transformation plan can be undone if an organization overestimates its capabilities.

One mining company felt that its health and safety capability was strategically important, and was convinced it was best in class. But this belief didn't stand up to close examination. It turned out that the company's capability was only slightly better than the average for the industry, and certainly not distinctive enough to act as a platform for attracting skilled labor. If the company wanted to turn its health and safety capability into a source of competitive advantage, it had a lot of work to do.

A global manufacturer fell into the same trap. Having designed a growth program that depended on sharing best practices across its plants, it was dismayed to discover that its track record in this supposed strength was patchy at best.

So objectivity is vital. You'll need to conduct a thorough analysis to determine how far your capabilities secure cost advantages or deliver superior products and services. You'll also need to establish whether the capabilities are truly *institutional*—in other words, embedded as a permanent feature of your organization. Will they endure as generations of employees come and go? Or do they depend on a particular individual or group to maintain them?

In our experience, genuinely institutional capabilities are supported by three systems within an organization: technical, management, and behavioral, as shown in Exhibit 4.1.

To make this point clearer, we sometimes use a fishing analogy. When you go fishing, the technical system is about having the right equipment: a sturdy rod, a good reel, the right bait. The management system is about having the right structures and incentives: a fishing permit, a boat if you need it, a market for the fish, and a way to get them there. The behavioral system is about knowing how to fish, using the right techniques, and understanding the habits of the fish that you're likely to encounter.

Exhibit 4.1
Elements of an Institutional Capability

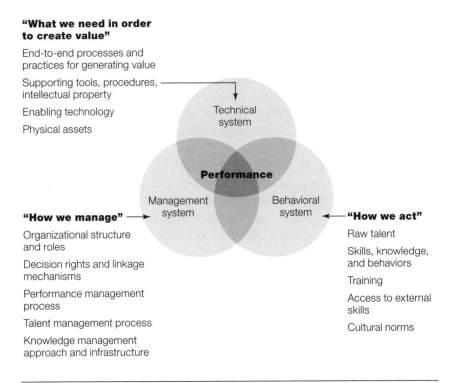

"What we need in order to create value"

End-to-end processes and practices for generating value

Supporting tools, procedures, intellectual property

Enabling technology

Physical assets

Technical system

Performance

Management system

Behavioral system

"How we manage" →

Organizational structure and roles

Decision rights and linkage mechanisms

Performance management process

Talent management process

Knowledge management approach and infrastructure

← **"How we act"**

Raw talent

Skills, knowledge, and behaviors

Training

Access to external skills

Cultural norms

Back in the business world, consider an organization that wants to make pricing a strategic capability. What changes will it need to make to these three systems?

In its technical system, the organization could change its pricing model from adding a percentage to the cost of the product ("cost plus") to understanding what customers are willing to pay to have their needs fulfilled ("value to customer"); switch from order-by-order selling tools to account planning tools; and move from treating all customers the same to using customer prioritization tools. In its management system, it might want to reorganize from a regional sales structure to a national customer-segment structure; change from price setting by the sales force to price setting by a commercial manager; and switch from monthly to weekly sales reporting.

In its behavioral system, it could consider moving from generic sales training programs to individual needs-based learning; switch its policy from
promoting from within to hiring from industries with sophisticated pricing practices; and move from an all-purpose coaching approach to a new
mentoring program that pairs up novices with pricing experts.

The mining company, whose health and safety capability wasn't as
distinctive as it thought, set about bringing it up to expectations in much
the same way by focusing on its technical, management, and behavioral
systems.

To upgrade its technical system, it invested in state-of-the-art health,
safety, and crisis-mitigation equipment for all its mines. Teams were provided with specialized emergency kits in case they were stranded under-
ground.

To upgrade the management system, the health and safety team studied
more than 50,000 safety incidents from both inside and outside the company
before revising its crisis plan. The exercise revealed that the power to make
decisions on health and safety matters was left not to senior management
but to line managers, who would often cut corners to finish tasks on time.
So the roles and responsibilities of the health and safety manager were
overhauled and a new management infrastructure was created. In addition,
each mining team was assigned its own health and safety champion, who
reported directly to the health and safety manager and had the right to shut
down the team's operation if their actions appeared to be unsafe. What's
more, senior leaders were required to include at least one performance goal
related to health and safety in their annual objectives.

To upgrade its behavioral system, the company revised its health and
safety training curriculum with input from leading industry experts. It
launched an "intervene if you think it's unsafe" campaign to ensure that
a safety mindset became part of the culture. Miners received 30 hours
of mandatory health and safety training per quarter to ensure that every
member of the workforce was up to date on the company's health and
safety practices.

As these examples suggest, all three systems—the technical, the management, and the behavioral—converge to create and support an institutional capability. But that doesn't answer the next question: How can you
make a sober assessment of your capabilities? There's a vast array of tools
to help you do just that—far too many, in fact, to list here. Many of them
are geared to specific capabilities, but most fall into a small number of categories: performance metric assessments and benchmarking; process mapping and "pain point" analyses; and observational assessments (grids that

break an institutional capability down into its component parts and describe what "poor," "good," and "great" look like so that you can compare the description with the reality at your organization). By selecting and using the right tools, you can arrive at a clear, fact-based evaluation of the reinforcements and shifts you have to make to strengthen the capabilities you need to fulfill your performance aspirations.

By the time you've determined which capabilities matter most in achieving your performance aspirations and assessed what state they are in at present, you'll be ready to plan the actions you need to take to get them to the right level. We'll look at that topic in the next chapter. First, though, we tackle the big question of how you assess the mindsets of the people in your organization.

Health: Discovery Process

So far we've discussed how to measure organizational health and how to determine what good health looks like for your organization. But if we find symptoms of ill health, how can we trace them back to root causes? As with our personal health, this isn't always simple. However, experience can tell us, or our doctor, where to look—and with organizational health, the place to look is at underlying mindsets. Mindsets drive behaviors, and behaviors support (or obstruct) the management practices that lead to good (or bad) organizational health.

Of course, mindsets matter in human health, too. Consider the predicament of people with heart disease. Years of research have shown that most cardiac patients can live considerably longer if they change their lifestyle by cutting out smoking and drinking, eating less fat, reducing their stress levels, and taking regular exercise. Indeed, many make a real effort to do so. Yet study after study has shown that 90 percent of people who have undergone surgery for heart disease revert to unhealthy behavior within two years.

That's a situation that Dean Ornish, a professor of medicine at the University of California at San Francisco and founder of the Preventative Medicine Research Institute, was determined to change.[6] He decided to try a new approach. Rather than focusing on the behaviors patients should adopt to survive, he decided to tackle their mindsets instead. As he said, "Telling people who are lonely and depressed that they're going to live longer if they quit smoking or change their diet and lifestyle is not that motivating. Who wants to live longer when you're in chronic emotional pain?"

Having realized that trying to motivate patients with a fear of dying wasn't getting him anywhere, Dr. Ornish turned the conventional approach on its head: he started trying to inspire them with the joy of living. How much better would they feel if they could enjoy the pleasures of daily life—making love, taking a hike, playing with their children or grandchildren—without suffering any pain or discomfort? Dr. Ornish put his patients on a low-fat vegetarian diet and helped smokers quit their habit. To help his patients make the right choices, he also offered them support groups and classes in relaxation, yoga, meditation, and aerobic exercise. It worked: 77 percent of his patients managed to make permanent changes in their lifestyles, as against a normal success rate of 10 percent.

As with people, so it is with organizations. To improve health, you need to trace issues back to the behaviors that shape them, and then go further still, to their root cause in shared mindsets. Bringing these mindsets to the surface and working with them explicitly is the only way to make sustainable change happen. Missing this step will doom any transformation to failure. In our 2010 survey, none of the companies that did no work on diagnosing mindsets rated their transformation programs as "extremely successful." Moreover, companies that did go below the surface to identify deep-seated mindsets were four times more likely than those that didn't to rate their transformations as "successful."

Now let's take a look at why mindsets matter. We'll also describe the scientific evidence underpinning our approach and explain how to uncover underlying mindsets by using the discovery process.

The Hidden Drivers of Outward Behavior

Having set clear aspirations for organizational health that target changes in specific management practices, surely we're ready to start changing people's behavior? Not yet.

If we tackle behavior head on, we're likely to waste time and energy, alienate those around us, and suffer a host of unintended consequences. At this point, we may well concede that the skeptics were right to claim that there's no reliable way to manage the soft stuff. So where have we gone wrong? We've overlooked a vital fact: people's behavior is driven by their mindsets.

We define a mindset quite simply as a fixed mental attitude or outlook that predetermines how people interpret situations and respond to them. In an organization, the interactions between members, leaders, and the external environment go to make up a set of shared mindsets that underpin "how things get done around here." These mindsets in turn spawn a myriad of predictable behaviors.

That's why mindsets are the highest leverage point for management time and energy. Chasing behavioral change *without* addressing mindsets is like playing Whac-A-Mole in an amusement arcade. You pound one mole into its hole only to find many more moles popping up all around you.

To see how much mindsets shape our actions, let's take an example: the assumption that our colleagues are well intentioned and capable. This mindset creates trust and encourages behaviors such as sharing information, asking for and offering help, and being decisive. When it's absent, people hoard information, seek control, and suspect others' motives. Employees who lack this mindset don't seem to miss it, or notice negative consequences like these. But if we can show them the damage the mindset causes and persuade them to adopt a different perspective, countless tiny day-to-day actions can be transformed for the better.

Take a company that wants to introduce a lean production system. Part of the change will be about defining new processes, systems, and behaviors to eliminate waste and reduce variability, and then embodying them in standardized working methods and manuals. But if the transformation stops there, its effect is unlikely to last for long. It will be all too easy for people to lapse back into old familiar working patterns, and any benefits will be short lived.

Now consider how different things would be if the company also addressed people's mindsets. If employees were encouraged to see inventory not as an asset but as a liability, how would their behavior change? If managers stopped seeing reporting as a quarterly activity and understood it as a real-time management tool, how would it affect the way they work? What if the organization no longer saw people as an expense, but recognized them as an asset? If it regarded the purpose of frontline jobs not as execution, but as the engine of continuous improvement? If it saw improvements in cost, quality, and service not as trade-offs, but as elements that could be successfully combined?

We once worked with a retailer that was struggling to improve the performance of its sales staff. When we explored employees' mindsets, we found that average performers and high performers had very different ways of looking at their work. The first important difference was in their view of customers. Many average performers believed that customers had decided before they even came through the door whether they were going to make a purchase or simply look at the merchandise, head home, and do their shopping online. These average performers also felt they were highly skilled at identifying which customers were which. In sharp contrast, high-performing sales staff believed that *everyone* who walked through the door might make a purchase.

The second key difference related to how staff viewed coaching from their boss. Average performers viewed it as something that happened when they'd done something wrong, and avoided it as far as they could. But high performers actively sought out coaching from their boss. They believed that as in sport, the coach is more likely to spend time with the star player than with someone who's about to be dropped from the team.

The Power of Mindsets

Any skeptics still unconvinced of the power of mindsets should consider Roger Bannister's story. Until the mid-1950s, the four-minute mile was regarded as beyond human achievement. Even medical journals judged it unattainable. Yet in May 1954, Bannister smashed through the barrier with a time of 3 minutes, 59.4 seconds. How did he do it? In his memoirs, Bannister explained that he spent as much time conditioning his mind as his body. He wrote that "the mental approach is all-important ... energy can be harnessed by the correct attitude of mind."[7]

What is perhaps more amazing is that two months later the four-minute barrier was broken again, by Australian John Landy. Within three years, 16 other runners had followed suit.

So what had happened? A sudden spurt in human evolution? A new super-race of genetically engineered runners? Of course not. It was the same physical equipment, but with a different mindset: one that said, "This can be done."

Are there any four-minute miles in your organization? If a few people could break through them, would you be able to unleash a new level of performance, just as Roger Bannister's attitude of mind unlocked a new level of achievement among athletes?

That's exactly what happens at successful organizations. In 1997, when Coca-Cola faced limited growth options in a mature market, it shifted its mindset from "We sold 1 billion servings of soft drinks this year" to "We've got 47 billion servings of beverages yet to go" (the number of worldwide beverage servings including bottled water, coffee, and tea). This way of thinking opened the door to a new set of growth opportunities that the company had never considered before.

Another vivid illustration of the power of mindsets involves a man named Abraham Wald who was in charge of assessing how vulnerable airplanes were to enemy fire during World War II. Statistics showed that some parts of planes were hit more often than others. Military leaders wanted to have these parts reinforced to minimize damage. Wald took a different view, arguing that the parts hit *least* often should be the ones that were protected. He surmised that if planes were hit in a critical area, it was unlikely they would make it back to base. Those planes that were able to return probably hadn't been hit in a critical area. Thus, he reasoned, reinforcing parts of planes that had sustained many hits would be unlikely to pay off.

How many well-intentioned people are hard at work reinforcing damaged parts of your organization? And how much more productive would their efforts be if they challenged prevailing assumptions about how and why work gets done?

Look at the case of the CIO of a large financial services firm in the midst of one of the largest mergers in the sector's history. As employees grappled with the challenge of reducing the cost base of the combined entity by one-fifth, the CIO turned the problem on its head. He asked, "If we double our transactions [as the firm did thanks to the merger], by what percent will our costs rise in the two legacy organizations?" Since the infrastructure costs were largely fixed, the answer was quite small. When employees started thinking about the challenge from this different perspective, it suddenly seemed much more modest, and perfectly achievable.

In *Competing for the Future*, Gary Hamel and C. K. Prahalad describe a hypothetical experiment that powerfully illustrates how today's experience becomes tomorrow's theology. Four monkeys sit in a cage that has a bunch of bananas hanging from the roof, accessible by a set of steps. Whenever the monkeys try to climb the steps to get to the bananas, they are blocked by a blast of cold water. After a few days, the monkeys give up climbing the steps. Researchers then remove the water hose and replace one of the original monkeys with a new one. Seeing the bananas, it starts up the steps. What happens? The other monkeys, being social creatures, pull it down before it gets blasted with water. This happens again and again until pretty soon the new monkey doesn't bother to go for the bananas either.

Over the next few weeks, the researchers remove the rest of the original monkeys one at a time and replace them with new monkeys who've never seen the jet of water. Even though there's no longer anything to stop the monkeys reaching the bananas, the new monkey is always pulled down by the others before it gets to the top of the steps. By the end of the experiment not a single monkey has ever seen a jet of water, but none of them tries to climb the steps. They've all learned the rule that "You don't grab the bananas around here."

How many of your employees are holding back from taking steps that would improve the performance of your organization simply because they've become accustomed to "the way things are done around here"?

Sometimes you need to make a decisive break with the past, as IBM's history illustrates. It had developed a proud technocratic tradition at a time when the market was ruled by mainframe computing. As the market shifted, however, it had to recognize and challenge the mindsets that were preventing it from moving to a new focus on customer solutions. Looking back, CEO Lou Gerstner observes that "I can recall numerous occasions in the early days when I would outline a change I thought was necessary, and my team would say: 'Oh, we tried that before and it didn't work.'" But Gerstner had to stick to his guns: "I couldn't explore the 'befores' or I'd learn all the reasons not to change."[8] By making a determined effort to stop looking back and look forward instead, IBM was able to enter the next era of growth and profitability.

In companies with long histories and long-serving employees, we find it can often be helpful to encourage people to think in terms of eras so that they understand that ways of thinking that served them well in the past may not work so well in the future.

The Evidence that Mindsets Matter

Advances in neuroscience have made it possible to undertake direct observation of the human brain, generating a vast amount of experimental data and a range of theories to explain what's going on inside our heads. Complex though an individual human brain is, an organization is even more so. When groups of people get together to negotiate and make decisions, a whole host of unique mindsets come into play. And groups are also susceptible to "groupthink" and other biases that can limit their flexibility and hinder their performance.

Leaders who want to understand the scientific arguments for why mindsets matter to performance have a considerable body of work at their disposal. In their book *The Unbounded Mind*, Ian Mitroff and Harold Linstone examine the need to change key assumptions to move from old ways of thinking to "unbounded systems thinking." Peter Senge analyzes how mindsets can limit or contribute to organizational learning in books such as *The Fifth Discipline*. Carol Dweck's book *Mindset: The New Psychology of Success* compares the impact on performance of "fixed" versus "growth" mindsets in the arenas of business, education, parenting, and relationships.

Edward Russo and Paul Schoemaker emphasize the impact of mindsets on the quality of decision making in *Decision Traps* and *Winning Decisions*. In *Creating the Corporate Future* and other works, Russell Ackoff argues that planning should be approached by challenging fundamental mindsets through a process of "idealized design": starting with the desired end state and working back to the objectives needed to reach it. More rigorous academic analysis can be found in the research of Chris Argyris, particularly in his accounts of the "ladder of inference" (showing how subconscious thought processes are biased by preconceived beliefs) and "double-loop learning" (explaining how underlying mindsets and assumptions affect the learning process).[9]

Some of the best-known research on the power of mindsets was done by Timothy Gallwey in his investigation into how people develop excellence in a variety of sporting and working contexts. He posited that our performance is equal to our potential minus the interference that gets in the way (sometimes expressed in the equation $P = p - i$), and argued that much of this interference is created by self-imposed constraints that come from fear, self-doubt, lapses in focus, and limiting assumptions. These mindsets fill our heads with self-criticism, hesitation, and over-analysis, making our actions awkward, mistimed, and ineffective. As Gallwey explained, "There is always an inner game being played in your mind no matter what outer game you are playing. How aware you are of this game can make the difference between success and failure."[10]

Uncovering underlying mindsets and shifting them is at the heart of making change happen. It also accounts for much of the frustration experienced by those who try to lead change in organizations. As George Lakoff, a professor of cognitive science and linguistics at the University of California at Berkeley, states, "Concepts [or mindsets] are not things that can be changed just by someone telling us a fact. We may be presented with facts, but for us to make sense of them, they have to fit what is already in the synapses of the brain. Otherwise, facts go in and then they go right back out. They are not heard, or they are not accepted as facts, or they mystify us: Why would anyone have said that? Then we label the fact as irrational, crazy, or stupid." According to Lakoff, political debates fall foul of the same syndrome. Conservatives and liberals don't understand each other and may even think the other side is mad because they are approaching the facts with different mindsets.[11]

Underlying mindsets can do more than form obstacles that block change efforts; they can also unravel them, sometimes in baffling ways. In a series of studies conducted at the University of Michigan in 2005 and 2006, researchers found that when misinformed people were exposed to accurate information in news stories, they rarely changed their minds. On the contrary, they often became even more strongly wedded to their beliefs. Far from *curing* misinformation, the facts were actively perpetuating it.

According to the lead researcher on the study, political scientist Brendan Nyhan, "The general idea is that it's absolutely threatening to admit you're wrong." He describes this phenomenon, known as "backfire," as "a natural defense mechanism to avoid that cognitive dissonance."[12] How many leaders have been surprised by backfire from their organizations when attempting to make change happen? Our guess would be many, perhaps even most—especially in the 70 percent of change programs that fail.

Given the wealth of scientific evidence for the power of mindsets, we might expect every business school or management seminar to teach leaders how to address them effectively. Far from it: in fact, leaders of transformations have little in the way of established methods or proven tools for assessing the mindsets in their organization. Although such methods and tools do exist, and are well tested in other fields, they have yet to be widely applied in the business world. We suspect that the reason, ironically enough, may lie in a prevailing mindset: the conviction that such investigations should be left for the psychologist's couch rather than undertaken by leaders in the workplace.

To be sure, working with mindsets will always have a degree of art to it—probably more, in fact, than any other aspect of managing a transformation. But that shouldn't deter leaders from venturing into unfamiliar territory. Remember, perfection is not the goal. Plenty of us take art classes without expecting to end up like Picasso or Rembrandt. We may not paint masterpieces worth millions, but by learning the basics of composition and technique, we can become better artists.

Too many managers think that shifting mindsets is beyond them—something that can be done only by masters of the art. Their reticence dooms their efforts to little more than the change-management equivalent of finger painting. If instead they are prepared to learn about mindsets and follow a few basic steps, they can greatly increase their ability to make change happen.

Approaches to Assessing Mindsets

So how can leaders uncover shared mindsets in their organizations and understand how they are linked to behaviors and ultimately to performance? To provide an answer, we developed what we call the discovery process—a

Exhibit 4.2
The Discovery Process

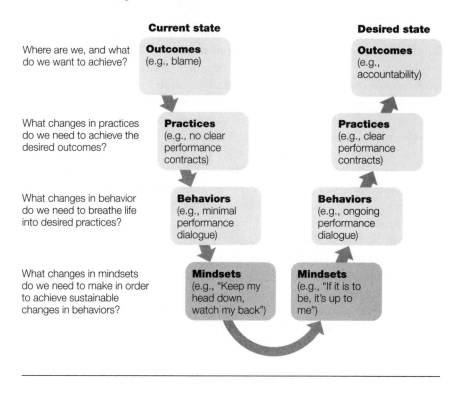

deep dive into an organization's inner workings that is summarized schematically in Exhibit 4.2.

As the diagram shows, using the discovery process involves looking at both your current state of health and your desired state as you defined it during the "aspire" stage of your transformation. Your state of health encompasses both *outcomes*—elements of health such as accountability—and the *practices* that underlie them, such as performance contracts and consequence systems. These practices are brought to life by employees' behaviors, which are in turn governed by their underlying mindsets.

The discovery process enables you to determine what behaviors you need to shift to allow your organization to adopt the desired practices. It then helps you to look beneath these behaviors into the root-cause mindsets that explain why hard-working and well-intentioned people are choosing to behave in the way that they do. Many ingrained mindsets are held at the subconscious or unconscious level, so the goal of the discovery process is to bring them to the forefront of consciousness where they can be examined.

Because mindsets lie below what we can readily observe, they are seldom scrutinized. The business thinker Chris Argyris calls them the "undiscussables." Yet they represent the highest leverage point for interventions to improve organizational health. What this means in practical terms is that engineering small shifts in mindsets enables companies to bring about much bigger shifts in behavior to support the practices they want to adopt to reach their desired state.

So why are mindsets so powerful? By way of analogy, consider the following text:

Aoccdrnig to rsceearh at an Elingsh uinervtisy, it deosn't mttaer waht oredr the ltteers of a wrod are in so lnog as the frist and lsat ltteers are in the rghit pcleas. The rset can be a toatl mses and you can sitll raed wuothit a porbelm.[13]

Just as a bit of context enables us to make sense of writing that's full of errors, so our mindsets tend to interpret the huge amounts of information available to us by filtering out some things and amplifying others—especially those that reinforce our existing beliefs.

In order to help managers navigate through the discovery process and get below the surface to uncover mindsets, we've developed a number of tools and approaches. The first is an interview-based technique called "laddering." The second takes place in focus groups using techniques such as collages and card sorting. The third involves analyzing patterns of words in texts created by or about an organization. Taken together, these tools enable leaders to bring a far greater degree of rigor to bear on the "soft stuff" than they were ever able to apply in the past.

Let's begin with the interview-based technique called "laddering." This approach is grounded in the theory of personal change set out by Dennis Hinkle in his 1965 doctoral thesis entitled *The Change of Personal Constructs from the Viewpoint of a Theory of Implications*. Hinkle argues that the more abstract or deeply held a personal construct (or mindset) is, the harder it is to change. In order to probe an individual's personal constructs, Hinkle developed a method of inquiry he described as "laddering," which essentially involves asking someone *why* they hold a particular opinion over and over again.

A greatly simplified version of a conversation using the laddering technique is shown in Exhibit 4.3. It works like this. Interviewees are asked about

Exhibit 4.3
Drilling Down to Underlying Mindsets

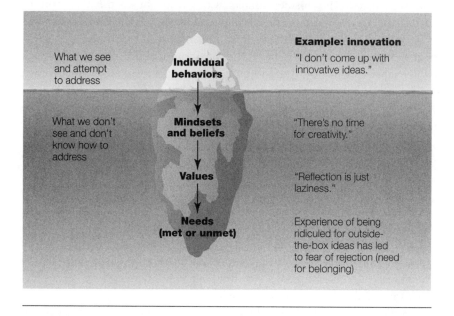

their observed behavior through a series of why questions that probes beneath the surface. The idea is that the "ladder" of questions prompts people to reflect on their deepest motivations, and eventually leads them to state the values and assumptions through which they construct their personal world. The technique originated in clinical psychology, but has been applied in business in both marketing and the field of organizational change.

Even the hardest-nosed business operator can feel comfortable with this technique. That's because it closely resembles the "five whys" approach that lean organizations use to get to the root causes of performance problems. Before they try to fix a given issue, lean practitioners ask why as many times as it takes to understand the problem fully. (Five questions are often enough to do the trick, hence the five whys.)

Take a classic textbook example. If a motor breaks down, a lean-minded operator won't just replace it but ask why. "Because it overheated," comes the reply. Why? "Because it wasn't properly ventilated." Why? "Because the machine is too close to the wall." The operator then moves the machine away from the wall before replacing the motor.

Without the probing for why, the fix would have been only temporary. The new motor would have soon burned out for lack of ventilation. Addressing the root cause produces a better and more durable solution. In much the same way, asking why about mindsets leads to insights into the points that offer most scope for improving organizational health.

So how can we drill down to the mindsets that shape individuals' understanding of the world? We're talking about people here, so naturally it's a bit more complicated than finding out why a motor keeps breaking down. The questions still revolve around why, but they involve a range of different techniques: *storytelling* (eliciting a colorful and detailed narrative by asking about heroes, legends, or war stories); *provocations* (making deliberately exaggerated statements to prompt an emotional reaction); *role playing* (putting the interviewee into a realistic work situation or someone else's shoes); *circling* (closing the loop between the current conversation and previous statements); and *hypotheticals* (describing imaginary scenarios and asking how they would play out).

An example will bring the discovery process to life. A bank conducted a benchmarking exercise and found that its sales per banker were lagging the competition. By posing a few fairly superficial why questions, management discovered that bankers weren't spending enough time with customers, largely because administration took up much of their day. So the bank set about reengineering its loan-origination process to minimize paperwork and maximize customer-facing time. In addition, it gave bankers new sales scripts and more easy-to-use tools to help them put the extra customer contact to good use. After training the bankers in the new processes and tools, executives thought they had the problem licked.

Six months later, they were dismayed to discover that the level of improvement was much lower than they had expected. Frustrated, they applied the discovery process using the laddering technique to drill down to the root causes of the disappointing results. They asked a sequence of carefully constructed questions such as "What does it feel like to do administrative tasks? . . . Who decides how much time you spend in front of customers? . . . Don't you want to spend more time with customers? . . . Let's role play—you are selling me a loan that is 0.9 percentage points higher than the competition. . . . How did that feel? . . . Do you enjoy being a salesperson? . . . What are the best and worst parts of your day?"

A simple but hitherto unsuspected reason for the poor sales soon emerged: most of the bankers preferred paperwork to people. Interacting with customers made them uncomfortable, so they actively sought reasons to avoid it. Further investigation uncovered the causes of the bankers' discomfort: a combination of introverted personalities, poor interpersonal skills, and a sense of inferiority when dealing with customers who had more money and a better education than they did.

To make matters worse, most supervisors had started out as bankers, and tended to be equally insecure in their selling and interpersonal skills and equally focused on managing paper-based activities. Moreover, most bankers hated thinking of themselves as salespeople. They thought it made them sound like hucksters at a used-car lot. To them, the bank's efforts to create more time for them to sell felt like a violation of their professional identity.

Armed with these insights into the root causes of poor sales performance, the bank adjusted its change program to address the mindset challenges directly (Exhibit 4.4). Not only did this put the program back on track within six months, it also delivered sustainable sales gains in excess of the original targets.

As the bank could confirm, laddering is a powerful technique for identifying mindsets that may be blocking change. However, in large and diverse organizations, it isn't always practical to use an approach that involves working with individuals. Our second technique provides a way of working with groups of employees instead.

Focus groups are a valuable tool, but they have their shortcomings. Chief among these is the risk of eliciting "groupthink" responses. Fortunately, there are a few approaches that a savvy organization can use to bypass groupthink and cut straight through to genuine personal perceptions. An approach that we've often seen work well is to lay a selection of pictures on a table and ask participants to choose two images: one that represents how the organization appears to them and another that represents how they would like it to be. Where appropriate, this approach can be targeted to specific business challenges. For instance, frontline employees can be asked "Which image represents what it's like to sell to customers?"

The benefit of using pictures is that they trigger a much more honest and visceral conversation than asking stock questions like "What's it like to work around here?" ever could. When someone chooses a picture of a traffic jam for the way things are and a picture of a free-flowing motorway for the way they'd like them to be, the message comes over loud and clear. A handy side-benefit is that the images representing employees' ideal organization can be adopted in the communications program later, thus forging a link between people's passions and the themes in the change effort. After people have chosen images individually, the wider group can go on to create collages that summarize how they collectively feel about their work.

Exhibit 4.4
Linking Laddering to Business Realities

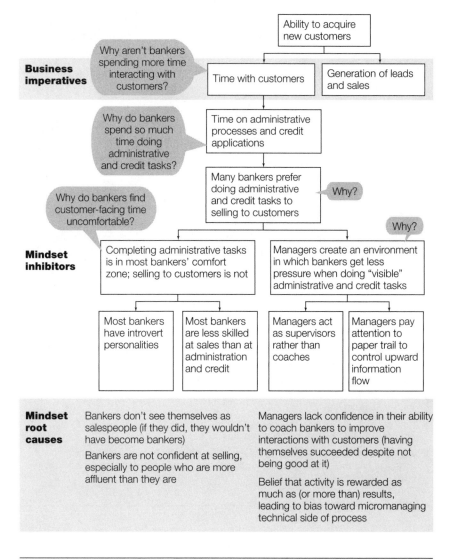

A Focus Group Collage

1. "It's a zoo out here!"
2. "Stressed is how you feel most of the time. You constantly face roadblocks, and have to jump through hoops for people."
3. "If you do a good job, it definitely makes you happy."
4. "We have pride in our product. We build a great product. You won't find a better one in the world, guaranteed."
5. "Kids get sick, and you want your boss to care about your kids. They need to stop worrying about who they can fire for what."
6. "Managers don't get in trouble; just the workers do. All they care about is their schedule and their paperwork. They claim they care about quality, but schedule is the most important thing."

Another useful method to cut to the chase in focus groups is card sorting. Here, up to 50 statements that list various reasons for why the organization might be facing its current situation are printed on separate cards. Participants are asked to divide them into vital, interesting, and unimportant. They then talk about the reasons behind their choices. This enables the organization to explore critical areas in depth, to establish overall group priorities, and to identify areas of misalignment.

One manufacturing organization used the card-sorting exercise with great success to explore why it was suffering repeated shutdowns. It started by using employee focus groups to help identify possible reasons. The groups came up with a list of 30 statements ranging from "The right way to do things exists in the heads of a few experienced individuals" to "Standard procedures are considered optional" to "Operations, maintenance, and technical groups don't all work seamlessly as one team." Each reason was put on a card, and then a cross-section of the organization was asked to sort the cards in the way we've just described. When the company knew which statements most staff classified as important, it followed up by probing them in more depth. The "Aha" moment came when it uncovered the prevailing mindset that maintaining a quick production turnaround always took priority, even if it meant factory workers had to sidestep a few maintenance procedures.

Whether conducted through interviews or focus groups, the discovery process represents a change intervention in itself. Both interviewer and interviewee come away with a much better understanding of the mindsets that help or hinder performance. Once subconscious elements are brought to consciousness, it's possible to examine an individual's current and potential role in maintaining constructive mindsets and shifting unconstructive ones.

Using a skilled and objective third party to help with interviews and focus groups can be helpful, but we often suggest that the leadership team should take part too. This is what lean manufacturing executives call *genchi genbutsu* or "go and see": head for where things are happening and find out what is actually going on.

The third tool for understanding mindsets comes from the social science methodology known as qualitative data analysis (QDA). This method can be utilized at scale to help large organizations mine rich sources of textual data such as reports, websites, advertisements, internal communications, and press coverage. QDA uses a number of techniques ranging from the tracking of word patterns to deeper linguistic analysis, all designed to discover themes emerging from texts created by individuals or organizations.

One technique involves analyzing how often words are repeated in a particular text or texts as a proxy for what matters to an organization. The results are then processed by visualization software to generate a "word cloud," in which the size of each word reflects how often it has been used.

The value of word clouds comes not just from the insights that they yield individually, but also from the conclusions that can be drawn by putting together word clouds from different sources: public or private, formal or informal. Setting two examples alongside one another can expose blind spots—places where an organization espouses one set of values or standards but enacts another. There's a good chance that blocking mindsets will be at work somewhere in this conflict.

Another revealing technique is to set word clouds developed from internal texts alongside an organization's stated values and formal leadership standard. One large public sector institution had spent a lot of time defining and communicating a set of values concerned with quality, collaboration, accountability, customer focus, and efficiency. To see what impact these efforts had had, the organization distilled its broadcast online communications—manager blogs, broadcast e-mails, discussion boards, internal websites—to produce a word cloud.

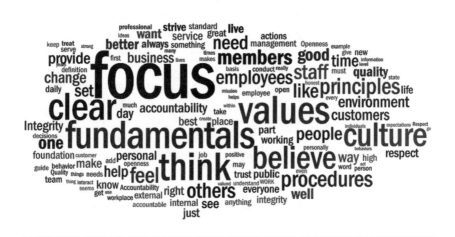

The results (see above) came as a shock to executives. Some of the core values were barely featured in the word cloud; others weren't there at all. After so much effort, why weren't people talking about them? And if they weren't *talking* about the values, they probably weren't *thinking* about them either—or, more to the point, *living* them.

Drastic action was clearly needed: not just an overhaul of communications, but a raft of measures that would make the values part of people's lives. So the organization introduced new training programs, made changes in performance evaluation, and asked its senior team to act as role models so that employees would see them embodying the values as they went about their daily work.

Focusing on the Vital Few

The goal of the discovery process is to identify mindsets that should be strengthened and reinforced, as well as those that might create barriers to organizational health. However, the latter are particularly important because of our tendency to cling to mindsets that used to be valid in the past. If the transformation program requires people to abandon old mindsets and adopt new ones, it must address the shift explicitly. Without correction, old mindsets can make it impossible to adopt new practices.

Shifting mindsets is a gradual process, and we'd advise organizations not to take on too many at once. Tackling three to five "from/to" shifts over a 12- to 18-month period would be a reasonable target. Keeping the list short acknowledges that you have limited time and resources to do the work involved, and allows you to focus on the desired end state.

So how do you choose the shifts that matter most? It takes reflection, discussion, and judgment. You need to understand your performance and health aspirations, the state of your health, and what your employees really care about.

One global financial services institution was grappling with traders' less than constructive attitude toward risk taking. On numerous occasions, it had found itself in peril after a succession of separate actions by different traders had caused a slow build-up of risk over time. Whenever such a situation arose, the bank would heroically save itself—which served only to reinforce traders' mindsets that they were free to take more and more risk.

Investigation revealed that traders saw generating revenue as far more important than the risk a particular trade might pose. At a deeper level, they found the buzz of last-minute risk mitigation exciting, and felt that all the firefighting gave them more status in the eyes of others. Once this mindset had been properly understood and brought to awareness, work could begin on developing the more constructive mindsets needed in the future. The organization developed a set of "from/to" statements that included shifting from "brilliant risk trouble-shooting in response to a crisis" to "vigilance and measured action in anticipation of potential risks" and from "degree of hunger for all revenue opportunities" to "fundamental loss of appetite for revenue with inappropriate risk."

In another case, a large retailer bent on delighting the customer empha-sized perfection in everything it did. Any decision connected with getting products into customers' hands had to be vetted by multiple stakeholders via multiple rounds of consultation. Although the aim was to make customers happy, no one had stopped to ask whether all this activity genuinely boosted customer satisfaction or sales.

Many consumer panels later, the retailer learned that far from being excited by its products, customers saw it as reliable but dated. So it decided to shift from a perfectionist mindset to one focused on progress. "Delighting customers" was redefined as moving ahead with good ideas and getting innovative products to the customer at the right time. This approach helped the retailer establish a successful online presence well ahead of its competitors, and dramatically improved its customer preference ratings.

If we look back on all the work we've done on mindsets, the "from/to" shifts that recur most often are those that relate to moving from a transactional to relational way of working, from working in silos to collaborating where it counts, and from assigning blame to taking accountability. Typical examples of these shifts are illustrated in Exhibit 4.5.

It's important to note, though, that the shifts don't always have to be *from* one mindset *to* another. For many organizations, the choice is not "either/or" but "both/and." This is especially true for those aiming for a "good to great" transition rather than a turnaround. Instead of losing the benefit of existing mindsets, they need to build on them to take the organization to the next level.

Some organizations get the best results by combining from/to mindset shifts with the both/and variety. Consider the National Health Service (NHS) in England, a complex group of government-funded organizations providing health-care services that are in most cases free to the patient at the point of delivery. The NHS is a massive entity employing over 1.3 million people, and with a budget of £110 billion (US$176 billion). Since becoming its CEO in September 2006, Sir David Nicholson has been working to improve the performance and health of the system, in part by focusing on a clear set of mindset shifts that combines either/or with both/and approaches.

Having used the discovery process to assess mindsets, Sir David and the NHS Management Board found that there was a strong sense of accountability in each of the individual organizations that make up the NHS. Though positive in itself, this mindset had the unintended consequence of not supporting the kind of collaboration between organizations that would bring further benefits to patients. So the need here was to achieve a both/and shift in mindset: *both* to retain the strong sense of individual accountability *and* to expand the view of what that accountability was for so that it became "what is best for the patient."

Exhibit 4.5
Focusing on a Few Critical Shifts

From transactional . . .

"I am responsible for quickly and efficiently meeting the needs my clients express."

"Probing my clients about their financial situation would be prying into their private affairs."

"Account opening is a chore to be done by junior sales staff."

. . . to relational

"I am responsible for bringing the best of my company to clients and addressing their needs whether articulated or not."

"I need to understand my clients' full situation before I can give them the best advice."

"Account opening is potentially the most important client interaction of all."

From silos . . .

"My success depends on optimizing my area."

"I know what's right for my area and no one else can achieve what I can."

"I view other areas as a hindrance— they are incompetent and selfish."

. . . to collaboration

"My success depends on optimizing my company's results."

"I can learn from others and there is great value in 'mining the seams' together."

"There is no 'they'—I assume that other people are competent and show goodwill."

From blame . . .

"The problems we face are beyond my control."

"There is a lack of clarity regarding accountabilities around here."

"I show up at every meeting so I can watch my back."

. . . to accountability

"If I'm not part of the solution, I'm part of the problem."

"I seek to clarify my and others' accountabilities if they are unclear."

"I trust others to do what they are supposed to do in a fair manner."

This collaborative mindset proved helpful in planning for the Quality, Innovation, Productivity and Prevention (QIPP) initiative in 2008, which aimed to identify £15 to £20 billion (US$24 to US$32 billion) of productivity improvements in the space of four years. Local NHS organizations worked together—often for the first time—to develop regional plans, while hospitals and social care providers ceased competing with one another and began sharing best practices and transferring knowledge. The effort helped the

NHS identify opportunities to reduce the risk of stroke in patients with atrial fibrillation by 50 percent to 70 percent, which is expected to save up to 4,000 lives a year and deliver savings of £134.5 million (US$215 million).

By contrast, another prevailing mindset—that "innovation is risky"—was holding back improvements in care. Here, there was a clear need for a from/to shift, to "innovation is necessary." Innovation was central not only in improving productivity but also in areas as diverse as waste management, breast-cancer screening, the prevention of hospital-acquired infection, and catheter management. Having adopted the "to" mindset, an acute medical unit at Ipswich Hospital introduced a system for managing pulmonary embolism on an outpatient basis. The system is now used in 95 percent of cases, saving the hospital 1,000 bed days a year. The unit has gone on to devise tools and techniques to roll out the innovation on a national scale. If successful, it could save the NHS 217,000 bed days and £65 million (US$104 million) a year.

The transformation of such a huge and complex entity as the NHS will take some time to complete. However, early results have been highly positive. One example can be seen in the ratings of NHS Trusts. These are independent health-care entities such as hospitals, ambulance providers, and payors that are regulated by the government, but have their own board and CEO, and enjoy relative freedom to define their agenda and manage budgets. The number of trusts rated as "excellent" rose more than sixfold between 2006 and 2008, and those classed as "weak" fell from nearly 10 percent of the total in 2006 to just 5 percent.

A final consideration for organizations tackling mindset shifts is the *sequencing* of the shifts. The trick is to start with the fundamental shifts that will make the biggest difference. When universal bank ANZ faced this decision, the senior team chose to focus for the first 18 months on establishing a shared direction, creating a baseline of trust, and developing a sense of personal accountability. Once these elements were sufficiently embedded, the team worked on mindsets related to innovation, people development, and customer focus for the next 18 months. Attempting to tackle all six themes at once, or in a different order, could easily have fragmented the effort and weakened its impact.

The Process of Assessment

In 210 BC, a Chinese commander named Xiang Yu led his troops across the Yangtze River to attack the army of the Qin dynasty. Camping for the night on the bank of the river, they awoke to find their ships on fire. They rushed to take on their attackers, only to find that it was their own leader who had set the ships ablaze. Not only that, he'd had all their cooking pots smashed. Without the pots and the ships, he knew that his army had no choice but to fight their way to victory or die trying. Xiang Yu's seeming sabotage created tremendous focus in his troops, who fought ferociously and won nine consecutive battles, obliterating their opponents.

That's a perfect example of what's often referred to as "deficit-based" change: "We've got a problem, let's fix it." This model identifies the problem ("What is the need?"), analyzes causes ("What's wrong here?"), considers possible solutions ("How can we fix it?"), and then plans and takes action ("Problem solved"). Advocates of this approach argue that its linear logic—dissecting things to understand them—is at the heart of all scientific progress made by western civilization.

Deficit-based change has become the dominant model taught in business schools, and the default option for most organizations. However, there are drawbacks to this approach. Research by David Cooperrider, Suresh Srivastava, Diana Whitney, and others in the field of appreciative inquiry—a discipline concerned with how to engage people in an organization to make change happen—has shown that a relentless focus on what's wrong is unsustainable, invokes blame, and creates fatigue and resistance. People have no opportunity to use their passions and experience, or to celebrate their successes.

Hence a rival model has arisen: the "constructionist" approach to change. Here, the plan is to find out what is working well today, imagine what life would be like if it happened more often, put plans in place to make it so, and then execute them. Result: you get more of what works.[14]

In a study carried out at the University of Wisconsin, two bowling teams were filmed in action. Each team was then given its own video to study. One team got a video that showed only its mistakes; the other got a video that showed only its successes. After seeing the videos, the team that studied its successes improved its score by twice as much as the team that studied its mistakes.

The moral of the story is that it's better to focus on the positive than the negative when it comes to changing human behavior. The deficit-based approach works for technical systems, but a constructionist approach revolving around what's going right pays dividends where people are concerned.

So should enlightened leaders focus *only* on where things are going well, and forget about identifying and solving problems? We think not. Strange though it may seem, people are more averse to risk when choosing from options framed as gains than from those framed as losses.

What would you do if offered a choice between a sure gain of US$100 and a 50 percent chance of gaining US$200? Social science experiments show that most individuals are cautious and choose the sure gain. But what if you had to choose between a sure loss of US$100 and a 50 percent chance of losing US$200? Most of us are happy to take the risk and choose a 50 percent chance of losing US$200.[15]

The message here is that a single-minded focus on what's possible actually *prevents* us from achieving radical change because it tends to bias us toward conservative choices. As humans, we instinctively dislike losses more than we like gains, so we tend to think more boldly when looking to solve problems or fill gaps than we do when building on our strengths.

Both the deficit-based and the constructionist approach have their limitations as well as their merits. It's clear that dwelling on problems creates more fatigue and resistance than conjuring up visions of a positive future. But it's equally clear that when it comes to behavioral change, some anxiety is good. An excessive emphasis on the positive can lead to watered-down aspirations and diminished impact.

Our view is that the field of change management has drawn an artificial divide between the deficit-based and constructionist approaches. The best solutions combine both. If the University of Wisconsin had got a third bowling team to study both its successes *and* its mistakes, we suspect it would have beaten both the other teams. When leaders assess their organizations we advise them to investigate "What's wrong, and how do we change it?" and "What's working, and how do we get more of it?" with equal focus and vigor.

Our 2010 survey confirms this view. It shows that transformations that emphasize a company's strengths as well as its weaknesses are three times more likely to be successful than those that focus on one or the other.

One leader who advocates precisely this approach is T. H. White, former president of GTE Telephone Operations: "If we dissect what we do right and apply the lessons to what we do wrong, we can solve our problems and energize the organization at the same time. . . . We cannot ignore problems, but we just need to approach them from the other side."[16]

■ ■ ■

At the end of the "assess" stage of transformation, you'll have answered the question "How ready are we to go there?" in relation to your performance and health aspirations. You'll have identified the critical few strategic capabilities required to fulfill your performance aspirations, and taken a long, hard look at the state of these capabilities in your organization today. You'll also have uncovered the mindsets you need to support the level of health you hope to achieve, and determined the critical few mindset shifts you need to make to drive the right behaviors. You'll have taken a balanced approach to this inquiry, unlocking bold ideas as well as building energy for change.

Be warned, though: getting to this point involves a lot of effort. The journey through the "assess" stage can be the most challenging in the whole transformation. Organizations begin it with clear aspirations and a sense of excitement about the changes in store. It feels like it's time to act. But instead, people are being asked to explore their unspoken assumptions and views of the world. "What's happening? Let's just get on with it" is what we often hear at this point.

So it's hardly surprising that some leaders wonder if they can skip this stage. The answer is always the same: "You can do it now, or you can do it later." In our view, it should be now. If an organization doesn't tackle mindsets before it moves on to the "act" stage, it's sure to have to do so months or years down the line, after its transformation has stalled, and it doesn't know why. At that point the work will be harder, because high hopes will have given way to cynicism and disengagement.

The truth is, though, that the assess stage is always hard. That goes for leaders as well as their organizations. Bombardier CEO Pierre Beaudoin speaks frankly about how uncomfortable self-assessment can be: "We really had to force ourselves to look in the mirror and say, 'The first thing you have to recognize, if we're going to fix this organization, is that you, as a leader, have things to address.' Asking leaders to make themselves vulnerable is not that easy."[17] But as Bombardier's story shows, it's worth it.

Having assessed how ready you are to make the journey, you're now prepared to tackle the question in the next stage of the transformation: "What do we need to do to get there?"

CHAPTER 5

Architect

What Do We Need to Do to Get There?

When Alan G. Lafley took the helm at Procter & Gamble in June 2000, the global consumer goods giant was floundering. His predecessor as CEO had issued three profit warnings in four months, and Lafley vividly recalls being "the deer in the headlights, being grilled about the company and about why it was doing so badly. And the stock price had gone down a few bucks that day because I was a total unknown."[1]

Jump forward five years to 2005, and the company's fortunes had been transformed. Profits had soared by 70 percent to US$9.8 billion, and revenues by almost 30 percent, to US$51 billion. Jump forward another five years to 2010, the year Lafley retired, and his legacy was plain to see. P&G's portfolio of billion-dollar brands had grown from 10 to 22, the number of brands with sales between US$500 million and US$1 billion had increased fivefold, overall sales had doubled, profits had quadrupled, and market value had increased by more than US$100 billion.

Impressive though they undoubtedly are, the numbers don't tell the whole story. Under Lafley, P&G had also become a more consumer-driven and externally focused company. Between 2002 and 2007, the billion dollars it invested in consumer research went not only on traditional techniques such as focus groups, but on studying consumers in more detail by living and shopping with them. Lafley also drove innovation through the organization by looking externally for ideas and making it clear that "innovation is everyone's job."

So how did Lafley and his leadership team do it? As with any transformation, the journey was a sequence of complex interlocking decisions about brands, people, technologies, and markets. Lafley committed P&G to "stretching but achievable double-digit earnings-per-share growth" and a relentless market focus. "I wanted to put consumers front and center and get back to asking, 'Who are they and what do they want?' Find out what they want and give it to them. Delight them with P&G products."

But P&G's secret sauce lay not so much in the nature of its goals as in its choice of actions to achieve them. Although that might sound obvious, it doesn't happen easily. As Lafley noted, "Most human beings and most companies don't like to make choices. And they particularly don't like to make a few choices that they really have to live with. They argue, 'It's much better to have lots of options, right?'"

Lafley rejected this line of thinking and opted instead to make explicit and categorical choices about what P&G should do. At such a vast and diverse organization it was impossible to tackle every market and operation at once, so he and his senior management team decided to give priority to four core businesses and 10 out of more than 100 countries. Many companies talk about their core businesses, but few define them as stringently as P&G. Their core businesses had to be global leaders with the best structural economics in their industries, and demonstrate an ability to grow consistently at a certain rate while delivering a certain return on investment. The businesses that qualified were fabric care, baby care, feminine care, and hair care.

As well as drawing up a "to do" list focusing on these priority areas, Lafley also took the more unusual step of drawing up a "not to do" list. One item on this latter list was P&G's "skunk works": experimental technology projects outside the mainstream businesses. These projects—which had an annual budget that went as high as US$200 million—were driven by technology rather than customer needs, and culminated in products and services that had to be "pushed" to consumers in the hope they would be taken up. Lafley, on the other hand, wanted the organization to concentrate on products that clearly fulfilled consumer needs—those "pulled" by consumer demand. P&G also abandoned some regional advertising and marketing promotions in favor of more unified and coordinated global efforts. The "not to do" list was rigorously enforced: "If we caught people doing stuff that we said we were not going to do, we would pull the budget and the people and we'd get them refocused on what we said we were going to do."

As well as working to shape P&G's portfolio of business improvement initiatives, Lafley took every opportunity to role model what it meant to have a consumer-centered mindset. Best known for his work with Tide washing powder, he sometimes encountered skepticism over his plans to roll out proven P&G approaches across different product categories. One senior manager in Japan told him that cosmetics was nothing like laundry products. Undeterred, Lafley spent much of the next month talking with customers in shops and in their homes.

Not only was this the best way to find out what they really cared about, it also gave Lafley an early chance to role model P&G's intense new customer focus. He came back with a renewed sense of purpose. "Do you know what I've learned after 30 days?" he asked his team. "Cosmetics is everything like laundry detergent! You need to know who your customers are—intimately. You need to understand not just their habits and practices but their needs and wants, including those they can't articulate. Then you've got to delight them with your brands and your products."

Aware that having a clear strategy would mean nothing if people didn't understand it, Lafley communicated the game plan with "a *Sesame Street* level of simplicity" to get through to managers who "have so many things going on in the operation of their daily businesses that they don't always take the time to stop, think, and internalize."

Formal systems were also adjusted to reinforce the company's new direction. Planning processes now started with understanding consumer trends. Technology investments were shaped not by innovation for innovation's sake, but by a clear idea of what consumers were looking for. Rather than abandon the organizational structure introduced by the previous CEO, Lafley reframed it with a stronger consumer orientation. In practice, that meant that the first "moment of truth" in the customer relationship—the purchase decision—became the responsibility of the new market-development operation, while the responsibility for the second moment of truth—when the customer uses the product—fell to the new global business units. An inherited organizational structure that might have been a liability had thus been turned into an asset now that it had "a simple reason for being," as Lafley put it.

Lafley also invested in building the skills to support the culture he was trying to create by founding an in-house college for general managers and ensuring that P&G's consumer focus pervaded every aspect of the curriculum. In addition, he dedicated a substantial part of his own time to coaching, holding monthly private sessions with line presidents and functional leaders, for instance. As a result of this emphasis on individual leadership development, P&G consistently comes close to the top of the *Fortune* list of the best companies for leaders.

In addition, Lafley built on his predecessor's efforts to harness external sources of expertise with the intention that "half [of new products and technologies] would come out of P&G labs and half would come *through* P&G labs, from the outside."

Told in these terms, P&G's journey looks like a classic turnaround story. Lafley knew his starting point and he knew the destination he was aiming for. But things are never as clear-cut at the time as they look in retrospect. How did Lafley work out what choices he needed to make to take P&G from its shaken state in 2000 to its new-found (and enduring) confidence in 2005?

That's the theme we turn to here. First we take a brief look at how you can develop a portfolio of performance initiatives. Then we discuss in much more detail how you can choose appropriate steps to shift mindsets and behaviors in your organization. We give this more space than any other topic in the book because leaders keep telling us that it's the hardest part of a transformation, and the one where they need the most help.

It's just as well, then, that at this stage in the journey an organization's efforts to improve performance and health start to come together. They interlock and reinforce one another as the portfolio of initiatives becomes the main vehicle for shifting mindsets.

Performance: The Portfolio of Initiatives

By this stage, you know your aspirations and the facts about your capability platform, so it's time to work out exactly what you need to do to get from where you are now to where you want to be. To make the transformation manageable, you'll need to break it down into a portfolio of change initiatives. Companies that follow a portfolio approach and set clear targets, benefits, milestones, resources, and leadership for each initiative are 3.5 times more likely to have a successful transformation according to our 2010 survey.[2]

Identifying the right set of initiatives is not always straightforward. Again, there's a close analogy with human health. When you feel ill and visit your doctor, he or she will ask about your symptoms, conduct an examination, eliminate possibilities, and if necessary use tests to form a judgment on your disease or condition, the course it will take, and the treatment most likely to prove effective. Translated into a business context, this might sound something like: "This is where we are heading if we carry on as we are. Unless we address X and build on Y, we won't be able to get to where we want to go."

Just like the human body, organizations are dynamic and interconnected. We need to understand the whole entity reasonably well. If we

Exhibit 5.1
The Portfolio of Initiatives

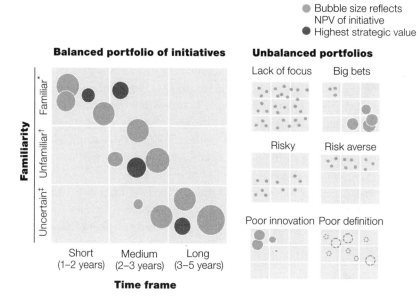

⬤ Bubble size reflects
NPV of initiative
● Highest strategic value

Balanced portfolio of initiatives   **Unbalanced portfolios**

Lack of focus   Big bets

Risky   Risk averse

Poor innovation Poor definition

Familiarity

Familiar* Unfamiliar† Uncertain‡

Short (1–2 years)   Medium (2–3 years)   Long (3–5 years)

Time frame

---

*$**Familiar:**$ distinctive knowledge (superior to competition); initiative already possessed or easily acquired; some execution risk

†$**Unfamiliar:**$ knowledge surpassed by competitors; attempt small to moderate investments to gain familiarity

‡$**Uncertain:**$ difficult to estimate probability of success; combat uncertainty by diversifying and learning from experience; attempt small initial investments to gain familiarity

---

don't, we may end up treating a symptom while missing a cause, or create unintended consequences in some other part of the system.

To help companies devise a holistic set of actions to meet their performance goals, we've developed an approach that we call the "portfolio of initiatives." To follow it, organizations develop a list of potential initiatives to take and then plot them on a grid with two axes, time and familiarity, as shown in Exhibit 5.1. The grid they produce will reveal at a glance whether the initiatives are balanced, like the large grid in the exhibit, or unbalanced, like the six smaller grids on the right. It's worth looking at the grid in a little more detail.

The *time* axis helps ensure that the portfolio is balanced between efforts that meet current earnings expectations, efforts that yield medium-term impact, and efforts that create long-term value.

The *familiarity* axis ensures that the portfolio isn't biased toward big bets on the future on the one hand, or incremental improvements that stay too close to the core on the other.

The *value-creation potential* of each initiative is denoted by the size of the circles plotted on the grid.

Adopting a portfolio-driven approach doesn't just help organizations to balance time and risk. It also helps them guard against fragmenting their change program across too many initiatives, and weigh their expenditure of money and resources against expected risks and rewards. For instance, they can choose to make small staged bets on less familiar opportunities rather than wait for these opportunities to become clear—when it will be too late to capture competitive advantage.

The unbalanced portfolios on the right-hand side of Exhibit 5.1 illustrate six patterns that organizations would do well to avoid: lacking focus or depending on too many big bets, taking too many risks or being risk averse, and showing poor innovation or poor definition.

A portfolio of initiatives should embody all the actions that your organization needs to take to meet your medium-term performance aspirations. That means looking at all the main levers available to improve performance:

- *Improving customer productivity* via price optimization, sales stimulation, product development and innovation, trade promotion effectiveness, product and customer mix profitability, brand portfolio reshaping, and so on.
- *Improving cost productivity* via site-by-site cost-performance enhancement, logistics redesign, sourcing leverage, sales and marketing spend effectiveness, overhead reductions, labor contracts, and so on.
- *Improving capital productivity* via site configuration, throughput debottlenecking, outsourcing, capex controls, working capital discipline, and so on.

Any initiative adopted will need a well-defined project plan incorporating a charter, timelines, milestones, resourcing, accountabilities, measurement mechanisms, involvement model, dependencies, and so on.

Every organization needs to draw up its own portfolio of initiatives to suit its own circumstances. There is no magic formula to follow, but seeing the portfolios of initiatives that other organizations have adopted can help to make the concept more concrete.

Take the experience of EMC, a maker of information storage equipment, as an example. When Joseph M. Tucci became CEO in 2001, the company was posting record losses. Five years later, record losses had turned into record gains, and annual net income was in excess of US$10 billion. So what was the portfolio of initiatives that brought about this remarkable turnaround?

EMC first embarked on a number of cost-cutting initiatives, exiting non-core businesses and carrying out two waves of downsizing. One medium-term initiative was to exploit a previously neglected networked storage product and a newly developed system for retaining and protecting fixed content such as check images, X-rays, and e-mail archives. EMC supported this initiative by developing an integrated solution to combine its range of high- and mid-tier data-storage products with leading-edge software and services. Another initiative involved overhauling its flagship offering to increase the role of software and services in its revenue mix. Building new sales partnerships and distribution channels with Dell and others and acquiring organizations such as VMWare took EMC into less familiar territory that it explored for longer-term impact.[3]

Another company that adopted the portfolio of initiatives approach was Tata Motors. As we saw in Chapter 3, it had suffered a shocking loss of 5 billion rupees (US$110 million) in 2001, and managing director Ravi Kant and his team had developed a set of aspirations to "stem the bleeding," consolidate Tata's position in its home market, and expand internationally. These aspirations were translated into a portfolio of initiatives that included slashing costs across the whole supply chain, improving product quality and features, intensifying product development efforts, introducing new sales planning processes built on sharper customer segmentation, tightening credit norms, improving dealer profitability and liquidity, extending the distribution network, and making targeted acquisitions in key markets and segments. Five years later, Tata's fortunes had been transformed, with profits of 19 billion rupees (US$423 million). By then it was the world's fifth-largest manufacturer of medium and heavy trucks, owned a 60 percent share of its home market, and had the second-highest passenger vehicle sales in India.[4]

The most valuable aspect of the portfolio of initiatives approach to driving performance is that it makes choices explicit, as we saw in P&G's experience at the beginning of the chapter. That means organizations are forced to have robust discussions about what they will focus on—and, equally important, what they won't. Organizations that pursue too many initiatives can easily lose focus.

So how many initiatives should an organization take on? That depends on its capacity to drive the changes. It will already have a good idea of this from the work it has done during the "assess" stage of the transformation. In our experience, the biggest constraint is likely to be how much time and energy senior managers can devote to sponsoring the effort so that it delivers real impact.

Health: The Influence Model

Once you've decided on the vital few shifts in mindset that you need to make to achieve your performance and health aspirations, your next priority is to devise a set of interventions to influence them. Taking deliberate steps to move the needle on the soft stuff is a vital element in organizational transformations, though it's often overlooked. In our 2010 survey, we asked senior executives if they pursued any initiatives that were intended not to improve performance directly but to change employees' mindsets and behaviors. Those who did were twice as likely to report that their transformations were successful.

Let's now look at how to influence wholesale mindset shifts in your organization. In doing so, we'll also explore some counterintuitive insights about people's predictable irrationality. Understanding when doing the logical thing might create unintended and unhelpful consequences could save you a lot of time and frustration when you come to pursue your own transformation.

Creating the Right Context

The key to influencing mindsets lies in making meaningful changes to the context in which people work. To see why, imagine that you go to the opera on Saturday and a football game on Sunday. At the climax of the opera, you sit silent and rapt in concentration. At the climax of the football game, you leap to your feet, yelling and waving and jumping up and down. You haven't changed, but your context has—and so has your mindset about the behavior that's appropriate for expressing your appreciation and enjoyment.

To continue with the analogy, organizations that are unhealthy are often caught between an opera house and a football stadium—not a comfortable place to be. Asking employees for a football-stadium mindset is no use

Exhibit 5.2
The Four Levers of the Influence Model

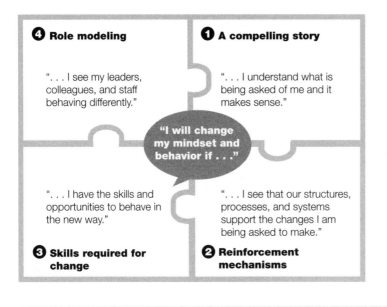

❹ **Role modeling**

". . . I see my leaders, colleagues, and staff behaving differently."

❶ **A compelling story**

". . . I understand what is being asked of me and it makes sense."

"I will change my mindset and behavior if . . ."

". . . I have the skills and opportunities to behave in the new way."

". . . I see that our structures, processes, and systems support the changes I am being asked to make."

❸ **Skills required for change**

❷ **Reinforcement mechanisms**

if your evaluation systems and leadership actions communicate that your organization is still an opera house. If you want your people to think like football fans, you need to provide plenty of cues to remind them they are in a stadium.

Through years of research and practical application, we have developed what we call the "influence model." It identifies four major levers that leaders can use to shift employee mindsets on a wide scale (Exhibit 5.2):

- **A compelling story.** Can employees say, "I know what is expected of me, I agree with it, and I want to do it?" The key elements in a compelling story are its content, the way it is communicated, and the embedding of its message through rituals.
- **Reinforcement mechanisms.** Do the organization's formal mechanisms reinforce the shifts in mindset that employees are being asked to make? To make sure they do, organizations need to link performance and health with rewards and consequences, leverage nonfinancial

incentives, and adjust their management processes, structures, and systems.

- **Skills required for change.** Do employees have the skills they need to think and behave in the new way? The right skills can be developed by adopting a "field and forum" approach, working on the required relational as well as technical skills, and refreshing the talent pool.
- **Role modeling.** Do employees see their leaders, colleagues, and staff thinking and behaving in the new way? Effective approaches to role modeling include having the top team undergo a visible transformation, taking symbolic actions, and selecting and nurturing influence leaders.

To see how the four elements fit together, imagine that we want you to develop a mindset of "Sky-diving is worth the risk." To make that happen, we sign up to a charity initiative where for every jump we donate US$100,000 to cancer research, a cause dear to your heart. That makes for a *compelling story*. We promise to multiply your bonus by 10 this year if you do the jump, but say we'll withhold it altogether if you don't. To make sure you're safe, we also ensure that you have state-of-the-art equipment. Those are powerful *reinforcement mechanisms*. In addition, we get a champion sky-diver to give you an in-depth training program. Now you have the *skills* you need. Finally, your boss and two of your closest colleagues did the same jump last year, and had such a great time and raised so much money for charity that they've agreed to do it again this year. That takes care of *role modeling*. Wouldn't all those changes make you more likely to adopt the mindset we are looking for? The research on influencing mindset shifts suggests that they would.

Indeed, so strong is the intuitive appeal of the influence model that it can lead managers astray. It's obvious, they think: all we need do is apply the model using plain common sense. But that's not the way to get good results, for the simple reason that people don't always behave rationally. Subconscious thought processes influence our behavior even when a moment of objective analysis would tell us they shouldn't.

When we're in a hurry, how many of us circle around a parking lot looking for the most convenient space when we'd have been much quicker walking from the first one we saw? Why might we think nothing of spending US$3,000 to upgrade to leather seats for our new US$25,000 car, but consider it extravagant to spend it on a leather sofa that all the family will use every day? Why are we happy to spend a small fortune during the sales, but reluctant to spend so much on full-price goods? How come we'd take home a pencil from the office for our kids without a thought, but be shocked at the idea of raiding the petty cash to buy them one? In certain situations, we are all susceptible to irrationality in our decision making.

Don Ariely, author of *Predictably Irrational*, drives this point home by showing his audiences an optical illusion.[5] It's a powerful way to demonstrate that knowing something to be true doesn't necessarily make people believe it—a prime example of irrationality. Have a look at the two tables in the picture. Which is longer? Easy: the one on the left. Now take out a ruler and measure them. Lo and behold, they are exactly the same length. Now look at the picture again. Which table is longer? Still the left! It's as if you've not learned anything in the past few seconds.

How do we know which table you see as longer? Because there are certain predictable ways in which our eyes deceive us, and this is one of them. What's most striking about optical illusions like the "two tables" or Shepard illusion is that processing visual information is one of the things human beings do best: the visual cortex is the biggest part of the brain. So if we make mistakes in vision—something that by and large we are very, very good at—what are the odds we'll make mistakes in something that we aren't so good at, like change management?

The social, cognitive, and emotional biases that lead to irrational decisions are already well understood in the field of economics. In our view, it's high time they were also appreciated in the field of change management. With that in mind, our exploration of the influence model looks at areas of human irrationality that any effective change program will need to take into account.

A warning: Dealing with the irrational side of change is not easy. As Nobel laureate Murray Gell-Mann once said, "Think how hard physics would be if particles could think."

Now let's look at each of the four dimensions of the influence model in turn.

A Compelling Story

The first lever for influencing mindsets is to create a compelling story and tell it whenever you can, wherever you can, and to whomever you can. That's because people need to understand not just the facts about the change you're planning, but the thinking behind it. The advantage of a story—as opposed to a report or an analysis—is that it can convey emotions as well as facts. For that reason, we respond to it in a different way; we don't just process the information intellectually, we relate it to our personal experiences and beliefs.

The work of Stanford social psychologist Leon Festinger demonstrates the great need people have to align their actions with their beliefs. Half a century ago, Festinger proposed the theory of "cognitive dissonance": he observed that individuals seek consistency among their thoughts, opinions, and beliefs (or cognitions), and try to eliminate any inconsistencies or dissonance between them. Festinger noted, "It's difficult to behave in a different way if the behavior is inconsistent with your view of the world." Seen in this light, the purpose of a compelling story is to give people a clear view of what's possible for their organization in the future, and to prepare them for the role they are expected to play in creating that future.

According to our survey, programs that communicate an emotionally compelling narrative about the transformation are 3.7 times more likely to succeed than those that don't. The secret of telling a compelling story is to get the content right, to adopt the right storytelling process, and to embed the story in the organization's language and rituals.

WHAT'S THE STORY? We use stories to transmit meaning. Every transformation needs a story that explains why the change makes sense both for the organization as a whole and for the individuals in it. Indeed, so great is this need that if the leader doesn't provide a story, employees will create their own. For instance, an innocent comment from a leader about the need to be more cost conscious can spark near hysteria as it spreads through an organization. Before long, it can turn into a story like "All the work in

Exhibit 5.3
Elements in the Transformation Story

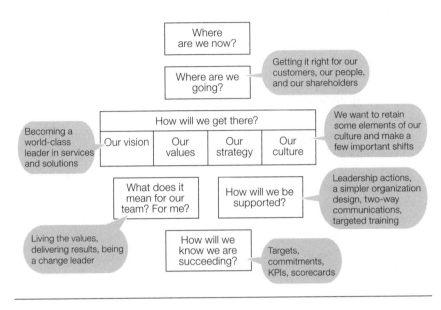

our division is going to be outsourced and we'll all lose our jobs." Sounds far-fetched? Not at all—we've seen it happen.

With better communication, this kind of misunderstanding would never have arisen. Good change stories use language that is concrete, evocative, and immediate. They answer employees' fundamental questions: Why do we have to change? What are we changing to? How do we get there? By when? (A fuller list of questions appears in Exhibit 5.3.)

In addition, stories operate at an emotional level by revealing what the transformation means to the person who tells the story, and clarifying "gives" ("What changes am I expected to make?") and "gets" ("What's in it for me? How will I be supported? What *won't* change?"). A story helps employees to see the objectives they are working toward and shows them how the tiny changes they make in their day-to-day working lives will benefit the whole organization. As Corrado Passera, the CEO of Italian bank Banca Intesa, notes, a good story is "not like an analyst's presentation, with figures and graphs," but is rather "a book written in human language, telling people where we were, where we wanted to go, and how we were going to get there."[6]

This much is hardly news to savvy business leaders, you might think. But there's more. To achieve maximum impact, stories need to be carefully framed to appeal to their audience on several different dimensions at once. Not many leaders realize that. As a result, they tend to fall back on a couple of classic narratives. One of these narratives is "good to great," which goes something like this: "Our historic advantage is being eroded by intense competition and changing customer needs. If we change, we can regain our leadership position, dominate the industry for the foreseeable future, and leave our competitors in the dust."

The other narrative is "the turnaround," which goes something like this: "We're performing below the industry standard, so we need to transform ourselves to survive. Incremental change won't be enough; investors won't keep pouring money into an underperforming company. Given our assets, market position, size, skills, and staff, we can do much more. We can become a top-quartile performer in our industry by exploiting our current assets and earning the right to grow."

These stories seem plausible enough, so what's wrong with them?

Research by a number of leading social scientists such as Danah Zohar, Chris Cowen, Don Beck, and Richard Barrett suggests that such stories tap into only a fraction of the energy that people can bring to change.[7] That's because these classic narratives revolve around the *company*—beating the competition, leading the industry, attracting investors—which is only one of the sources of meaning that motivate people to change. There are at least four others. People also want to hear about the impact changes will make on *society* (improving people's lives, building a community, stewarding resources), the *customer* (providing superior service, better products, closer relationships), the *working team* (creating a sense of belonging, a caring environment, harmonious working conditions), and *me personally* (better development opportunities, increased pay and bonuses, more empowerment to act).

In surveys of hundreds of thousands of employees to discover which of these five sources of meaning motivates them most, the surprising result is a consistently even 20 percent split between dimensions. Regardless of level (senior management to frontline), industry (health care to manufacturing), and geography (developed or developing economies), the split stays broadly the same.

The implication for leaders is profound. It suggests that what *they* care about and typically put at the heart of their story—namely the company—will tap into only about 20 percent of what motivates their workforce. To get people truly on board, leaders need to be able to add that missing 80 percent and draw on *all* of the sources of meaning that their employees care about. In other words, they need to be able to *tell five stories at once*. If they can pull that off, they'll unleash tremendous amounts of energy in the organization. But if they can't, it will remain latent.

When a large U.S. mortgage company embarked on a program to increase its efficiency by reducing overheads and reengineering processes, it devised a story that ticked all the boxes according to conventional wisdom on change management. Costs were up and revenues were down, so the burning platform seemed obvious, and so did the message: if we don't get leaner, we won't survive. Three months into the effort, though, the story didn't seem to be working. Employee resistance was holding the program back. Hardly anyone was submitting improvement ideas, and people were still keeping performance information to themselves.

Desperate to break through the barrier, the team recast the story. Instead of focusing on the company's need to stem the unsustainable growth in expenses, they broadened the story out to include elements on the missing four factors. The new story touched on the benefits change would bring for individuals through the creation of bigger, more attractive jobs and opportunities to shape the whole organization. It touched on a better life for working teams, with less duplication of effort, greater delegation of responsibility, and a stronger sense of accountability. It touched on the improvements that customers would experience in the form of greater simplicity, fewer errors, and more competitive prices. And it touched on the benefit for society: affordable services that would enable more people to own their own homes.

This simple and easy-to-achieve shift in approach had a dramatic impact. Within a month, employee motivation levels had soared from 35 percent to 57 percent. What's more, the program went on to achieve efficiency improvements of 10 percent in the first year—far surpassing the company's initial expectations.

We should make it clear that "telling five stories at once" is not about spin. The message that a leader communicates must be true to the actions being taken. It must also offer *reasons* for those actions that are wholly credible and likely to appeal to different perspectives. And it must be sincere. John Mackey, CEO of Whole Foods Market, notes that any "lack of honest, authentic communication and transparency usually boomerangs... and undermines trust and creates cynicism."[8]

HOW SHOULD WE TELL THE STORY? Too often, executives make the mistake of not communicating the change story enough. That's because they fall victim to the phenomenon known as "the curse of knowledge." Because they themselves know the story inside out, they assume that other people will take it in quickly and see all the implications that they can see. But that's not how it works. When people hear a story for the first time, they are so busy processing what they hear and trying to work out what it means that they can't possibly appreciate all the nuances. Leaders who have to tell and retell a story over and over again can easily lose sight of what it's like to hear the story for the first time.

Consider an experiment that involved a group of people divided into two sets, "tappers" and "listeners."[9] Tappers were asked to beat out the rhythm of a well-known tune such as "Happy Birthday to You"; listeners had to guess what it was. Tappers were asked to predict what proportion of their listeners would guess correctly. They predicted half; the actual result was just 2.5 percent. Only one person in 40 correctly identified the tune.

Why the huge gap between expectation and reality? It's because once we know something, we find it incredibly hard to imagine *not* knowing it. It's easy for us to hear the tune as we tap, but the listener hears only a sequence of apparently random beats. Similarly, leaders must take care that the carefully crafted messages that make so much sense to them aren't heard by employees as a string of seemingly disconnected ideas.

One of the choices leaders must make when telling a story is which channels to use: speech, print, online channels, actions, symbols, new-minted language, and so on. Using multiple channels enables leaders to show that there is a consistent message. Employees may hear from their leader at an off-site working session that a transformation is under way, then read about it on the company home page as they log in. At lunch, they see posters on the walls. At home, they read about the plans in the press. As time goes on, they notice how the environment is changing. People work in open-plan offices, not behind closed doors. The corporate jet goes up for sale. All of these things combine to convince employees that the story is real.

As well as deciding *how* to tell the story, leaders need to think about *when*: do we launch it at a big event, for instance, or should we let the narrative unfold gradually? The best approach depends on the circumstances. In an organization that has already gone through multiple change programs, a gradual approach may be advisable. For organizations that need to change fast, it will probably make sense to go for the "big bang" option.

A key characteristic of a good change story is that it encourages employees to feel a sense of authorship, like the lottery-ticket writers in Chapter 3.

Exhibit 5.4
The Interactive Cascade Process

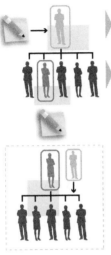

CEO as author
CEO drafts a personally meaningful change story taking on board input from the organization and agreements made with senior team

CEO as "teacher," senior managers as "students"
Senior managers participate in an interactive session with peers to listen to, understand, and give feedback on CEO's story

Senior managers as authors, CEO as coach
Managers prepare their own versions of the story that are relevant to their units, using the CEO's story as context and receiving coaching from the CEO as needed

Senior managers as teachers, next-level managers as students
Senior managers facilitate an interactive story session for their employees (with the CEO attending at least for the kick-off)

Next-level managers as authors, senior managers as coaches
. . . and so on

That's the thinking behind the "interactive cascade" approach illustrated in Exhibit 5.4, which turns writing and telling a story into a job for people at every level of an organization.

The story cascade begins with the senior leader writing down their own story about why the transformation is necessary, how it will be accomplished, why they are personally committed to it, and what they need to change in their own thinking and behavior to make it happen. The CEO then tells this story to direct reports, who ask questions and discuss what transformation means for them and for their areas of responsibility.

Once they fully understand the story and its implications, these managers write a version of their own that will make sense to their teams. They tell it, and then the team members who have heard the story tailor it to their areas in turn. Level by level, the process cascades throughout the whole organization. Being involved in writing the story builds conviction among the "authors" as well as ensuring that the story is applicable to every part of the organization and every person in it.

One company that has used the cascade approach successfully is Symantec, the manufacturer of Norton antivirus software and a global leader in IT security, storage, and systems management. After senior managers had spent several months defining a transformation story, they held a series of four-day events to communicate it to the company's 14 divisions. During the first two days of each event, managers were exposed to the new strategic vision, the core initiatives, and the values, behaviors, and culture that the company wanted to develop. The managers also grappled with the question "What does it mean for us in our division?"

In the last two days of each event, everyone in the division right down to the front line came together to translate the company's direction into job-level objectives for all employees. The entire process was completed in 13 weeks, and then the content from the cascades was built into the company's orientation program for new hires.[10] The impact was felt almost immediately. Symantec went on to gain the number one spot in the worldwide security market, and increased its market share by 6 percent within a year.[11]

Cascading the story in such an interactive way undoubtedly takes longer than pushing it directly through the organization. However, savvy leaders realize that even if it takes twice as long, it's likely to have far more impact in building people's commitment to the outcome. Indeed, if the lottery-ticket experiment is any guide, the impact could be as much as five times higher—which makes the cascade approach a solid return on investment by any standard.

HOW DO WE EMBED THE STORY?   To have a sustained effect, the change story must be told over and over again to remind employees where they are heading, and to highlight places where the transformation is already achieving results. Recognizing how important this is, organizations such as technology company 3M and NASA (National Aeronautics and Space Administration) go to the lengths of building storytelling skills into the curriculum of their leadership development programs.

At 3M, the business units abandoned conventional business plans in favor of business narratives. These narratives set the scene, state the challenges, and finally offer possible resolutions. When the organization relocated its U.K. headquarters in 2003, it asked employees to help create a story about what the new office would look and feel like for a customer and an employee. The story was repeated to the wider workforce through town halls, artists' interpretations, and written communications.

When NASA was approaching its fiftieth anniversary, it approached a master storyteller to turn its history, achievements, and future challenges into a compelling narrative. The story then became a play and was performed for employees. NASA also shares knowledge in story form in its *ASK* (Academy Sharing Knowledge) magazine, a compendium of vivid first-person stories told by NASA project managers about the work they have been doing.[12]

When we are telling stories, the words we use are critical. As Robert Kegan and Lisa Lahey write in *How the Way We Talk Can Change the Way We Work*, "Leaders have exponentially greater access and opportunity to shape, alter, or ratify the existing language rules. We have a choice whether to be thoughtful and intentional about this aspect of our leadership."[13] Choosing the right words is just as important when you are telling employees how you see the future of the organization as it is when you are making a presentation to investors or launching an innovative new product in the marketplace.

Capturing a key message in a memorable phrase is a good way to make it part of the culture. Consider Walmart's "10-foot rule," which reminds frontline employees of the company's customer service aspiration: whenever you are within 10 feet of a customer, look them in the eye, smile, and ask how you can help. For phrases to be memorable, they must be simple. As Willie Walsh, CEO of British Airways, explains, "The simpler the message, the easier it is to deliver. The simpler the message, the more likely it is to be consistent. The simpler the message, the easier it is to control and manage the communication."[14]

The language *not* used can be just as powerful. When Australian telecommunications and media company Telstra wanted to improve internal collaboration, it banned people from using the word "they" in conversations about other teams and units so as to remind employees to work as one organization. Posters proclaiming "No 'they'" appeared everywhere, and people started to call attention to references to "they" and "them" even in casual conversations.

Stories can also be embedded through a company's rituals. Consider the "Workout" town-hall meetings that GE holds to promote continuous improvement, as mentioned in Chapter 3. After groups of employees have spent a couple of days brainstorming, they take part in a review session where they present ideas to the plant manager and his or her boss. The employees present one idea after another, and the plant manager has to approve or reject them on the spot. Any idea that gets the green light is implemented according to an established process. The ritual is a powerful way to make sure that plant managers know their business, and that employees have the scope and skill to develop and present ideas. Having the plant manager's boss in the room signifies that the ritual is taken seriously.

Some manufacturing and mining companies make a point of opening all meetings with an announcement about emergency exits and safety hazards. Viewed as a one-off activity, this might seem a waste of time given that serious accidents don't often happen in meeting rooms. Regarded as a ritual, however, it serves a valuable purpose in reinforcing the mindset that safety matters.

When we were on our way to a meeting at Shell one day, an executive asked us to hold the handrail as we climbed the six steps to the imposing front door. Strange though the request seemed at the time, it was a great example of walking the talk.

Reinforcement Mechanisms

The second lever that leaders can use to influence shifts in mindsets is formal reinforcement mechanisms. Unless individuals feel they have support from their organization in transforming their mindset and behavior, the result will be massive cognitive dissonance: the feeling that "I'm being asked to do one thing but rewarded for another." As Paul Allaire, former CEO of Xerox, notes, "If you talk about change but don't change the recognition and reward system, nothing changes."[15]

B. F. Skinner and other behavioral scientists have argued that human behavior is a reaction to stimuli such as praise, rewards, punishments, and so on. When the stimulus changes, so does the behavior. According to Skinner, our environment sends us signals that make us more likely to behave in certain ways. However, fixed rewards and consequences lose their power to shape behavior over time. This limits the long-term impact of reinforcement mechanisms, which must be used in conjunction with the other three levers if they are to remain effective.

In practical terms, the key reinforcement mechanisms to put in place are linking performance and health to rewards and consequences, leveraging nonfinancial incentives, and adjusting management processes, structures, and systems.

LINKING PERFORMANCE AND HEALTH TO REWARDS AND CONSEQUENCES

As the U.S. novelist Upton Sinclair observed, "It is difficult to get a man to understand something if his salary depends upon him not understanding it."[16] It's hardly news that financial reward has a big effect on our behavior. Yet not all change programs create a direct link between the organization's aspirations and the incentives and performance targets that it gives to individual employees. Those that do are four times more likely to be successful.

So our advice would be to hardwire the mindset changes you want to see into the rewards and consequences you offer your employees. A straightforward mechanism for doing this is illustrated in Exhibit 5.5. The matrix is used to evaluate individuals in terms of both their business results (the horizontal axis) and their leadership behaviors and ability to "live the values" (the vertical axis). Each cell in the matrix carries clear implications for a set of rewards and consequences. The rewards include short-term incentives, promotions, and high-profile special assignments, and the consequences include formal warnings, remedial coaching, and demotion or termination.

We arrived at a nine-cell matrix after trying out a range of options. We found that using fewer than nine cells offers too little differentiation, demotivating high performers and putting insufficient pressure on low performers. Conversely, using more than nine cells introduces too much complexity.

Assessing how well an individual has delivered against expected business results is generally straightforward: it involves reviewing actual results against predetermined targets in terms of key indicators such as increasing sales, meeting budgets, and maintaining quality levels. However, a complication sometimes arises when employees don't have the necessary *decision rights* to influence their targets. For example, if a safety manager has the authority to report how safe the workplace is but not to design and enforce programs to make it safer, then it's hardly fair to hold that manager personally accountable for the company's overall safety record. People must have the power to make the decisions that affect the outcomes for which they are accountable.

Where decision rights and accountabilities are blurred, companies can use a tool called the RACI matrix to bring clarity. The matrix has five columns. Column one is for listing key decisions and activities; column two

Exhibit 5.5
Linking Behavior to Rewards and Consequences

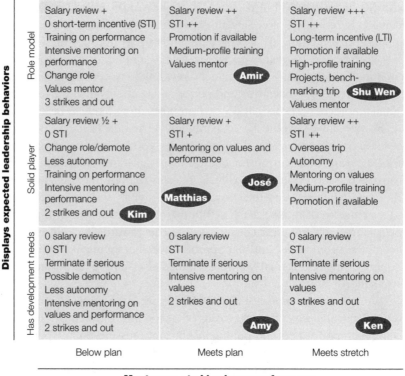

<table>
<tr><td rowspan="6">Displays expected leadership behaviors</td><td rowspan="2">Role model</td><td>
Salary review +
0 short-term incentive (STI)
Training on performance
Intensive mentoring on performance
Change role
Values mentor
3 strikes and out
</td><td>
Salary review ++
STI ++
Promotion if available
Medium-profile training
Values mentor Amir
</td><td>
Salary review +++
STI ++
Long-term incentive (LTI)
Promotion if available
High-profile training
Projects, bench-
marking trip Shu Wen
Values mentor
</td></tr>
</table>

| | | Below plan | Meets plan | Meets stretch |

Role model

Salary review +
0 short-term incentive (STI)
Training on performance
Intensive mentoring on performance
Change role
Values mentor
3 strikes and out

Salary review ++
STI ++
Promotion if available
Medium-profile training
Values mentor **Amir**

Salary review +++
STI ++
Long-term incentive (LTI)
Promotion if available
High-profile training
Projects, bench-
marking trip **Shu Wen**
Values mentor

Solid player

Salary review ½ +
0 STI
Change role/demote
Less autonomy
Training on performance
Intensive mentoring on performance
2 strikes and out **Kim**

Salary review +
STI +
Mentoring on values and performance **José**
Matthias

Salary review ++
STI ++
Overseas trip
Autonomy
Mentoring on values
Medium-profile training
Promotion if available

Has development needs

0 salary review
0 STI
Terminate if serious
Possible demotion
Less autonomy
Intensive mentoring on values and performance
2 strikes and out

0 salary review
STI
Terminate if serious
Intensive mentoring on values
2 strikes and out **Amy**

0 salary review
STI
Terminate if serious
Intensive mentoring on values
3 strikes and out **Ken**

Below plan   Meets plan   Meets stretch

Meets expected business performance

is headed "Responsible" (referring to the person who makes a recommendation on a decision or course of action and is tasked with executing it); column three is "Approval" (the person who approves the recommendation); column four is "Consult" (those who need to be consulted before the recommendation is made); and column five is "Inform" (those who are informed of the decision or actions afterward, and shouldn't expect to be involved in advance). By putting the relevant names in each cell, an organization can clarify where roles and responsibilities lie for particular decisions or actions.

Clarifying decision rights and aligning them with accountabilities is one essential step for organizations using the matrix in Exhibit 5.5. That step ensures that the business results axis can be evaluated fairly. But what about the leadership behaviors axis?

The key here is to be explicit about the expected leadership behaviors. Although it can be tempting to use an off-the-shelf model of leadership competency for this purpose, we advise organizations to create a leadership standard or model that is tailored to the mindset shifts they seek to achieve.

Exhibit 5.6 shows a sample leadership standard for an organization that has set its sights on six mindsets: results orientation, accountability, innovation, trust, collaboration, and passion. The organization has then translated these mindsets into specific observable behaviors. To evaluate an individual using the leadership standard, it gathers feedback about the extent to which they exhibit the desired behaviors from their peers, subordinates, and, if appropriate, external or internal clients, as well as their manager (or managers, in a matrix organization). From these many points of view,

---

Exhibit 5.6
A Sample Leadership Standard

Results orientation
- I know what's expected of me and my team
- I share objectives with my team and encourage them to meet those objectives
- I make good decisions in a timely manner
- I focus on the most important issues and establish priorities

Accountability
- I assume responsibility for problems and focus on solutions
- I admit mistakes and turn them into learning opportunities
- I know my emotions and channel them
- I hold others accountable

Innovation
- I question the status quo and provoke new thinking
- I propose and implement new ways of working
- I'm committed to my personal growth and transformation
- I take calculated risks and empower others to do so as well

Trust
- I do what I say I'll do
- I say what I think and feel
- I confront conflict constructively
- I care about the development of others

Collaboration
- I put the company before personal and departmental interests
- I ask for help and offer help to others
- I treat other people's time and opinions with respect
- I get out of the way to let others get the job done

Passion
- I'm proud of working for this company
- I do my best and encourage others to do so too
- I'm willing to go the extra mile when necessary
- I keep a sustainable balance between my passions inside and outside work

---

a clear pattern will typically emerge, enabling the organization to give the individual robust feedback and an objective evaluation.

Leaders need to face up to the fact that even when the organization's rewards and consequences are brought into line with its aspirations for change, some individuals may remain fixed in unconstructive mindsets. This means they will need to be dealt with—and the higher up they are, the more important this is.

Successful leaders don't shy away from this challenge. Cisco CEO and chairman John Chambers is known for withholding managers' bonuses if their behaviors aren't in line with expectations, even if they deliver results. Joseph M. Tucci, CEO of EMC, talks about "sorting out the skeptics from the cynics. The skeptics are your best allies, and the challenge is to win them over, to show them that the new habits are good and that it's ultimately their choice to adopt them. . . . The cynics are the real hardcore, arrogant individuals, and you have to get rid of them."[17] Dismissing employees is never easy, but as GE's Jack Welch reflects, "Anyone who enjoys doing it shouldn't be in the job, but nor should someone who can't do it."[18]

LEVERAGING NONFINANCIAL INCENTIVES Leaders of organizations that sustain excellent performance don't wait for formal reviews to reward desired behaviors. Nor do they rely exclusively on financial rewards. Offering big bonuses is the most costly way to persuade people to change. Other methods can be just as effective.

Researchers in one study measured how much a small unexpected gain increased people's satisfaction with their lives. In the experiment, a group of people were using a photocopier. Half of them found a dime in the coin return slot. When asked to rate their satisfaction level, those who got a dime scored an average of 6.5 on a 7 scale, while those who didn't scored 5.6.[19]

Why did such a tiny reward produce such a huge difference? It's been said that satisfaction equals perception minus expectation. If we aren't expecting a reward, even a small one can have a disproportionate effect on our state of mind. That's also true of employees during a change program.

When Continental Airlines made it to the top five for punctuality, CEO Gordon M. Bethune sent a US$65 check to every employee in the company. At ANZ Bank, John McFarlane gave every employee a bottle of champagne for Christmas with a card thanking them for their work on the change program. The CEO of Wells Fargo, John Stumpf, marked the first anniversary of its change program by sending out personal thank-you notes to all the employees who had been involved. Indra Nooyi, CEO of PepsiCo, goes so far as to send the spouses of her top team handwritten thank-you letters. After seeing the impact of her success on her mother during a visit to India, she began sending letters to the parents of her top team as well.

Some managers might dismiss these rewards as token gestures with at best a limited impact. Employees on the receiving end would beg to differ. They say that the resulting boost in motivation can last for months if not years.

So why are these rewards so powerful? It's because employees perceive them as a form of social—as opposed to market—exchange with their organization. To see the difference, imagine you are invited to your mother-in-law's house for a special dinner. She has spent weeks planning the meal, and all day cooking. After dinner you say thank you and ask how much you owe her. How would she react?

Chances are she'd be mortified. The offer of money changes the experience from a social interaction built around a reciprocal long-term relationship to a market transaction that is financially based, shallow, and short-lived.

But what if you had brought your mother-in-law a bottle of wine as a contribution to the feast? She'd probably have accepted it graciously. The offer of a gift rather than payment indicates that social and not market norms are in play.[20]

Consider another example. A daycare center decided to impose a US$3 fine when parents were late picking up their children. Instead of encouraging them to be punctual, it had the opposite effect. Late pickups went through the roof. Why so?

Before the fine was imposed, a social contract existed between daycare staff and parents, who tried hard to be prompt and felt guilty if they weren't. By imposing a fine, the center had inadvertently replaced social norms with market norms. Freed from feelings of guilt, parents frequently chose to be late and pay the fine—which was certainly not what the center had intended.[21]

When it comes to change, using social rather than market norms to shape behavior is not only cheaper, but often more effective. The American Association of Retired Persons once asked some lawyers if they would offer their services to needy retirees at a cut-rate price of around US$30 an hour. The lawyers declined. Then the AARP asked if they would offer their services for free. Most of the lawyers agreed.

So what was going on here? When compensation was mentioned, the lawyers applied market norms and found the offer lacking. When no compensation was mentioned, they used social norms and were willing to volunteer their time.

Reinforcement mechanisms need not always be material. Public recognition by peers and superiors has a powerful motivating effect. When Infosys Technologies hands out awards to recognize exceptional performance, it invites the nominees to present their work to a big audience that includes management council members and employees from all locations. This not only gives the award winners senior exposure and peer recognition, but serves as a role-modeling exercise and a demonstration of the value placed on behaviors such as collaboration and teamwork.

And let's not forget that words can be the most persuasive motivators of all. As Sam Walton, founder of Walmart, put it, "Nothing else can quite substitute for a few well-chosen, well-timed, sincere words of praise. They're absolutely free—and worth a fortune."[22]

ADJUSTING STRUCTURES, PROCESSES, AND SYSTEMS The structures, systems, and processes that underpin the activities of day-to-day working life have a profound influence on employees' mindsets and behaviors.

When a multinational energy company decided to instill a mindset of accountability, it reorganized around a larger number of P&Ls, creating dozens of business units where before there had been just a few. This was designed to give more leaders full control of the levers that drive performance so that they would have no excuses when it came to the results they posted. The company also wanted to encourage a collaborative mindset, so it expanded job descriptions to ensure that leaders from similar business units met regularly to discuss the strategic and technical challenges they had in common.

Organizations need to think about adjusting their systems as well as their structures. Do you want your frontline employees to develop customer-centered and empowered mindsets? Then give them customer relationship management (CRM) systems to help them engage with customers. Do you want your managers to become more attuned to people development? Then give them ready access to information about career opportunities.

Even seemingly innocuous systems can have a surprisingly powerful effect on mindsets. When PricewaterhouseCoopers was making the transition to a more entrepreneurial culture, one partner complained that although he liked what was happening, he felt he was treated not like a partner but like a salaried employee. If he wanted to give his assistant flowers for working until midnight, he needed three signatures for the expenses system. If he wanted to meet a client in another city, that was another three signatures.

He felt he wasn't trusted. It had never occurred to anyone that the expenses system was transmitting powerful behavioral cues that were incompatible with an entrepreneurial culture. To prevent mishaps like this, organizations need to review their reinforcement programs regularly, and revise them when necessary.

Processes can have a potent effect on mindsets, too. Consider the annual planning process. Managers often see it as the place where the rubber meets the road in terms of balancing short-term performance with long-term investment and showing the value that's placed on collaboration, honesty, and transparency.

To promote the mindset that long-term considerations are just as important as short-term issues, Emerson Electric, a provider of engineering services and one of the largest conglomerates in the United States, split its annual review cycle into two sets of dialogues. One examines how operational improvements can be achieved through initiatives in compensation management, productivity, asset management, and other areas. The other focuses on capturing long-term growth by expanding market share, introducing new products, reexamining channels and marketing, pursuing M&A, strengthening talent, and building capabilities.

Talent management processes such as recruitment, selection, induction, career paths, on-the-job development, formal training, and succession planning also send powerful signals that shape mindsets. Savvy leaders take every opportunity to use these processes to support the changes they want to see. One way to boost collaboration is to encourage high performers to make frequent moves between businesses so that they can develop skills and networks that help them solve problems across the organization. Orientation processes for new employees can be updated with new modules that showcase the desired culture and tell stories about what it feels like from the inside.

Similarly, career paths can be shaped to reflect new priorities and values. At companies such as 3M and oil and gas company Petronas, a "dual ladder" system of parallel career paths—management and technical—reinforces awareness that scientific innovation is central to the business. Even small actions, such as using a promotion announcement to comment on the behavior that earned the promotion, can have a discernible effect on mindsets.

Beyond talent management and planning, many other processes can influence mindsets and behaviors. Consider the public sector organization that decided to abandon the 1,500 pages of supply-chain reports it produced every month. It replaced these towering stacks of paper with a weekly meeting of 20 people from key areas in the supply chain. Each week, the group discusses how to keep improving the time from demand to delivery, and keeps a sharp eye on last week's results as well as longer-term trends. The new process encourages participants to develop new mindsets such as not tolerating bureaucracy, taking an end-to-end view of customers, and valuing collaboration. Introducing the process had a huge and immediate impact on performance, shaving more than 70 percent off delivery times in just three months.

It's worth bearing in mind that formal processes can affect mindsets and behaviors by their absence as well as their presence. Netflix, an online DVD rental company and video-streaming service, has no formal policy on vacations, for instance. Chief talent officer Patty McCord wryly observed, "There is also no clothing policy at Netflix, but no one has come to work naked lately." Organizations don't need detailed policies to cover every eventuality. Doing without them can help to stem bureaucracy.

When revamping structures, processes, and systems, savvy leaders go out of their way to ensure that employees see the changes as fair. One bank undergoing a major change program learned this the hard way. Having decided that its pricing did not fully reflect the credit risk it was taking on, it created new risk-adjusted rate-of-return models and new pricing schedules for frontline staff to follow. At the same time, it adjusted sales incentives to reward customer profitability rather than volume.

The result? Customers (profitable as well as unprofitable) deserted in droves. Price overrides soared, destroying a great deal of value. So what had gone wrong?

Looking at what's called an "ultimatum game" can offer us a clue. We give player A US$10 and explain that the money has to be shared with player B. Player A has to propose how the money is split, and if player B accepts the offer, they both get the agreed shares. If B rejects the offer, though, no one gets any money. Studies show that if player A offers a US$7.50/US$2.50 split, player B will reject it more than 95 percent of the time, preferring to go home with nothing than see someone else get three times as much for no good reason. And that isn't because the absolute sums are so small: even when the money on offer is the equivalent of two weeks' pay, the results are similar.[23]

There's a clear message here for organizations planning change. If employees are put in a position that violates their sense of justice and fair play, they will act against their own self-interest, and against whatever formal incentives are in force. This may seem irrational, but it's entirely predictable.

Let's go back to the bank. When it raised its prices and adjusted its sales incentives, frontline staff thought it was being unfair to customers—a case of greedy executives losing sight of customer service. Even though they were putting their own sales targets in jeopardy, many bankers bad-mouthed the new policies to customers, choosing to take their side rather than the bank's. They also used price overrides to show good faith to customers and take revenge on the "greedy" executives.

Ironically, their perception of injustice was misdirected. Customers were, after all, only being asked to pay a price commensurate with the risk the bank was taking on. The whole sorry saga could have been avoided if the bank had only paid enough attention to employees' sense of fairness when it was developing the communications and training that accompanied the price changes.

Skills Required for Change

The third lever that leaders can use to shape mindsets relates to the skills people need before they can change. Employees must be confident in their ability to think and behave in the way their leaders desire. As individuals, we like to do things we feel competent at, especially when others are watching. Those of us with no natural ability may try to avoid dancing, for instance, unless we've been talked into it or lost our usual inhibitions.

Academic support for the importance of this lever comes from a number of sources, including adult learning theorist David Kolb and organizational psychologist Chris Argyris, in work related to experiential and action learning. However, the "expectancy theory" of educational psychologist Victor Vroom is perhaps the most relevant thinking in this area. Vroom believes that if management wants to motivate employees, it must do three things: first, discover what employees value; second, discover what resources and skills employees need; and third, deliver on promises of rewards and make sure employees know about it. He thus puts building skills on an equal footing with offering rewards and tapping into employees' passions.[24]

Our survey confirms the importance of building skills: those change efforts that do so are 2.5 times more likely to succeed. In practice, we have found there are three key factors for success: adopting "field and forum" approaches, addressing both technical and relational skills, and augmenting the talent pool where necessary with skills from outside the organization.

THE "FIELD AND FORUM" APPROACH A Chinese proverb makes a good point about learning new skills: "Tell me and I'll forget; show me and I may remember; involve me and I'll understand." Studies of adult learners have established that if they take part in speech-based training sessions such as lectures, presentations, demonstrations, and discussions, they retain only 10 percent of what they have learned after three months. When they instead learn by doing—through role plays, simulations, or case studies—they retain 65 percent. And when they take what they have learned in the classroom and immediately put it into practice for a few weeks at work, they retain almost everything.[25]

Aware of the need for practical application, many organizations duly pack their skill-building programs with interactive simulations and role plays in a bid to ensure that time spent in the classroom is as effective as it possibly can be. Participants are often asked to make commitments about the actions they will take back to the workplace to embed their learning ("My Monday morning takeaway is . . . "). So far so good—except that come Monday morning, very few do what they have promised.

The gap between intention and action is highlighted in a social science experiment carried out at a Princeton theological seminary.[26] Students were asked questions about their personalities and religious beliefs before being sent across the campus. On their way, they encountered a stranger who was slumped over, groaning, and asking for help. Did the students who classed themselves as nice people help more? Not at all. Nor did those who professed religious commitment.

The only factor that had much bearing on the students' behavior was how much time they had. Half the students had been told they were late for an appointment on the other side of the campus; the others believed they had plenty of time. Sixty-three percent of those with spare time helped, as opposed to just 10 percent of those in a hurry. When short of time, even those with religious leanings didn't stop to help.

Human nature being what it is, we can't expect employees to practice new skills and behaviors in the workplace unless there are formal measures to encourage them to do so. No matter how good their intentions are, busy executives, like the seminary students, simply don't have the time and energy to learn to perform an activity in a new way or tackle an extra set of tasks, especially when they are playing catch-up after days away on training programs. Organizations that fail to create space for practice back in the workplace shouldn't be surprised if their training programs don't achieve the impact they intended.

In our view, day-to-day practice needs to become a fixture in the skill-building process. First, training shouldn't be a one-off event. We recommend a "field and forum" approach in which the forum—classroom training—is spread over a series of sessions and interspersed with fieldwork. Second, since skills are best learned through real-life application, trainers should set fieldwork assignments that are directly linked to participants' day jobs. People should practice new mindsets and skills in contexts for which they are accountable. Assignments should have outcomes that can be measured to indicate the level of competence participants have reached, as well as certification that recognizes and rewards the skills they have attained.

One manufacturing company employed such an approach to build lean skills in its workforce. The first forum focused on core skills and mindsets related to performance improvement. The fieldwork that followed involved meeting targets for cost, quality, and service over a three-month period. Anyone who made the grade was awarded a "green belt" in lean.

The next forum sought to develop deeper skills in designing technical systems and leading projects and teams. The fieldwork included redesigning areas of the plant floor and overseeing teams dedicated to specific improvements. Quantitative targets were set in terms of financial results and people and project leadership. Those who achieved these targets became "black belts" in lean.

The final forum built advanced skills such as shaping plantwide improvement programs to address strategic issues, applying improvement concepts to complex operations, and coaching and mentoring. As before, fieldwork was used to put these lessons into practice. Those who met the quantitative improvement goals emerged from the program as "master black belts."

PepsiCo adopts a field and forum approach in its Strategic Customer Leadership Forum, a program to help high-potential talent develop business knowledge and innovation skills. Participants attend a three-day classroom-based course where they work in teams on a business simulation. Teams are then assigned a high-profile executive sponsor who specifies a business development project for them to work on during the fieldwork phase. They spend six months developing these projects, with their executive sponsor providing mentoring and support. The program culminates with a final meeting where projects are presented to an executive panel and moved through to implementation.

Project pilots and final implementation have both delivered substantial benefits for PepsiCo. One team that worked on analyzing the company's relationship with Walmart identified an opportunity to market directly to the retailer's Hispanic customers. A seven-week trial resulted in a 50 percent growth in Walmart's sales of PepsiCo brand products, and a

45 percent increase in its net profits for Quaker, Tropicana, and Gatorade products.[27]

An Indian wholesale bank also adopted a field and forum learning program in combination with coaching and facilitation. At the first forum, the top 80 leaders were asked to review raw data from a strategic assessment, decide what the bank should do, and identify which behavioral changes would be needed. Smaller working groups then formed around each opportunity and were supported through real-time skill building in key behaviors such as engaging customers in discussions and collaborating with central product departments. This effort involved additional facilitated forums that introduced new concepts, explored them through role play, and then took them out into the world through fieldwork, with experienced coaches on hand to help leaders and teams reflect on and learn from their experiences. The feedback on the program was extraordinary. One participant said, "I have learned more in this program than in all of my career to date. In a very short time I have built a number of new skills that will be vital to lead the company into the future."

When skill building is done well, employees move through the full adult learning cycle from being *unconsciously unskilled* ("I didn't know this was important") to *consciously unskilled* ("I realize this is important and I can improve my performance") to *consciously skilled* ("I can do it if I concentrate on it") and finally to *unconsciously skilled* ("It comes naturally to me"). Once people reach the last stage, applying the skill takes little effort. That means they can put more energy into improving other skills that need work.

Learning to drive is a good example of the learning cycle in action. Some of us make the move from being unconsciously unskilled to consciously unskilled as teenagers, when it dawns on us that having to rely on our parents to act as taxi drivers is holding back our social life. Whatever our motivation, the first few months of learning will require our full attention: checking the mirrors, remembering to signal before turning, working out who has priority at a junction. With time and practice, we gradually become consciously skilled.

As we gain more experience, we find that driving requires less effort. We seem to be able to do everything we need to do without having to think about it first. Now we've become unconsciously skilled. At this point we can get from A to B safely while having a conversation, eating a snack, consulting the satellite navigation system, or even thinking up great solutions to nagging issues from work. Of course, multitasking while driving can be taken too far—you wouldn't want to cause an accident—but under normal conditions an experienced driver will be able to drive safely without having to concentrate as single-mindedly as a learner would.

Formal training programs are not the only way to build the skills required for change, of course. Other common approaches include introducing job rotations, offering informal coaching and feedback, setting up a mentoring scheme, and assigning special projects. One of the benefits of the field and forum approach is that it can serve as a device to bring together multiple approaches like these into a coherent program. For example, managers who are rotating into new roles or taking on special projects can learn about these opportunities in a forum and then apply what they have learned in fieldwork coupled with coaching and mentoring, 360-degree feedback, and so on.

TECHNICAL AND RELATIONAL SKILLS As Peter Gossas, president of Sandvik Materials Technology, a manufacturer of high-performance metal and ceramics products, notes, "Change must be driven by developing competence within the organization."[28] When it comes to shifting mindsets, relational skills are often more important than technical skills, though both need to be addressed.

Take an organization targeting a customer-service mindset. Frontline staff may need to develop their relational skills to help them pick up cues about the kind of behavior that particular customers would prefer. Do they want to cut straight to the transaction? Or would they prefer to exchange small talk first to establish a personal connection? On the other hand, an organization that needs to strengthen its performance ethic may need to help managers build their skills in coaching and conducting performance dialogues so that their interactions with employees come across as honest and compassionate rather than sugar-coated or harsh.

There are many more examples. If an organization is too inwardly focused, it will need to improve its ability to draw insights from outside, perhaps by honing its skills at segmenting customers and understanding their buying decisions. If empowerment is an issue, employees may need to develop problem-solving skills to help them find opportunities for improvement. These skills could include learning how to break down a problem into its component parts, how to generate hypotheses for addressing them, and how to test the hypotheses through analysis.

Motorola, a provider of telecommunications equipment, created a vice presidents' institute to help senior leaders deepen their technical and relational skills in the areas of collaboration (to foster networks across businesses) and innovation (to find ways to invent new technologies

and businesses). Infosys has created the world's largest corporate training facility in Mysore, India to help people develop the skills they need
for change. One of its projects provides high-quality training in technology
competency; another seeks to develop the client-focused mindsets and skills
at deploying institutional knowledge that are suited to a global consulting
organization.

How are relational skills built? The short answer is: by developing emotional intelligence. In the 1990s, Daniel Goleman analyzed the difference
between "good" and "high" performers in thousands of positions in hundreds of companies.[29] He found that 90 percent of the difference related
to emotional intelligence—EQ, not IQ. Goleman identified five characteristics that contribute to emotional intelligence: self-awareness, self-regulation,
motivation, empathy, and social skills. Further studies carried out at PepsiCo
found that in comparable bottling plants, teams with the highest EQ performed 20 percent above the norm, while those with the lowest rating
performed 20 percent below.

Goleman's most important discovery, however, was that EQ is *learnable*. If leaders reflect on their own capacity for the five elements that make
up EQ, they can improve their ability to connect with others at an emotional
level and so adopt the personal styles that will achieve the best results. In
a typical leadership development program, EQ skills are tackled with more
technical skills as part of a field and forum approach so that there is a direct
link between the "softer" side of skill building and the measurable impact
it has on an organization's performance and health.

REFRESHING THE TALENT POOL   Building skills sometimes involves bringing in new talent from outside the organization. This is especially true for
businesses facing major issues. As an analyst noted in an open letter to the
chief executive and board of directors of cellphone company Vodafone, "A
turnaround cannot be led by the same managers that led the business into
trouble in the first place."[30] In many cases, skill building will involve bringing in people with the necessary skills—and moving out those who lack
them. The matrix for evaluating individuals on their business performance
and leadership behaviors (described above in the section on reinforcement
mechanisms and illustrated in Exhibit 5.5) provides a good tool to determine
where talent may need to be refreshed.

If someone is performing badly, not exhibiting the expected leadership
behaviors, or both, something has to give. Field and forum programs to build
technical or relational skills may do the trick, but there isn't always time for
such measures. And sometimes an individual may lack the performance

potential required by a particular role. In such cases, the adage "If you can't change the people, change the people" applies.

On occasion, a change in strategy will make it necessary to bring in new people from outside the organization. When Apple decided it wanted to be able to add new features to its products without sharing detailed plans with external vendors, it hired people from the semiconductor industry to help it hone its skills in computer chip design. Two of the new hires were former chief technology officers at Advanced Micro Devices, Bob Drebin and Raja Koduri. Apple also sought out engineers with experience in creating the multifunction chips used in cell phones. In addition, in 2008 it acquired P. A. Semi, a designer of low-powered microchips—a move that analysts interpreted as a bid to customize key parts for its iPhone, iPod, and Macintosh products.[31] These infusions of talent brought Apple not just the technical skills but also the mindsets to support in-house innovation.

Companies such as Southwest Airlines maintain the distinctive skills they have acquired and built by hardwiring them into the recruiting process. As former chairman and CEO Herb Kelleher notes, "What we are looking for, first and foremost, is a sense of humor. Then we are looking for people who have to excel to satisfy themselves and who work well in a collegial environment. We don't care that much about education and expertise because we can train people to do whatever they have to do. We hire attitudes."[32] Southwest has found that it's hard to train employees to create an upbeat atmosphere; it's much easier to hire people with the right personality in the first place.

Hiring and firing are not the only mechanisms for refreshing the talent pool. Other ways to develop skills and confidence include bringing in external contractors, introducing job rotations, and expanding or shrinking permanent roles to make way for people with fresh perspectives.

Role Modeling

The final lever that leaders can use to influence mindsets is role modeling. Employees need to see the people they admire behaving in new ways. Respected people at every level must show that they are putting the desired mindsets and behaviors into practice in their everyday work.

Niall FitzGerald, former CEO of Unilever, makes this point well: "One of the things that leaders don't fully recognize is that when they speak or act, they are speaking into an extraordinary amplification system. The slightest thing you say, the slightest gesture you make, is picked up on by everybody in that system and, by and large, acted upon."[33]

Academics in the field of social psychology agree. Kurt Lewin argues that people's perceptions are strongly influenced by those in close psychological proximity to them.[34] Similarly, Konrad Lorenz, a professor of psychology, winner of a Nobel Prize, and founder of modern ethology, concludes from his work on imprinting that people take their cues from those they consider as "significant" and model their behavior accordingly.[35]

Our research into transformation programs bears out the importance of role modeling. Programs in which leaders model the desired changes are four times more likely to be successful.

In an organizational context, the key elements of role modeling are transformation among senior leaders, symbolic acts, and developing a cadre of "influence leaders."

SENIOR LEADER TRANSFORMATION   CEOs and other senior leaders have a disproportionate impact on a transformation. Both individually and collectively, they must be willing and able to live up to Gandhi's maxim, "Be the change you want to see."

That's a lot harder than it sounds. Most senior leaders accept the responsibility in principle, yet do little to change in practice. Why? Because they don't see themselves as part of the problem. Deep down, they don't really believe that it's they who need to change. Executives who seem perfectly happy to characterize their organization as low in trust, lacking in customer focus, and plagued by bureaucracy are much less willing to apply these judgments to their own behavior. How many executives would say yes if asked, "Are you bureaucratic?" or no to "Are you trustworthy?" Not many, we bet.

The fact is that most well-intentioned and hard-working people believe they are doing the right thing, or they wouldn't be doing it. However, most of us have an unwarranted optimism about our own behavior, as study after study demonstrates.

An early example is a piece of research carried out in 1976 by the U.S. College Board. Students in a sample were asked to rate themselves in relation to others in the group in terms of a number of positive characteristics. When asked to rate their leadership ability, 70 percent of students put themselves above the median; when asked how good they were at getting on with others, 85 percent did so. Twenty-five percent rated themselves in the top 1 percent.[36]

In another study, students in Sweden and the United States were asked to rate their driving skills. As many as 93 percent of the U.S. sample and 69 percent of the Swedish sample put themselves in the top 50 percent of the group. Asked about how safe they were as drivers, 88 percent of the Americans and 77 percent of the Swedes ranked themselves in the top half.[37]

Excessive optimism is just as prevalent when people are asked about their health. One study asked participants to estimate how often they and their peers took part in various forms of healthy and unhealthy behavior. Participants reported that they took part in healthy behavior more often than their average peer, and indulged in unhealthy behavior less often. This was true whether they were reporting past behavior or talking about how they expected to behave in the future.[38]

In fact, in many aspects of behavior, people consistently believe they are better than they are—a phenomenon that psychologists call "self-serving bias." In working life, this bias can block leaders from using their personal actions to transform the performance and health of their organizations. At one company, we asked employees to estimate how much time they spent tiptoeing around other people's egos: making a manager feel that "my idea is yours," for instance, or taking care not to tread on someone else's turf. Most said 20 percent to 30 percent. Then we asked them how much time other people spent tiptoeing around *their* egos. Most were silent.

A powerful way to expose and defeat self-serving biases is to use 360-degree feedback techniques via surveys, conversations, or both. When eliciting feedback, the best approach is not to ask about general leadership competencies—"off the shelf" descriptions of what good leadership is—but to ask about specific leadership behaviors related to the mindset shifts you are seeking to achieve. We looked at this earlier when describing how to link performance and health to rewards and consequences. Keeping the feedback specific also serves the useful purpose of reinforcing the transformation story and leadership standard.

It's often revealing to engage an objective third party to observe senior executives going about their day-to-day work. The feedback can be enlightening: "You say you aren't bureaucratic, but every meeting you attend spawns three more, and no decisions are ever made." Another revealing technique is calendar analysis: "You say you're customer focused, but last month you spent no time meeting customers and only two hours reviewing customer data."

So how can leaders get it right? Kevin Sharer, the CEO of biotechnology company Amgen, took the direct route. He asked each of his top 75, "What should I do differently?" and spoke candidly with them about his development needs and commitment. The top team at Bombardier Aerospace adopted a technique called "the circle of fire." As part of the change effort, every team member was given on-the-spot feedback from their colleagues on "What makes you great?" and "What makes you small?" The leaders at a multiregional bank made time after each major event in their change program to conduct a short survey on how well they had modeled the desired behaviors. This ensured that feedback was timely, relevant, and actionable.

SYMBOLIC ACTS   Senior leaders' acts have powerful symbolic value. They help to create stories about the new mindset and behavior that will spread from person to person through the whole organization.

When McDonald's founder Ray Kroc noticed litter in the parking lot at one of his restaurants, he called the manager and his driver over, and the three of them picked it up together. As word of the incident spread, so did the realization that cleanliness and order really mattered. In a similar vein, the founder of IT company Hewlett-Packard, Bill Hewlett, once took a bolt-cutter to a lock on a supply-room door to signify that management and frontline staff could trust one another.

Sam Walton, the founder of Walmart, was a keen pilot. Whenever he flew over a town, he habitually checked out the parking lot at K-Mart and Walmart. If he thought his store wasn't getting a fair share of the action, he would call in unannounced.[39] When N. R. Narayana Murthy, chairman of Infosys, takes his wife on business trips, he pays the difference between a single and a double hotel room out of his own pocket, so setting a symbolic example of integrity—a value highly prized in his company's leadership model. As he puts it, "Credibility comes from eating one's own food before recommending it to others."[40]

Symbolic actions can take place at any level of leadership and through actions of any kind. The U.K. supermarket chain Sainsbury's moved to open-plan offices to symbolize the breaking down of barriers between silos. It also banned meetings on Fridays to allow managers time to prepare stores for the weekend rush, thus reinforcing the focus on customers.

When a struggling airline made an investment in a new computer system that would take a long time to pay back, the action sent a message to employees that the company was serious about capturing efficiency gains. A manufacturer redesigned production layouts by moving from functional groupings to a single integrated flow line, relocated all tooling and consumables next to the line, and removed surplus equipment from the production floor to make it clear that capex constraints were real. And a sales organization reinforced the importance of being responsive to customers by equipping its sales force with wireless-enabled laptops so that they could connect with its IT systems from the field.

INFLUENCE LEADERS   Successful transformations start at the top, but don't stop there. Another key role is played by "influence leaders": people who, regardless of their official title or status, have a wide circle of personal contacts who respect and emulate them. Our 2010 survey showed that transformations that engage influence leaders to help motivate employees were 3.8 times more likely to be successful.

A powerful testament to the importance of influence leaders comes from the story of Blake Mycoskie. While traveling through Argentina, he noticed that many of the children he saw had no shoes. Not long after, he founded TOMS Shoes, a company that promises that for every pair of shoes purchased by a customer, it will give away a pair of new shoes to a child in need. By targeting influence leaders at college campuses and using innovative marketing techniques such as asking customers to go without shoes for a day, TOMS attracted a lot of attention. Key influence leaders would be invited to accompany Mycoskie on "shoe drops" to Argentina, Haiti, or Ethiopia.

Newspapers and magazines soon started featuring celebrities wearing TOMS and covering events like the company's "a day without shoes." This coverage attracted more celebrities, influence leaders, and social sector organizations to the cause, creating a virtuous cycle. Designer Ralph Lauren collaborated with TOMS to produce a limited-edition rugby shoe. A band called Hanson hosted barefoot mile-long walks before every concert to show its support. The company has distributed more than a million pairs of shoes to needy children, and had AT&T cover its millionth shoe drop in a television commercial.

But how do you find influence leaders in the first place? An analytical technique known as social network analysis (SNA) can be used to help identify who they are and who they influence. The SNA is like a CAT scan of an organization's brain that shows which areas are being connected up to perform a given task. It maps who interacts with whom and on what issues to make decisions or get work done, and also measures the quality of these connections in terms of frequency, helpfulness, and other criteria.

A simplified network map is shown in Exhibit 5.7. It would have been impossible to identify Smith as an influence leader from the formal organization structure on the left. However, the SNA shows the web of connections that make Smith the most influential person within the group, and thus the highest point of leverage for positive role modeling (or the highest point of vulnerability in the case of negative role modeling).

Most leaders we encounter feel they already have a good idea of who the influence leaders are in their organizations. However, the results of the

Exhibit 5.7

Identifying Influence Leaders Using Social Network Analysis

Hypothetical example

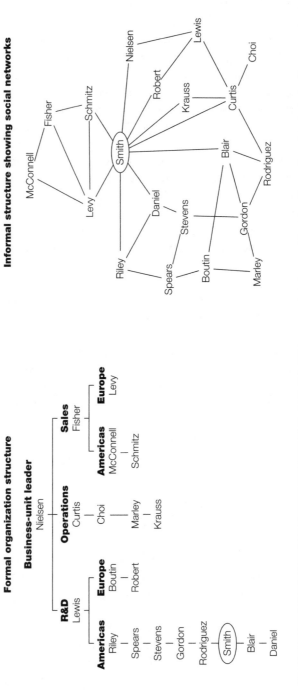

Formal organization structure

Informal structure showing social networks

Source: Adapted from Rob Cross and Andrew Parker, *The Hidden Power of Social Networks* (Boston: Harvard Business School Press, 2004)

SNA take many of them by surprise: the real informal organization often looks very different from what they were expecting. Our experience with clients from many industries shows that identifying influence leaders is harder than it looks. When leaders are asked to do it, they get it right less than 40 percent of the time. This is true at all management levels, from CEOs to business-unit leaders, heads of manufacturing plants, store managers, and so on.

As well as establishing who the influence leaders are, the SNA can estimate how much authority they have (how many people do they reach? how great an influence do they exert?) and their willingness to transform and lead (can they become role models?). Once identified, the influence leaders can be set to work to role model the desired shifts in mindsets and behaviors.

Some organizations have been able to achieve significant shifts through the help of influence leaders. When the private wealth management business of investment bank Goldman Sachs was trying to increase its contribution to the firm's earnings, it identified "positive deviants"—influence leaders who exemplified a different and better way of doing things—and mobilized them to help roll out the new practices to all investment teams, showing not just *how* to adopt them but *why*. The tactics buzzed throughout the business and were adopted so fast that average productivity per team doubled.[41]

Although the impact of influence leaders shouldn't be underestimated, it shouldn't be overestimated either. As Malcolm Gladwell argues in his book *The Tipping Point*, influence leaders should be seen as one intervention among many, not an all-purpose catalyst for making change happen. After all, not everything that influence leaders say, wear, or do catches on in the way that TOMS footwear did. Influence leaders are not a panacea. They are one tool in a transformation, not the whole toolkit.

Using Performance Initiatives to Influence Mindsets and Behaviors

Each of the four levers in our influence model affects mindsets in a particular way. An individual transformation program may rely on some levers more than others, but using all four together sets in motion a powerful system that maximizes a company's chances of getting new patterns of thought and behavior to stick. Executives often ask us which lever is the most important. We reply that the key is to take a few high-impact actions on each lever simultaneously.

Some of the interventions pursued to shape mindsets will be freestanding, separate from the slate of initiatives in the broader transformation program. The cascading of the change story is one example; others include adjustments to performance management processes and broad-based leadership development programs.

However, a great deal of mindset-influencing activity can be woven into performance initiatives. In fact, *every* performance initiative that touches employees—be it a customer service enhancement, a sales force effectiveness drive, an IT upgrade, or a cost-cutting effort—creates an opportunity to influence mindsets. By carefully engineering initiatives like these so that they shape the culture as well as accomplish their primary objectives, organizations can do the bulk of the work involved in shifting mindsets not by doing new things, but by doing the things they are already doing in a new way.

When the Taiwanese bank Taishin launched a program to transform its retail banking, an initial health check uncovered deep-rooted mindsets that were holding employees back in executing key business initiatives. For instance, branch staff felt that cross-selling might alienate some of their best customers, that customers didn't want other products, and that the products didn't live up to expectations. So the bank crafted a series of toolkits for cross-selling, account opening, and teller referrals to support its initiatives and tackle employees' concerns head on. It also introduced storytelling and dialogues—between consumer finance and the branches, for instance—to explain products more clearly, elicit suggestions for improvement, and communicate the benefits of cross-selling for both customers and bank. The impact was immediate and dramatic: for instance, the volume of loan products cross-sold to banking customers tripled within three months, hitting a record high.

New customers were a key focus, as COO Greg Gibb explains: "The first 60 days of a customer relationship matter most in terms of cross-selling.... After two or three months things become 'business as usual' and cross-selling becomes much harder."[42] To capture the opportunity, the bank designed a "day one bundle" to encourage every new customer to open four or more accounts. Take-up rates have been impressive, at some 50 percent to 60 percent of all new branch customers, and the initiative has driven up average product holdings per customer as well as customer profitability, which is "roughly four to six times greater for customers with a well-executed day one bundle."

When introducing the new approach, Taishin began not with the biggest branches or those most in need of reform, but with those most likely to embrace the change and spread the word. It tracked progress at branch level so that successes could be celebrated and lagging branches supported. Frontline staff saw the benefits of cross-selling at first hand, and the shifts in their mindsets contributed to the success of the transformation as a whole.

When U.S. financial services provider Thrivent Financial for Lutherans undertook a performance initiative to adopt lean methods in its insurance operations, it engineered the effort to address health at the same time. Its *kaizen* events not only empowered frontline employees to use their ideas to improve operations but tackled cultural issues such as increasing trust between the front line and management. Thrivent's lean training programs weren't confined to technical skills but explored emotional intelligence and how individuals could connect their work to their personal legacies. The change story spoke of how leaders and frontline employees were expected to live the new values as well as what changes the transformation would bring.

By the third year of the program, Thrivent had achieved a 20 percent reduction in costs, raised service and quality standards, and improved its health on all measures, especially those related to key mindset shifts. Employees' sense of empowerment rose by 32 percent, for example, and the feeling of trust between the front line and management improved by 48 percent.

To ensure that performance initiatives are leveraged to influence mindset shifts, a company can adopt a simple analytical tool like that illustrated in Exhibit 5.8. Each major initiative is plotted on a matrix, with the four levers of the influence model down the side and the particular mindsets or cultural themes targeted by the organization across the top. This creates a grid in which the company can log ideas for adjusting implementation by drawing on the examples and suggestions in this chapter. Ensuring that each cell of the matrix contains at least one powerful idea will "hot-wire" the implementation approach to achieve an impact on both the business and employees' mindsets.

By tying the vast majority of the work on shifting mindsets directly to business initiatives, organizations can maintain a strong link—what we call a "red thread"—to performance so as to ensure that health-related activities are not performed only for health's sake.

■ ■ ■

At the end of the "architect" stage of your transformation, you'll know "What do we need to do to get there?"—in other words, how to bridge the gap

Exhibit 5.8
"Hot-Wiring" Performance Initiatives to Influence Mindsets

Example: bank

Initiative 7: Simple product portfolio			
Initiative 2: Customer intimacy			
		Mindset themes	
	Customer focus	Collaboration	Strategic thinking
A compelling story	"Day in the life of a customer" vignettes created to understand customer's experience more fully	Collaboration emphasized as an enabler of rapid impact via communications and success stories	"Balcony" and "dance" imagery introduced to emphasize balance between short- and long-term thinking
Reinforcement mechanisms	Customer feedback and loyalty scores represent ultimate measure of initiative success and are tracked regularly	Cross-functional core team created to drive initiative	↑ Analytical models adjusted to consider lifetime value of customer; staff also trained to use this in decision making ↓
Skills required for change	For each issue, customer handoffs across silos are process-mapped to gain better understanding of customer experience	Start with easier cross-silo issues to build confidence and skills before tackling more difficult customer pain points	
Role modeling	Executive sponsors ask, "What is the impact on the customer of that recommendation?"	Initiative co-sponsored by executives from two business units that seldom work together	Leaders challenge ingrained mindsets and explore unintended consequences of trade-offs

(row label at left margin: **Influence levers**)

between your organization's current capabilities and mindsets and the ones you need in order to achieve your performance and health aspirations. You'll have made strategic choices that culminate in a concrete plan for both performance and health.

On the performance side, you'll have constructed a portfolio of clearly defined performance improvement initiatives that are well balanced in terms of timing and familiarity. That means avoiding traps such as making excessively big bets on the one hand or being unduly cautious on the other.

On the health side, you'll have planned a coherent set of actions to bring about the desired shifts in mindsets and behaviors. These actions will draw on the four levers available to leaders to influence their organizations: telling a compelling story, establishing reinforcement mechanisms, building the skills required for change, and setting a strong example through role modeling. As far as possible, you'll have integrated the actions you take on mindsets into your plans for executing the portfolio of performance initiatives. That way, work to improve performance and work to improve health will be experienced by employees as a single unified program.

At this point, in the words of P&G's Alan G. Lafley, "it's about executing with excellence."[43] In architecting a program of this kind, we should live by the adage that a good plan today beats a perfect one tomorrow. As we see in the next chapter, a "test and learn" approach to execution, coupled with rigorous monitoring and a robust governance model, will enable you to refine your plan as the journey unfolds.

We now move on to the central question of the next stage of transformation: "How do we manage the journey?"

CHAPTER 6

Act

How Do We Manage the Journey?

When Julio Linares took over as executive chairman of Telefónica de España in January 2000, Spain's incumbent telecom operator was in a perilous situation. The fixed-line business was in decline, and gross earnings had fallen for three years running. Between 1997 and 1999, the company's earnings before interest, taxes, depreciation, and amortization (EBITDA) had shrunk by 10 percent, and its cash flow by 15 percent. At the same time, the sector was liberalizing, competition was intense, and growth opportunities were unclear. Not surprisingly, employee morale was low. The future looked uncertain.

As Linares admits, "the company needed to change completely."[1] But with such strong industry headwinds and a demoralized workforce, how could he and his senior team motivate the organization to go the extra mile? Simply running the business would be tough enough; how could they transform it too, and keep the effort going not just for months, but for years?

It was clear that Telefónica's transformation program would need to be handled with great care. Above all, employees needed to be able to make sense of what was going on. With that in mind, Linares and his team created a structure emphasizing three themes—growth, competitiveness, and commitment—that would run through the whole transformation.

The team developed a range of actions to improve performance and health and grouped them under these themes. For instance, developing new distribution models and improving customer segmentation came under the heading of growth. Moves to adopt lean work processes and enable online transactions were about competitiveness; embedding a new set of company values and reorganizing business units related to commitment. Linares explains that the approach was "a useful communication device—it helped people understand how the project they were working on would contribute to that year's targets and, therefore, to the overall transformation program."

Another key element in execution was Telefónica's ownership model, designed to foster both top-down accountability and bottom-up involvement. To achieve this, transformation initiatives were owned by the line with support from the program management office, rather than the other way around. In addition, a broad group of leaders helped the program to evolve. Linares and his senior team brought the top 500 managers together every January to help design the program for the coming year. They explored a host of questions about the progress of the transformation: Which initiatives can we celebrate as victories? Which new initiatives should we pursue? What else can we change to help us reach our goals?

And the involvement didn't stop there. Linares knew that in an organization with more than 200,000 employees, it would take too long (and be too complex) to engage every individual in shaping the program, so his objective was to "give relevant people at different levels of the organization an opportunity to participate in the transformation program's (re)design and then to complement that with a strong communication program."

The third key aspect of execution was the way that Telefónica constantly monitored and reviewed progress so that the program could be adjusted over time. Regular events were set up to measure improvements by means of a wide range of performance and health metrics. Linares explains, "I don't think you can succeed with a program that is very stable or rigid. People need to feel the transformation effort is changing and moving forward; otherwise they will believe that there has been no progress and that they are not changing."

The choices made by the CEO, his leadership team, and the wider organization have paid dividends. Within four years of Linares' appointment, the impact of the transformation was evident. Cash flow had climbed, the downward slide in earnings had been reversed, and the return on invested capital (ROIC) had almost doubled. Health was now a priority for the whole organization. As Linares explained: "We have all understood the need to balance the focus on short-term results with efforts to gradually change our capabilities and attitudes." And still Telefónica's upward trajectory continued. By 2010, net income had tripled, earnings per share had almost tripled, and total returns to shareholders were far above global industry averages.

Executives sometimes say that managing a transformation is like trying to change the wheels of a bike while you're riding it. You have to make sure that your organization is still performing its usual functions and tasks, but at the same time you are taking them all apart, looking at them closely, and reassembling them in a new way. How do you summon up the energy—not to mention the balance, dexterity, and control—to do both at once?

Telefónica de España's experience shows that it can be done. But how do you do it at your organization? That's what we turn to now. We'll dig deep into how you take your game plan and convert it into impact.

At this stage in your transformation, the distinction between the things you do to improve your performance and the things you do to improve your health starts to blur. Performance initiatives are "engineered" to promote health as well. Your program management office supports activities on every front across the entire effort. Monitoring and review take place for health as well as performance.

This breaking down of boundaries means that employees experience implementation as one seamless integrated program. Which elements we classify as performance and which as health becomes a matter of emphasis rather than substance. This is all to the good: programs where there is a sharp divide between the two are far less likely to succeed. Remember that in the phrase "performance and health," the most important word is "and."

Performance: Delivery Model

Through long experience, we've found that the best way to implement initiatives in a transformation is through a three-phase approach: test, learn, and scale up. When you try out a prototype in a pilot location, you can learn from it and refine your approach before you start rolling it out more widely. If things go well, successes can be replicated elsewhere; if things go awry, you can confine mistakes to a small area and limit any damage. Early results also help to build people's appetite for change, smoothing the way for full-scale implementation.

But as you'd expect, there's more to it than that. Too often, organizations are impatient to get a pilot under their belt so they can press on with the rest of the implementation. Driving it too fast or without sufficient care and attention can quickly lead to unintended consequences, however.

Consider the experience of Eureko, a large Netherlands-based insurance group. In 2006, spurred by radical reforms in the health-care market introduced by the Dutch government, it launched a transformation of the health division within its Achmea brand. The leader of the division at the time was Jeroen van Breda Vriesman. He charged his managers with a stretch target: to improve the efficiency of their areas by 25 percent within three years.

To make this happen, one of the managers adopted a culture-focused approach in his call centers. His approach was successful: he met his 25 percent efficiency goal and improved the customer experience at the same time. This proved that the target savings were achievable, giving the health insurance division and Eureko the confidence to extend the efforts into other areas.

Before long, though, they ran into a roadblock: the approach taken by the manager who led the effort was hard to replicate elsewhere because he had achieved mindset and behavior changes through his personal influence, rather than by introducing systems to support the desired shifts. As Jeroen van Breda Vriesman wryly admitted: "We couldn't duplicate the improvement achieved by the manager who did it on his own."[2]

Eureko's experience provides an important lesson: a successful pilot doesn't necessarily make for a successful rollout. To be robust, the pilot phase should consist of not one but two tests—a double pilot, in fact.

The first pilot is a *proof of concept* designed to establish whether the idea you are testing truly creates value. Conducted properly, this pilot will make considerable demands on your attention as well as your resources. After all, if an initiative has made it into your portfolio, that must mean you expect it to deliver significant value, so investing in a field trial will be of the utmost importance. You'll probably need to allocate more time than you might imagine, too, because you'll be testing every aspect of the initiative for the first time. And some types of pilot may require you to put temporary workarounds in place so that you can clearly understand the opportunity for value creation.

Let's say the first pilot goes well. What's to stop you jumping straight from proof of concept to scaling up? We'd strongly advise against it. In our experience, it leads to lackluster results and what we call the "Nice pilot, but . . . " syndrome. That's because you've tested the idea, but not the robustness of the rollout approach. Whether it will work at scale will be a matter of hit or miss.

Instead, we recommend you complete a second pilot—a *proof of feasibility*—to work out how you can capture the bulk of the desired impact in such a way that it is fully replicable. This pilot needs resources on a par with those you'd dedicate to the real scale-up effort, plus a sustainable level of senior management attention (not an initial surge of interest that fades as time goes on). The pace of the pilot needs to be well judged, reflecting how long the scale-up approach is likely to take to deliver its contribution toward broader transformation goals. This time, any workarounds should be minimal, since the aim is to find long-term sustainable solutions.

Back at Eureko, another manager in the Achmea health division had taken a different approach. With the concept proven, the approaches were made replicable in a second pilot. This focused not just on realizing impact but on codifying the emerging method and helping change agents become skilled at using lean approaches systematically to achieve results. The feasibility pilot was conducted via a "train forward" approach in which people were brought in to learn the process so that they could go on to lead the rollout in subsequent waves of implementation.

This new approach proved successful in the health-care division: throughput rates rose, error rates fell, and quality shot up, enabling the division to reduce its workforce by one third. On the basis of this success, Eureko decided to roll out the improvement approach across all the divisions within the Achmea brand. Over time more than 200 leaders were "trained forward" to be lean experts.

The double-pilot approach also proved its worth at the NHS, the English health-care provider featured in Chapter 4. One of the transformation projects it undertook was a frontline initiative aimed at increasing the proportion of time that ward staff spent on patient care. After piloting the initiative successfully in one location, the NHS slowed the rollout to ensure that it could develop a scalable model, and to build "pull" for the project from other parts of the NHS. The second pilot built on the success of the first, but refined the approach to create an "industrial-strength" model robust enough to be rolled out more broadly.

This "go slow to go fast" pacing proved a major factor in the uptake of the program. Easy-to-use learning modules were swiftly incorporated into multiple parts of the NHS. They were propelled by stories from nurses and ward staff and shared with the wider body of employees through the intranet, communities of practice, and informal networks.

As these examples suggest, piloting both the proof of concept and the proof of feasibility will help get implementation off to the best possible start. And as Aristotle said, "Well begun is half done."

That takes care of testing and learning. But how do you go about the third and final phase—the actual scale-up?

After carrying out detailed reviews of dozens of successful implementation programs and observing hundreds at a distance, we've identified three broad "flavors" for scaling up program initiatives (Exhibit 6.1). Which you choose will depend on a number of factors, and you may find it helpful to use different methods for different projects, like the energy company we feature in the following pages. The three models are linear, geometric, and "big bang":

Exhibit 6.1
Three Models for Program Scaling

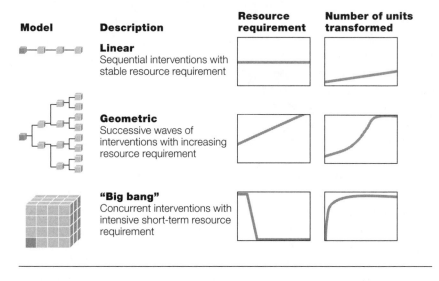

Model	Description	Resource requirement	Number of units transformed
	Linear Sequential interventions with stable resource requirement		
	Geometric Successive waves of interventions with increasing resource requirement		
	"Big bang" Concurrent interventions with intensive short-term resource requirement		

- In **linear** scale-ups, the second pilot (proof of feasibility) is replicated in one area after another across the organization. This approach is the best choice if an initiative is to be rolled out in only a few areas; if capable team members are in short supply; if the company is not facing a crisis; if the stakes (risk or rewards) are high; if deep, expert-led dives are needed; if there is strong resistance to change; or if the toolkit and solutions being used need extensive customization.

  A multinational energy company used the linear approach to roll out a unified people-management software system that was replacing an array of freestanding national systems. Senior management were aware that if they switched to the new software in all their global operations in one go, or even if they proceeded on a regional basis, they might create serious technical repercussions and overload the project team with demands for troubleshooting. Since changing to the new software would be a major shift, the company also wanted to ensure that all its country-level organizations would buy into the effort, and that any concerns that might emerge at one location could be fully addressed before the rollout moved on to the next. In addition, implementation called for considerable support from an external provider that had limited resources to devote to the effort.

All these factors prompted the organization to follow a linear scaling-up approach, with each successive effort building on the lessons from the one before. A project team comprising dedicated internal staff and outside experts moved from country to country to ensure that deep expertise was brought to bear from the beginning of each implementation. The organization was delighted to find that by following this approach, it was able to complete the project six months ahead of its original three-year schedule and save a fifth of its planned budget.

- In **geometric** scale-ups, implementation takes place in waves, with each successive wave much bigger than the last (say, two sites in the first wave, four in the second, 16 in the third, and so on). This approach makes sense if multiple areas share a few common features; if many areas need to be transformed and a linear approach would take too long; if capable implementers are readily available; and if the organization has the capacity to absorb the changes.

Whereas the energy company chose a linear approach to scale up its software project, it deployed a geometric approach when implementing its new global procurement strategy. By conducting an analysis of vendor relationships, it had uncovered similarities between markets in terms of buying patterns, levels of procurement sophistication, and vendor choice. Grouping markets that shared these similarities into clusters would enable it to increase its leverage with vendors. Once it had identified these clusters, it used the geometric approach to roll out the project within individual regions and countries. This enabled the procurement teams to get up to speed quickly, allowed approaches to be refined as the effort progressed, and ensured that cost savings could be captured from an early stage.

- In **"big bang"** scale-ups, implementation takes place across all relevant areas at once. That takes many resources, but only for a relatively short time. This approach makes sense if multiple areas share many common features; if the need for transformation is urgent; if little resistance is expected (or an appetite for change already exists); and if a standard toolkit and approach can be employed.

At the energy company, a big bang model wouldn't have worked for the rollout of the new global procurement strategy because each cluster of markets had unique requirements that a one-size-fits-all approach couldn't have accommodated. However, the company did adopt this model when it needed to overhaul its public relations process in response to a crisis. It knew it had to act fast to regain public confidence, so it specified new values and behaviors and revised its organization structure to create more transparency and accountability. It then implemented a big bang rollout across almost 100 countries within four months. The staggering scale and speed of the effort ensured that the organization not only restored its reputation, but did so much faster than competitors.

The three implementation models apply to both performance and health initiatives. For health-based interventions, there are two further mechanisms you can use to test, learn, and scale up. One is to leverage *pivotal individuals* such as influence leaders (as we saw in the last chapter), high-potential employees, or peers in grass-roots movements. At GNP, for example, 30 individuals were hand-picked to receive in-depth training on how to live the company's leadership standard so that they could act as role models, ensure that health initiatives were taking hold, and help create a two-way communications channel between the CEO and managers deeper down in the organization.

The second additional scaling-up mechanism is to leverage *critical interactions*—such as those among the top team, or vertical interactions within a business unit—for cascading a compelling story, conducting performance dialogues, developing skills, and so on. At GNP, top-team meetings have regular slots for learning health-related leadership skills, and subsequent meetings are observed by a team coach who provides on-the-spot feedback on how well team members are incorporating what they have learned into their ways of working.

Health: Change Engine

Transformation requires work. Work requires energy. Leaders need to find ways to unleash energy in the organization over and over again as employees carry out the routine tasks of running the day-to-day business while at the same time fundamentally rethinking many of them.

Organizations that are effective at mobilizing energy tend to succeed in their transformations. In our 2006 survey of 1,536 business executives, 89 percent of those who reported that their transformation was "completely" or "mostly" successful said that their organization was "completely," "mostly," or "somewhat" successful at mobilizing energy during the transformation.[3] Among the same group, 86 percent said their organization was also

Exhibit 6.2
The Change Engine

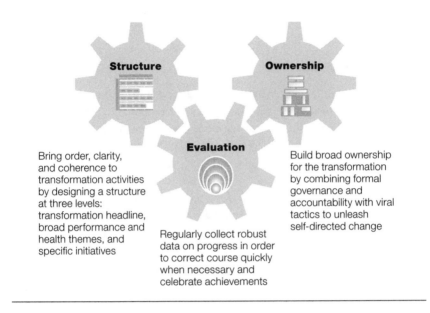

Structure

Bring order, clarity, and coherence to transformation activities by designing a structure at three levels: transformation headline, broad performance and health themes, and specific initiatives

Evaluation

Regularly collect robust data on progress in order to correct course quickly when necessary and celebrate achievements

Ownership

Build broad ownership for the transformation by combining formal governance and accountability with viral tactics to unleash self-directed change

"completely," "mostly," or "somewhat" successful in sustaining energy during the transformation.

To help leaders generate and manage energy in their organization during the hectic execution stage, we've developed a tool called the change engine (Exhibit 6.2). It applies equally to performance and health initiatives, and consists of three linked elements:

- **Structure.** Programs are more than six times more likely to be considered successful if they are well structured according to our 2010 *McKinsey Quarterly* survey.[4]
- **Ownership.** The same survey found that programs that energize employees through communications and personal involvement are twice as likely to be considered extremely successful. (Note that ownership shouldn't be confined to employees: the more that external stakeholders are involved—be they customers, users, patients, suppliers, or other partners—the more energy for change will be unleashed.)

- **Evaluation.** Programs that rigorously track progress and impact through clear metrics and milestones are more than seven times more likely to be considered extremely successful.

Now let's take a closer look at each of these elements.

A Structured Approach

Compiling a portfolio of performance and health initiatives and deciding how to scale them up are both necessary steps, but they aren't sufficient in themselves to make execution happen. If your initiatives aren't carefully structured into a coherent program, you'll find it exceedingly difficult to execute them. Having a portfolio isn't the same as having a game plan. Without structure, you run the risk of the "100 lost projects" syndrome: many initiatives embarked on but few completed thanks to a lack of leadership, control, and coordination. The results are predictable: poor outcomes, no confidence that progress is being made, and a lack of motivation just when you need it most, as the grind of implementation starts to set in.

Structure is essential. Without it, things fall apart. Here's an experiment that shows why. Take a look at the picture on the left in Exhibit 6.3. What does it show? Some abstract shapes? A pattern of light and dark? What if we

Exhibit 6.3
Seeing the Big Picture

asked you to talk about the picture for a few minutes? Could you find much to say, or summon much enthusiasm?

Now look at the larger picture on the right of Exhibit 6.3. If we gave you that to talk about instead, would it make any difference?

We'd be willing to bet that it would. You'd be able to describe the house and its reflections in the water and the trees in the foreground. Seeing the big picture—literally—of how everything fits together helps us create meaning. And meaning gives us energy.

Vital though structure is, it can be overdone. Micro-programming every facet of a transformation will only bog the effort down in energy-sapping bureaucracy. What we're after is coherence without rigidity. We want to be able to turn a portfolio of initiatives into an integrated whole, and then link it to our desired medium-term state (and long-term vision if we have one). To make this easier, we've developed the three-level structure illustrated in Exhibit 6.4.

Let's start at the top and work down:

- **Level 1** is the *transformation headline*—a phrase that sums up the organization's aspiration and suggests the rationale behind it. A good example might be IBM's aspiration to transform itself from a manufacturer of PC hardware and software into a complete IT solutions provider. The level 1 aspiration should remain recognizable throughout the transformation, although it may gradually evolve as circumstances change and themes from the next level start up or come to an end.

- **Level 2** involves a few broad *performance and health themes*—usually four to eight at a time—which serve as chapters in the transformation story. Each theme should be distinct (so as not to create complexity or require undue coordination across themes) and should apply to the organization as a whole rather than reinforcing any silos that exist (except where a particular business unit faces a specific challenge that it needs to tackle individually). Themes relating to performance might include extending geographic reach, achieving operational excellence, and building a service business; themes relating to health might include collaboration, market focus, and alignment. Level 2 themes provide a consistent underpinning for the initiatives in level 3. They should stay valid, and broadly unchanged, for two to three years.

- **Level 3** consists of *specific initiatives* that transform the story into a frontline reality. They typically target particular topics or areas in the organization: back-office operations, branch or store layouts, supervisor development programs, changes to performance management systems,

Exhibit 6.4

The Three-Level Change Structure

Example: energy company

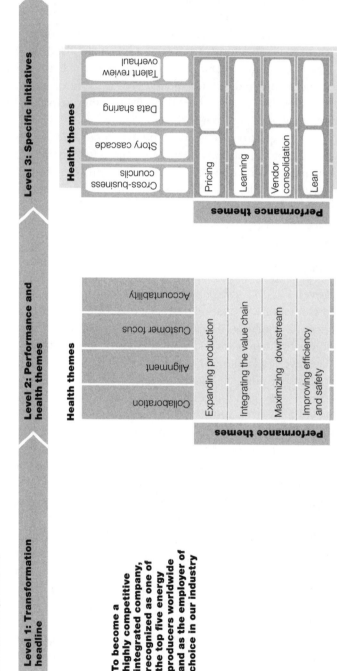

| Level 1: Transformation headline | Level 2: Performance and health themes | Level 3: Specific initiatives |

Level 1: Transformation headline

To become a highly competitive integrated company, recognized as one of the top five energy producers worldwide and as the employer of choice in our industry

Level 2: Performance and health themes

Health themes

	Collaboration	Alignment	Customer focus	Accountability
Performance themes				
Expanding production				
Integrating the value chain				
Maximizing downstream				
Improving efficiency and safety				

Level 3: Specific initiatives

Health themes

	Cross-business councils	Story cascade	Data sharing	Talent review overhaul
Performance themes				
Pricing				
Learning				
Vendor consolidation				
Lean				

and so on. Most initiatives will rely on proven methodologies such as lean process reengineering. Each one should further a level 2 theme. Unlike the level 1 headline and level 2 themes, which remain constant for several years, level 3 initiatives are usually completed in a matter of months.

What are the advantages of this three-level structure?

First, it fits the time frames that many companies use in managing their business. The level 1 transformation headline matches strategic eras (typically five to 10 years); the level 2 themes correspond to managerial time horizons (typically two to three years); and the level 3 initiatives slot into project lifecycles and budgeting processes (typically six to 24 months).

Second, the three-level structure enables companies to move fast without losing control of the effort. A relatively rapid succession of level 3 initiatives is compatible with a slower pace in level 2 themes and stability in the level 1 transformation headline.

Third, structuring implementation in this way helps managers shake off the harmful habit of confining initiatives within organizational boundaries. This ensures that economies of scale and skill are captured across business lines so that performance and health are improved for the whole organization, not just part of it. This is especially important when tackling cross-cutting issues such as customer focus, cost reduction, and leadership development.

Finally, adopting this approach can help employees deep down in an organization to appreciate how their efforts are contributing to the success of the transformation. At a time when heavy workloads and constant change often create frustration and disillusionment, knowing that their work is making a difference can give people a new sense of energy and purpose.

One organization that used the three-level approach to great effect is the South African Revenue Service. SARS was created in 1997 to collect and administer all government income. Some 10 years later, rapid growth in collections and a decline in tax rates had put its operations and capacity under strain. So it decided to modernize its systems and processes to provide a platform for sustainable revenue collection.

In implementing the three-level structure, SARS developed a level 1 headline that was about preparing for the next wave of performance and increasing compliance and tax growth nationally. Its level 2 themes were to build a new operating model, to create a solid organizational foundation, and to pursue additional government priorities, such as implementing a national social security tax and wage subsidy and strengthening border controls. Each theme was translated into a cluster of level 3 initiatives. For instance, the theme of creating a solid organizational foundation was advanced through the initiatives of transforming the culture, making management processes and governance more professional, improving the infrastructure, and ensuring effective communications and change management.

The program enabled SARS to make enormous strides in increasing the revenue it collects. By March 31, 2009, it had collected R625.10 billion (US$64.3 billion) in revenue, less than 1 percent short of its revised revenue target despite rapidly deteriorating global economic conditions. It had also improved its efficiency in dealing with taxpayers; its audit, investigative, and enforcement capabilities for detecting and deterring noncompliance; and its quality of service for taxpayers and traders. In addition, SARS had enhanced its trade facilitation and customs compliance to keep pace with soaring trade volumes, expanded the tax base across all tax types, and improved voluntary compliance in general.

Broad Ownership

People who feel a sense of personal ownership put more effort into making their company profitable. As Richard Evans, former chairman of United Utilities, a water services provider, remarks, "If people don't take ownership, they don't deliver to their full potential."[5]

Ownership can come from two sources: the formal accountabilities given to leaders and the use of "viral" tactics to mobilize self-directed change deep in the organization. To make the distinction more vivid, we can compare the first to a military campaign and the second to a marketing campaign. To achieve broad ownership, you need both.

THE MILITARY CAMPAIGN   Who is formally accountable for a transformation effort will usually depend on the hierarchy of the organization concerned. Hierarchies vary, but most program governance will include the following four elements:

- **An executive steering committee (ESC)** typically made up of the CEO and a senior executive team.[6] The ESC sets the direction for the transformation and makes critical decisions such as approving execution plans, allocating resources and capital, resolving issues across businesses or initiatives, and shaping the portfolio of initiatives over time.

- **A program management office (PMO)** charged with coordinating the overall program, tracking its progress, and ensuring that issues are followed up and resolved. Its role also involves facilitating transparent and effective interactions between the ESC and all relevant initiatives. The PMO sometimes assists with implementation by brokering the sharing of best practices across the portfolio and acting as a consultant and thought partner to initiative teams. It seldom leads initiatives itself except in rare cases where there is no natural owner for them elsewhere.
- **Executive sponsors** who provide guidance, judgment, and leadership to initiative teams by reviewing and validating execution plans and keeping a tight focus on business impact. They may be members of the ESC or senior leaders a level down who have direct line ownership of a particular initiative (or bundle of initiatives serving a level 2 theme).
- **Initiative teams** who are responsible for actually executing the initiatives. Team members are typically from the line, but may include change agents from staff functions. They are involved in formulating execution plans, identifying resource and capital requirements, and developing timelines and milestones. They operate as "task and finish" teams.

Within this structure, accountability for impact should rest as far as possible with line management and be built into the relevant budgets. We use the cheesy-sounding formula BBB—"benefits baked into budgets"—as a reminder that no aspect of a transformation is complete until its benefits have been fully reflected in the relevant budget. This also helps ensure that the PMO provides support and oversight, but the line has ownership.

Our 2010 survey shows that putting these structures into place provides clear payoffs. Programs that are characterized by clear roles and responsibilities are six times more likely to be successful than those that aren't; programs with effective steering committees are three times more likely to be successful than those without; and programs that have effective PMOs are twice as likely to be successful as those that don't.

To see how the military campaign aspects of ownership come together, consider the case of a retailer that was restructuring its global operations. It had embarked on a transformation program in the wake of three consecutive quarterly losses, and after an OHI survey had identified a number of health issues that had worsened with the onset of the 2008 recession. During the "act" stage, the CEO set up an executive steering committee comprising senior leaders from both the retailer and its parent company. An external board member and the CEO of a different company in the group were also asked to sit on the ESC to ensure that the retailer's health issues didn't affect the quality of its decision making.

The retailer then created a program management office and asked the widely respected senior manager of the most profitable business line to head it up. He promptly enlisted a top performer from his own department as well as two highly regarded middle managers from other departments. He also hired an external change expert and a retail turnaround specialist to work on the project so that best-in-class advice would be readily to hand. Otherwise the staffing of the PMO was kept light to ensure that it didn't become a permanent structure within the organization or prevent project ownership from lying where it should, with the initiative teams.

Each initiative in the program had an executive sponsor who supported the PMO in ensuring that the relevant team was fully committed to delivering against targets and had the resources it needed to do the job. The initiative team also identified a "project amplifier" whose role was to propagate the initiative at grassroots level and relay the concerns of the wider organization back to the initiative team.

Adopting such a clearly structured ownership model helped the retailer to reorganize its 75,000-strong workforce and cut costs by 12 percent within six months. The company also saw significant improvements in its health across the board. The light yet robust program structure proved easy to dismantle, and the responsibility for continuing to deliver and track the initiatives was then placed firmly in the hands of the business.

THE MARKETING CAMPAIGN   Important though the formal ownership structure is, it won't be enough to create the energy to transform everyday functions and tasks while simultaneously keeping the business on track. Organizations also need to enlist the active involvement of staff at every level.

Programs that mobilize frontline employees to feel ownership of change are four times more likely to succeed, programs that empower employees to use their own initiative to achieve aspirations for change are five times more likely to succeed, and programs that make the organization feel engaged and energized through communications and involvement are four times more likely to succeed than programs that don't do these things.

Even when an organization has done everything it can possibly do to generate maximum energy for change—involving staff in setting aspirations, balancing urgent issues with a positive view of the way forward, and using the influence model from Chapter 5 to promote frontline engagement—it may still run up against obstacles at the implementation stage. Common roadblocks include:

- **Cynicism.** Past failures feed a conviction that what began with a bang will end with a whimper, creating pain but no gain.
- **Local loyalties defeating allegiance to the wider organization.** When messages from the top seem remote and unremitting, people stop taking any notice.
- **Difficulty in communicating on a broad scale.** It's hard to get a lot of people to pay attention at one time.
- **Poor understanding of an organization's emotional state.** When leaders don't have real-time feedback channels, they can't tap into how people are thinking and feeling.

These symptoms tend to be most acute during the phase between piloting and scaling up performance initiatives—a phase we sometimes characterize as "the valley of desolation" (Exhibit 6.5).

Exhibit 6.5
The "Valley of Desolation"

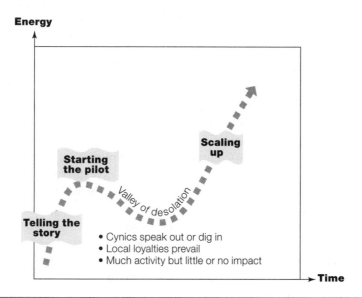

Organizations that would prefer to avoid plumbing the depths of this valley can borrow tactics from the field of viral marketing. The key elements of the viral approach are that it:

- Draws attention to what's happening right here, right now.
- Uses raw, direct personal messages.
- Revolves around "What's in it for me?" (not "What executives want").
- Relies on direct communication between peers (not corporate channels).
- Spreads through curiosity and a desire for information (not a push from the top).

Admittedly, viral marketing efforts can be kicked off by the corporate center, but after that they must be left to spread through the organization under their own steam. To get them started, some infrastructure and funding may be needed. Companies often give an influence leader in each area a small budget and freedom within a framework—scope to decide how to create energy for change in accordance with guidance about which aspects of the transformation story to emphasize.

So how does this work? One large telecom company released a flood of communications to explain what was happening in the organization. There were limited print runs of edgy, unofficial-looking materials; a "rogue" comic strip that expressed and corrected cynical views of the change program; a fly-on-the-wall video of a senior team working session that was "leaked" to the intranet; blogs from influential leaders; and hidden intranet access points with a video game–style facility to unlock new areas of information.

Viral tactics may need to be extended beyond internal communications to the outside world. As Banca Intesa CEO Corrado Passera reflects, "Internal results undoubtedly matter, but even they won't count for much if everyone keeps reading in the newspapers that the business is still a poor performer, is not contributing to society, or is letting down the country as a whole."[7] Energy for change doesn't come only from employees; customers, users, patients, voters, and other stakeholders can also play their part.

Another example of viral communication was started by English filmmaker Rebecca Hosking. When she visited a remote Hawaiian atoll in 2006 to make a BBC TV program about wildlife, she was confronted by the sight of hundreds of dead albatrosses that had washed up on the beach after swallowing plastic waste. The sea held more horrors: dead humpback whales, seals, and turtles awash in a mass of plastic fragments. On returning to her home town of Modbury in Devon, she and a group of friends persuaded all

43 local shopkeepers to replace their plastic carrier bags with reusable cloth ones. The town became the first in Europe to ban plastic bags. As word spread, traders in scores of other small towns across Britain, as well as 33 London boroughs, said they would introduce similar bans. The movement hit the national headlines when the then prime minister said he would like to eliminate single-use plastic bags throughout the whole country.[8]

One of the most powerful and far-reaching examples of viral communications was Barack Obama's bid for the U.S. presidency. The campaign went far beyond national media, penetrating niche social networks catering to different ethnic groups as well as broader platforms such as Google, Facebook, Hulu, Twitter, and YouTube. That made it easy for supporters to stay connected ("Turn on your TV now, check out what Barack is doing") and get others involved ("Check out Obama's YouTube posting this morning").

Viral communication happens all the time, every day, in every organization, whether you're aware of it or not. Like Obama's external online director, Scott Goodstein, you can choose what to do about it: "We could either ignore that thing that was going on . . . or we could engage in it."[9]

As an IT solutions provider, IBM is well placed to engage with "that thing." It has developed a proprietary social networking tool called BeeHive for internal use. This allows employees to promote projects and generate followership by drawing on their informal networks within the company. For instance, users can create and share brief lists—called "hive fives"—to spread ideas about topics they are passionate about or projects that need wider sponsorship. Colleagues in their network can comment on the list or re-post it as part of their own profile, thus spreading the ideas virally across the organization.

Measurement and Evaluation

Rigorous monitoring makes transformations twice as likely to succeed according to our research. In the wry words of N. R. Narayana Murthy, chairman of Infosys, "In God we trust; everybody else brings data to the table."[10]

The portfolio of initiatives must be continually monitored and adjusted as new challenges and opportunities emerge over the course of the transformation. It's a bit like making a long road trip through unfamiliar territory. Even with the best-laid plans, the journey seldom goes as you expected. The weather changes without warning, heavy traffic holds you up, road works prompt a detour, your car breaks down, and after all that, you need a break.

Companies on a transformation journey face similar hitches and uncertainties. Julio Linares of Telefónica warns: "The market is going to change constantly, and because of that you need to make a constant effort to adapt your company to the market. Of course, some parts of the program will end, but new ones will come up."[11]

Managing the program dynamically in this way depends on good data. You have to be clear from day to day how much progress you've made against your plans. That means regularly measuring the impact of your transformation on four key dimensions (Exhibit 6.6):

- **Initiatives.** Track your progress not just in terms of time and budget, but also against key operational performance indicators such as cycle time, waste, wait times, and quality.
- **Health.** Are mindsets shifting to support the improvements in performance that you want to see? To look for evidence, use targeted surveys, focus groups, and observation.
- **Performance.** Measure key business outcomes such as revenue, cost, and risk to confirm that improvements are happening where you expect and not causing unforeseen consequences elsewhere in the organization.
- **Enterprise value.** Keep a constant eye on shareholder value as the ultimate business outcome, or monitor key stakeholder value in not-for-profit and governmental organizations.

Clearly, measurement has to be done in every area of business. But leading a transformation is a special case because it's a process that adapts and develops over time. If your personal fitness plan didn't give you the improvements in performance and health that you expected, you'd change it. So, too, a transformation program must be fine-tuned from time to time if it's to produce the desired results. Measurement and evaluation are not just a means to gauge how far you've come, but a compass to help you navigate each step along the road.

How often you need to measure will depend on what you're measuring. As a rough guide, initiative measures could be reviewed weekly by initiative teams, health and performance monthly or quarterly by sponsors and steering committees, and enterprise value once or twice a year by everyone involved in the transformation. Reviews serve two purposes. One is to enable you to enforce accountability, identify issues, and determine remedies; the other is to identify best practices to share,

Exhibit 6.6
Measuring Impact in Four Dimensions

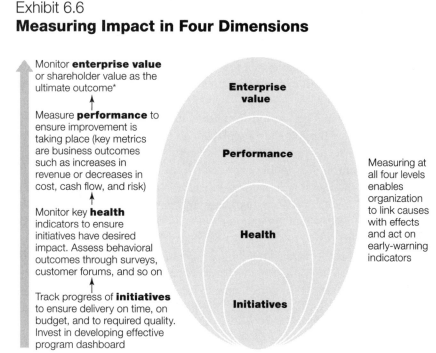

Monitor **enterprise value** or shareholder value as the ultimate outcome*

↑

Measure **performance** to ensure improvement is taking place (key metrics are business outcomes such as increases in revenue or decreases in cost, cash flow, and risk)

↑

Monitor key **health** indicators to ensure initiatives have desired impact. Assess behavioral outcomes through surveys, customer forums, and so on

↑

Track progress of **initiatives** to ensure delivery on time, on budget, and to required quality. Invest in developing effective program dashboard

Enterprise value

Performance

Health

Initiatives

Measuring at all four levels enables organization to link causes with effects and act on early-warning indicators

*Or impact on key stakeholders for not-for-profit and public sector organizations

spotlight successes to celebrate, and instill a culture of continuous learning and improvement.

■ ■ ■

Whereas the "aspire," "assess," and "architect" phases in a transformation typically take months, the "act" stage usually lasts for years. There's no denying it can feel like a long haul, especially when you are some way in but have no immediate end in sight. At this point, there's comfort to be had in Benjamin Franklin's adage that "Energy and persistence conquer all things."

When we're talking to companies about the act phase, we often liken it to what happens when a champion sports team takes the field. Aspirations have been shared, skill and will requirements are clear, and there's a game plan in place. But once the whistle blows, it's not often that the points scored come from well-rehearsed set plays. Whether it's a key rebound in basketball, a pass interception returned for a touchdown in American football, or a goal coming out of a full back's solo run in soccer, it's the improvising within the game plan that usually makes the difference between winning and losing. As for sports teams, so for organizations. Needless to say, the goal of everything you've just read is to help you position yourself to win.

When the going gets tough in the act stage, it's easier to carry on if everyone knows what role they are playing and you can be sure that you're on the right track. If you've followed the steps we've described here—test each initiative through a double pilot, scale it up via the appropriate model, impose coherence with a three-level structure, create ownership through a mix of formal leadership accountabilities and viral tactics, and use regular evaluations to adjust your program as you go—then you can be confident that all your efforts will bear fruit in the end.

So you're on the way to fulfilling your transformation aspirations. But what happens when you get there? How do you make sure you keep winning and stay on top? What does it take to reach the stage of transformation that Julio Linares describes as "a never-ending journey"? That's what we turn to next.

CHAPTER 7

Advance

How Do We Keep Moving Forward?

"Three and a half years ago, ANZ was the worst performer of [Australia's] big four banks, regarded as the highest-risk bank investment by the market, and in strategic disarray. The transformation [CEO John] McFarlane has rendered over that relatively short period by implementing some exquisite forms of work-harder and work-smarter techniques on his staff has turned ANZ from the industry's lame duck into a highly polished money-making machine with an eye to its customer needs."[1]

Such was the story reported in *The Australian* back in 2001 as ANZ finally turned the page on a dismal chapter in its history. In 1997, it had been grappling with almost A\$2 billion of bad debt and a cost-to-income ratio of nigh on 63 percent. By the end of 2001, it had cleaned up the riskiness of its portfolio, doubled its share price, and reduced its cost-to-income ratio to an industry-leading 46 percent.

ANZ's transformation had begun in 1998, not long after John McFarlane took charge. An initial focus on cost cutting and risk restructuring soon gave way to a broader performance and health program structured around three themes: perform, grow, and break out. The "perform" strand continued the bank's earlier focus on cost drivers and productivity. "Grow" was about transforming the customer experience so as to become "the bank with the human face." "Break out" was concerned with health, and aimed to create a high-performance culture.

One of the most innovative initiatives in the breakout theme was ANZ's leadership development program. It steered clear of traditional tools and approaches for setting direction, managing performance, managing time, and so on. Instead, it strived to embed deeper qualities of leadership such as self-awareness, resilience, and the ability to energize oneself and others. In the words of Siobhan McHale, head of breakout and cultural transformation at ANZ, "We realized the program had to be an 'inside/out' journey. In other words, it's the individual who transforms, and in turn, the organization. Achieving this would not only build a more positive culture, but improve our competitive advantage."[2]

Convinced that there is no better environment for developing leaders than a transformation, ANZ had more than 6,000 individuals take part in the program. The response was tremendous: participants spoke of its "profound impact" and described the experience as "life changing."

Some four years after ANZ's transformation had begun, the turnaround was declared complete, its goals having been met. But the story doesn't end there. Now ANZ ushered in an era of continuous improvement. For instance, under the breakout theme, there were grassroots business initiatives that ranged from delayering to bureaucracy busting, and from creating internal job markets to improving diversity. These efforts were supported by a central infrastructure of some 180 breakout champions who worked in the businesses to foster continuous improvement on top of doing their normal jobs. ANZ also held workshops designed to improve employees' leadership capabilities, cascading them right through the organization in a process that eventually touched more than 26,000 employees.

After 10 years in the CEO suite, John McFarlane retired from the bank in 2007. He left a remarkable legacy. In the years following the transformation, the emphasis on continuous improvement had enabled ANZ to continue its upward trajectory. Since 2002, profit after tax had grown at a cumulative average growth rate of 15 percent, putting ANZ well ahead of the industry pack. Market capitalization had doubled again, and customer satisfaction had soared from 65 percent to 78 percent.

The organization's health remained strong, too. Staff engagement was the highest of all peer organizations in Australia and New Zealand. Job satisfaction ran at more than 80 percent. The share of employees who agree that "we live our values" was 85 percent. Eighty-one percent of employees felt that "we are earning the trust of the community." This clarity of purpose and sense of pride soon led to recognition from the outside world: the accolades ANZ picked up at this time (in some cases for several years running) included *Money* magazine's Consumer Finance Award for Bank of the Year, *Personal Investor* magazine's Bank of the Year, *Asiamoney* magazine's Asia's Best Bank, and *Australian Banking & Finance* magazine's Best Bank in Australia. The "lame duck" of the 1990s had certainly come a long way.

ANZ's experience provides a vivid insight into how to make the transition from the intensive work and constant upheaval of a transformation to a period of continuous improvement. In this phase, a programmatic approach to improving performance and health gives way to a focus on, as John McFarlane put it, "unleash[ing] the potential of some very talented people by giving them a lot of freedom to take their businesses where they've got to go."[3]

How do you achieve this for your organization? You do it by focusing on two things: ensuring that continuous improvement is hardwired into your organization, and leading from a core of self-mastery and ongoing learning.

Performance: Continuous Improvement Infrastructure

Building the capacity for continuous improvement is a task that requires as much energy and focus as any other stage in a transformation. An organization that has come this far on its journey will have much to celebrate, but the work of transformation must still go on. The key to embedding a capacity for continuous improvement in your organization is to hardwire it into its infrastructure. According to our 2010 survey, companies that build the capacity for continuous improvement into their organization are 2.6 times more likely to consider their transformation program a success over the long term.[4]

The transformation program will already have helped develop many of the mindsets and competencies that are needed to support continuous improvement: stronger functional and problem-solving skills, confidence that improvement can be achieved, the breakdown of silo thinking, and so on. But structures, processes, and systems are a different matter. Here the organization will need to take specific steps to put a continuous improvement infrastructure in place. This comprises four main elements: systems for sharing knowledge and best practice, processes to identify and capture opportunities for improvement, methods to facilitate continuous learning, and dedicated expertise. Let's take a look at each of these in turn:

- Putting in place **systems for sharing knowledge and best practice** ensures that relevant improvements in one area are quickly adopted across the organization. Microsoft employees are familiar with the phrase "Knowledge shared is knowledge squared." As former CEO Bill Gates explains, employees "read, ask questions, explore, go to lectures, compare notes and findings . . . consult experts . . . communicate what we're learning and practice new skills."[5] In Germany, Volkswagen has created its own Lean Center, a model factory designed to spread best practices in manufacturing efficiency, ergonomics, and quality, and educate employees about lean, clean process flows that can be applied to all nine brands in the carmaker's group. As a senior executive explained, "Lean is a culture, not a specific process or plan. You have to develop a culture where continuous improvement is the goal."[6] P&G operates a web-based knowledge repository, stages regular reviews to share best practices between brand managers, and constantly updates its international training programs to reflect best practices. In industries characterized by partnerships with customers and suppliers, approaches like these are often extended beyond the company to allow knowledge to be shared and leveraged from one end of a process or relationship to the other.

- Developing **processes to identify and capture opportunities for improvement** enables employees at any level to change things for the better. A lean manufacturing environment is a great place to see this at work. If employees spot a problem on the production floor, they are expected to sort it out there and then: stop the line, get into a huddle to identify the cause, take corrective action, and track progress until the problem is resolved. Such processes can be adopted in any business setting. A notable example of an organization with a well-developed process for improvement is Caterpillar. As part of a transformation launched in 2001, it adopted a continuous product improvement (CPI) process that enables dealers and service representatives to communicate issues raised by customers to the wider organization. When a problem arises, a CPI team from Caterpillar contacts the customer to understand its scale and impact, launches an investigation, and in due course reports back to the aggrieved customer with its findings. It also shares the information with dealers worldwide so as to assist other customers facing similar issues, and with new product development so that relevant findings can be used to improve future product design and manufacture. Thanks to this and other elements in its change effort, Caterpillar was able to deliver an 80 percent increase in revenue from 2001 to 2005.

- Adopting **methods that facilitate continuous learning** gives an organization a chance to pause, step back, and take stock of what's working, what isn't, what it means, and what to do about it. The U.S. Army's After Action Reviews (AARs) serve precisely this purpose, and involve interested observers as well as soldiers from all ranks. They turn training activities into a learning process that asks what was planned, what actually happened, why, and what could be done better next time. The aim is not to judge success or failure, but to focus on learning from the experience so that the organization is better equipped to meet similar challenges in the future. To build its institutional capability in R&D, pharmaceutical company Pfizer holds periodic "lessons learned" sessions for researchers. Such sessions don't necessarily have to take place after the event; "premortems" can also be held to challenge assumptions. Psychologist Gary Klein describes a process in which managers ask members of their team to play devil's advocate and compete to articulate plausible ways that a project might go wrong. As he explains, the strength of the technique is that "The whole dynamic changes from trying to avoid anything that might disrupt harmony to trying to surface potential problems."[7] Moreover, learning shouldn't be confined within the walls of an organization. One international airline studied how pit stops were orchestrated in the Indianapolis 500-Mile Race to help it develop a more efficient luggage-handling system. In much the same way, a construction company took route-planning lessons from a pizza-delivery chain and was able to raise its rate of on-time cement deliveries from 68 percent to 95 percent.[8]

- Having **dedicated expertise** enables organizations to ensure that continuous improvement gets the attention it deserves. Although continuous improvement is everyone's job, companies that excel at it tend to charge certain people and groups—often former members of the program management office—with helping it to happen. Estimates suggest that two-thirds of Fortune 500 organizations have dedicated expertise, typically a core team of skilled individuals who direct and coordinate improvement activities.[9] Motorola has three such teams: *kaizen* teams that address relatively simple challenges; lean teams that focus on cross-functional projects; and Six Sigma teams that perform deep process analytics to resolve complex challenges. At Dutch insurer Eureko, the 200 lean experts trained as described in Chapter 6 continued in their roles and the company also put 20 experts on behavioral change in place to help the Achmea health division with continuous improvement. Public sector organizations are also beginning to invest in dedicated expertise. One Middle Eastern government is setting up an innovation unit to study excellence in government and to identify and share best practices. Expert teams will help government entities implement innovative ideas on the ground, and regular networking events will be staged to facilitate exchange between practitioners.

All four of these elements must be highly tailored to an organization's context. Some organizations will need to stress particular elements more than others. The key to success is to ensure that all the elements are thoughtfully designed and mutually reinforcing.

Let's now move from the organization to the individual, and the qualities of leadership you need to keep an organization constantly moving forward. But before we do so, a quick health warning: even the most capable leaders will struggle to drive continuous improvement if the infrastructure is lacking. To borrow a phrase from the father of modern continuous improvement processes, W. Edwards Deming, "A bad system will beat a good person every time."

Health: Centered Leadership

Creating a continuous improvement infrastructure lays the foundation for ongoing performance. But what about health? The core requirement here is the right kind of leadership.

It's partly a matter of mindsets. Eureko's executive board member Jeroen van Breda Vriesman observes that "It's very important that [leaders] understand that continuous improvement is not a program with an end point. It's about coming to work every day with a new mindset. To understand and really feel that distinction is very important. You can almost see in the results whether top management is implementing continuous improvement or just implementing a program."[10]

Naturally, leadership competencies are vital, too. Putting the right mindsets together with the right competencies is what breathes life into an organization's continuous improvement infrastructure. Although we've chosen to discuss leadership competencies as part of the "advance" stage, in practice the effort to build them takes place right from the beginning of a transformation.

Our research shows that change programs that explicitly address leadership competencies are 3.2 times more likely to succeed than those that don't. But that's not an easy thing to do well. In a recent survey of CEOs and senior executives, 76 percent cited leadership development as important, yet only 7 percent thought their organization was doing it effectively.[11]

So what competencies do you need to lead a continuously improving organization? To be sure, there are many ways to lead, and no shortage of models and theories to help (or confuse) actual and aspiring leaders. The literature on leadership is almost as extensive as that on change management, as a visit to Amazon.com will confirm. We don't propose to discuss technical skills such as goal setting, problem solving, communications, team building, and so on, as these topics are covered in great detail elsewhere. Rather, our aim is to distill the competencies and mindsets that matter most in driving continuous improvement.

These things don't just enable leaders to be effective in driving performance and health, but also keep them passionate about their work and satisfied with their lives. In this way, they help leaders avoid the traps of burnout and exhaustion that lie in wait when the adrenaline-fueled intensity of transformation gives way to the ceaseless effort of continuous improvement. We refer to these competencies and mindsets as centered leadership.

Centered Leadership Defined

The centered leadership model comprises five elements, which, when combined, give leaders the resilience and emotional capacity to continuously improve themselves as they continuously improve their organization (Exhibit 7.1).

Exhibit 7.1
The Elements of Centered Leadership

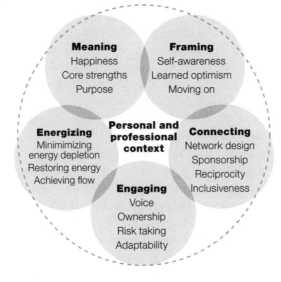

- **Meaning**
  Happiness
  Core strengths
  Purpose
- **Framing**
  Self-awareness
  Learned optimism
  Moving on
- **Energizing**
  Minimimizing
  energy depletion
  Restoring energy
  Achieving flow
- **Personal and professional context**
- **Connecting**
  Network design
  Sponsorship
  Reciprocity
  Inclusiveness
- **Engaging**
  Voice
  Ownership
  Risk taking
  Adaptability

These elements are:

- **Meaning:** finding and communicating personal meaning in work, and enabling others to tap into their own sources of motivation and purpose.
- **Framing:** discovering opportunities in adversity by viewing even the most difficult problems in a way that opens up constructive and creative solutions.
- **Connecting:** taking active steps to build a web of internal and external relationships.
- **Engaging:** generating the confidence to step up and act, involving themselves and others in the face of uncertainty and risk.
- **Energizing:** investing systematically in one's own physical, mental, and emotional energy and creating the practices and norms needed to energize others.

A *McKinsey Quarterly* survey of 1,147 executives found that the five elements of centered leadership are mutually reinforcing.[12] Respondents who reported that they frequently practiced four or all five gave high ratings to their passion for their work, their effectiveness as leaders, and their satisfaction with life (Exhibit 7.2).

We'll now take a closer look at these elements, bearing in mind that as important as each one is, it's the combination of all five that gives the centered leadership model its power.

MEANING In the centered leadership model, "meaning" relates to a leader's ability to motivate himself and others. Leaders who score high on meaning feel a deep personal commitment to the work they do, and pursue their goals with energy and enthusiasm. They know their strengths, use them to the best of their ability, enjoy their work, and inspire others to do the same. Of all the dimensions of centered leadership, meaning makes the greatest contribution to satisfaction with work and life. In fact, our survey shows that its impact on overall life satisfaction is five times more powerful than that of any other dimension.[13]

The idea that meaning is the prime source of personal energy is not new. Research by leading thinkers such as Danah Zohar, Don Beck and Chris Cowen, and Richard Barrett has shown that inspirational leadership is not about charisma and cheerleading—it's about engaging fully in one's own purpose and helping others connect with theirs.[14] People achieve the most extraordinary feats if their purpose is truly meaningful to them. Of

Exhibit 7.2
Multiplying the Benefits

Centered leadership Number of dimensions practiced frequently*	Percent of respondents achieving high level of success in each outcome, by number of dimensions practiced*		
	Passion for work	**Leadership effectiveness**	**Life satisfaction**
0 out of 5	14	12	15
1 out of 5	15	18	18
2 out of 5	24	29	25
3 out of 5	42	45	47
4 out of 5	50	63	53
5 out of 5	100	100	100

* Respondents answered a series of questions to assess how frequently they practice each dimension of centered leadership; "frequently" and "high level of success" both refer to the top 20 percent of respondents in each group.

Source: July–October 2009 McKinsey survey of 1,147 executives in the financial services industry

course, the opposite is equally true: when you can't help wondering "Why am I doing this?" it's hard to get great results.

Aristotle argued in the fourth century BC that people achieve "eudaimonia," a contented sense of flourishing as a human being, when they use their talents to the full, thereby satisfying their basic function in life. In the twentieth century, psychologist Abraham Maslow gave the concept the new name of "self-actualization" and put it at the top of his hierarchy of human needs.[15]

Meaning is closely linked to happiness and energy. Engaging in activities that you choose to do, that use your core strengths, and that give you a sense of purpose leaves you with a deep and enduring sense of fulfillment. When this happens, hard work energizes rather than depletes you. Similarly, when leaders connect to their own source of authentic purpose, they create positive energy around them, becoming more compelling as role models and more inspiring as communicators. As they get better at helping the people around them to do whatever they are doing, they unleash a huge amount of collective energy in their organization.

A strong sense of personal meaning boosts motivation, generates followership, and enhances personal and business productivity in ways that formal incentives or sanctions can't match. And leading from a place of meaning creates a virtuous cycle. The greater your contribution to something bigger than yourself, the deeper the sense of meaning you derive from it, the more you inspire others, and so on. As well as influencing others and improving outcomes, you also derive great personal satisfaction.

Research by psychologist Sonja Lyubomirsky indicates that short of undergoing brain surgery, finding meaningful work is the best way to increase happiness over the long term.[16] This is confirmed by thinkers in the field of positive psychology, which focuses not on treating mental illness but on making normal life more fulfilling. They define happiness in terms of three states: pleasure, flow, and meaning (which is foremost in the hierarchy).[17] The notion of "meaning making" is entering the business lexicon. Gary Hamel, a business thinker and the author of our Foreword, urges modern managers to see themselves as "entrepreneurs of meaning."[18]

But what does that involve in practical terms? CEO Tom Glocer can shed some light on this. Having taken the top job at Reuters during troubled times in 2001, Glocer got to work with his leadership team and turned the company around. So far, so good, but soon people started to wonder: What next? As Glocer comments, "The imminent threat of collapse had fueled all of us, but what was the rallying cry now?"[19]

Glocer proceeded to reflect on what the organization's deeper sense of purpose might be, and held many dialogues with other leaders to encourage them to do the same. Gradually a purpose emerged that everyone was passionate about: improving the quality of decision making for individuals, organizations, and society in general by providing the right information at the right time. When Reuters merged with Thomson in 2008, the organization acquired the enormous scale it needed to achieve this ambitious goal. Under Glocer's continued leadership, it has built on its strengths to become one of the world's leading sources of information for businesses and professionals, with 55,000 employees in more than 100 countries.

FRAMING   The frame we use to view the world and process our experiences can make a huge difference to personal and professional outcomes alike. Optimists who choose to focus on the opportunities in any situation have a clear edge over pessimists who focus on the threats.

Optimism correlates with success and much more: health and popularity, for starters. As Bill Clinton famously remarked, "No one in his right mind wants to be led by a pessimist." Of course, not everyone is a born optimist.

Many of us aren't, and researchers say that as much as 50 percent of a person's outlook is genetically determined. However, in *Learned Optimism*, Martin Seligman argues that optimism can be acquired.[20] Pessimists can't change their basic personality, but they can learn to apply the tools that optimists habitually use without even realizing it to put events and situations into their proper context.

It's easy to see how positive framing can improve leadership capabilities. Pessimists tend to view negative situations as permanent, pervasive, and personal. This can limit their range of thinking, preventing them from seeing strategic options and rapidly draining energy in a downward spiral. Conversely, optimists view negative situations as temporary, specific, and externally caused. This helps them see the facts for what they are, identify new possibilities, and act swiftly.

Imagine you're giving a presentation to your bosses. They seem distracted, and halfway through, the most senior leader gets up and leaves the room. At the end of your presentation, you get a subdued response rather than the fanfare you'd secretly been hoping for. As you leave the room, what are the thoughts that run through your head? Do you wonder if your content or delivery were off the mark? Do you start to worry that management has lost confidence in you? Could your career be starting to spiral?

Or does it cross your mind that the team may be grappling with an urgent problem that's only just arisen? Perhaps your presentation came at a bad time, and yet they value you so much that they didn't want to cancel your slot? You might even have taken the opportunity to stop and ask, "Should I carry on with this, or do you need to be somewhere else right now?"

We all constantly make assumptions about our environment, whether through an optimistic or pessimistic lens. For leaders, optimism, be it learned or innate, is at the heart of resilience: the ability to absorb shocks, assess their implications, and respond effectively. Taking risks, as all leaders must do, exposes us to the risk of failure. When things go wrong, it's positive framing that enables us to recover gracefully. Pessimism, on the other hand, can lead to a relentless dwelling on the negative that can paralyze a leader and stop the organization in its tracks.

To be clear, positive framing is *not* the same as what people call "the power of positive thinking." Research shows that talking yourself into a positive outlook has at best a temporary effect. In any case, genuine optimists tend to be realists. Perhaps surprisingly, they are more able to face the brutal facts than pessimists are. They are susceptible to a different kind of pitfall: persisting in trying to resolve an intractable problem long after it's become time to move on.

The need to strike a balance between hope and realism is vividly illustrated in the "Stockdale paradox" described by Jim Collins in his book *Good to Great*. Admiral Jim Stockdale was the highest-ranking U.S. military officer in the so-called "Hanoi Hilton" prisoner of war camp at the height of the Vietnam War. Imprisoned from 1965 to 1973, he was frequently tortured, and had no prisoner's rights, no release date, and no certainty that he would ever see his family again. How did he survive? "I never doubted not only that I would get out, but also that I would prevail in the end and turn the experience into the defining event of my life . . . [But] you must never confuse faith that you will prevail in the end—which you can never afford to lose—with the discipline to confront the most brutal facts of your current reality, whatever they might be."[21]

Australia's first woman prime minister, Julia Gillard, who took office in 2010, sums up the power of framing well: "If you worry about everything that can go wrong, you would never do anything. You've got to be able to focus on the things that really matter and not lose too much sleep on the rest. . . . in the exposure of national politics, if you got upset every time a newspaper columnist wrote something negative, or a voter came in to critique . . . then you wouldn't get through it."[22]

Leaders who frame things positively can sometimes snatch victory from the jaws of defeat. When Thomas Edison was 67, his laboratory was destroyed in a fire. His response as his life's work lay in ruins? "There's great value in this disaster. All our mistakes are now burned and we can start anew." Three weeks later, he produced his first phonograph.

Another leader who has triumphed over adversity by framing his experiences in a positive light is Steve Jobs. After co-founding Apple in 1976, he was forced out in 1984, an event that many an executive might have regarded as a career-ending body blow. But Jobs didn't see it that way: "Getting fired from Apple was the best thing that could have ever happened to me. The heaviness of being successful was replaced by the lightness of being a beginner again . . . it freed me to enter one of the most creative periods of my life."[23]

As well as creative, it proved highly lucrative. Not long after leaving Apple, Jobs made the most profitable investment of his life: picking up the computer graphics division from George Lucas's Lucasfilm for US$5 million. The company didn't succeed in turning a profit in its original capacity as a graphics hardware developer, but it did rather better in its subsequent incarnation as Pixar. After forming a partnership with Disney, it scored a massive public and critical hit with its first film, *Toy Story*, in 1995, where-upon Jobs engineered an exquisitely timed public offering that made him an instant billionaire. A handful of blockbusters later, Jobs sold Pixar to Disney in 2006, in a deal that netted him a seat on its board and a share of its stock worth more than US$3 billion.

Jobs didn't do too badly back at the old firm either. After returning to Apple as an adviser in 1996, he became interim CEO in 1997, and subsequently CEO and chairman. Under his leadership, Apple has produced a stream of products that transformed high-tech boxes into some of the most desirable goods on the main street. The elegant pared-down design and innovative features of the iPod, iPhone, and iPad have captivated consumers, and the almost 18-fold rise in Apple's annual net income from 2000 to 2010 has kept shareholders happy as well.

CONNECTING   Another mark of the centered leader is the ability to forge relationships with influential people from many different stakeholder groups. Centered leaders build complex webs of connections that both amplify their personal influence and accelerate their personal development because of the diversity of ideas and experiences that they encounter through their contact with others.

Relationships are essential to our well-being, of course, as well as our success. However, we don't always give them the attention they deserve. Ronald Heifetz and Marty Linsky argue that people who are thoughtful about personal relationships are more successful as leaders.[24] When it comes to building relationships, researchers have shown that women and men typically adopt different approaches.[25] Whereas women prefer to build a small number of deep relationships, men tend to build broader but shallower networks.

Organizations need both types of networks, in fact, and both can be mastered by anyone. Broad but shallow networks provide a wide range of resources that help us expand our knowledge and professional opportunities, and make it easy to enlist enough people to drive change. Narrow but deep networks can give us access to the "let me tell you how it really is" type of advice that comes from a more intimate relationship based on knowledge and trust. Psychological research shows that this kind of relationship is also one of our greatest sources of fulfillment.

When we advocate building a network of influential people, we don't mean one that consists only of our peers or superiors in the organization hierarchy. Junior employees should be included, too—a type of networking that Jack Welch called "reverse mentoring." He hit on the idea when he realized that he was struggling to use the internet effectively, and connected up with two much younger people at GE who could help him get up to speed. Finding the approach effective, he got his top 500 leaders to look for internet mentors of their own, recommending that they choose someone below the age of 30.[26]

The ability to connect and network requires a strong grounding in emotional intelligence: sensitivity to our own and others' emotional states. Thomson Reuters CEO Tom Glocer has observed that in his experience, truly exceptional leaders have "much higher amounts of emotional intelligence" than others.[27] Fortunately, EQ is learnable, as we saw in Chapter 5. Emotionally intelligent leaders quickly establish rapport with others through a combination of attention and empathy. Their relationships are based on reciprocity, with equal give and take. Social psychologist Johnathan Haidt notes that "Relationships persist to the degree that both people involved believe that what they are getting out of the relationship is proportionate to what they put in."[28] At work, such reciprocal relationships can have a powerful effect on performance.

Leaders can use their EQ to be strategic about where they connect. Approaches such as social network analysis (described in Chapter 5) enable them to work out where they may have gaps in their networks so that they can take steps to fill them. Networking consultant and executive coach Carole Kammen encourages leaders to seek out a whole host of benefits in their networks: wisdom and experience, a sympathetic ear, challenges and shifts in perspective, help in navigating the social system, nonstop coaching, visionary inspiration, and sponsors who will pound the table for you.

Organizations can do a lot internally to get the right people together and encourage them to pool their wisdom across geographies, hierarchies, and silos. At W. L. Gore, makers of Gore-Tex waterproof fabric, the founders banished formal structures outright to allow fluid working teams to form and thrive. As part of the system, new hires are expected to focus on building relationships during the first three to six months of their careers. HR leader Donna Frey explains, "Often new associates will say, 'I don't feel like I'm contributing. I've spent three months just getting to know people.' However, after a year they begin to realize how important this process was."[29]

Most senior leaders are used to delegating to a small team of top executives with well-defined roles. Cisco Systems does things differently. CEO John Chambers works with cross-functional "collaborative councils" to set and implement strategy. As we saw in Chapter 3, he admits that learning to work this way didn't come easily, but it has allowed Cisco to be far more nimble as a company. "The days of being vertically integrated and having

everything within your control will never return," he declares.[30] When senior leaders like Chambers take on the responsibility of "connector-in-chief,"
they start to think less about "who works for me" and more about "who
does what."

A final benefit of having a strong personal network is the learning and
growth that comes from exposure to a multitude of different perspectives. As
U.S. property and business magnate Donald Trump puts it, "Watch, listen,
and learn. You can't know it all yourself. Anyone who thinks they do is
destined for mediocrity."

ENGAGING   Engaging is about being willing to take bold action. We approach work and life with the mindset of "If it's to be, it's up to me." We
feel we are personally accountable and can positively influence our own
experience, our team, and our organization. On the other hand, people
who are disengaged tend to be passive and feel that events are out of their
control. Rather than trying to fix problems, they attribute blame. In our
survey on centered leadership, respondents who indicated they were poor
at engaging—with risk, with fear, or even with opportunity—also lacked
confidence: only 13 percent thought they had the skills to lead change.[31]

In the 1950s, psychologist Julian Rotter developed the theory that our
personalities are determined not just by our innate character traits but by the
way we engage with society. He introduced the concept of "locus of control"
and argued that people who have an *internal* locus of control understand
they are agents with the power to determine outcomes, whereas people
with an *external* locus of control believe that their actions have no bearing
on their fate.[32] Engagement differs from framing in that positive framing
enables us to *see* an opportunity, while engagement gives us the courage
to risk *capturing* it.

Writing in 1951, the mountaineer and author W. H. Murray sums up
one of the things that makes engaging so powerful: "Until one is committed,
there is hesitancy, the chance to draw back, always ineffectiveness. . . . the
moment one definitely commits oneself, then providence moves too." For
him, engaging sets in motion a whole chain of events that "[raises] in one's
favor all manner of unforeseen incidents, meetings, and material assistance
which no man could have dreamt would have come his way."[33]

So how can we expand our level of engagement? It helps if we have an
elementary grasp of how the physiology of the brain governs our instinctive
responses.

Put simply, the brain consists of three parts: the brain stem, which deals
with basic functions such as breathing; the limbic system, which regulates

emotions; and the neo-cortex, which governs logical reasoning and creativity. Within the limbic system is an organ called the amygdala whose function is to save us from physical or emotional harm. As information about our surroundings enters our senses, the amygdala tests it on the way to the neo-cortex to determine whether we have time to think. If it detects a threat, it short-circuits our rational thought processes and prompts an immediate reaction.

Should a car roar toward you as you cross the road, you instinctively leap out of its path. Only when you're safely back on the curb does your brain take the time to work out what's just happened. Thinking first and acting second would have ended in disaster, or so your amygdala tells you. But our instinctive reaction can often be out of proportion to the actual threat: cars don't as a rule try to mow down pedestrians. This "amygdala hijack"—the term given to what happens when our emotional response overwhelms our rational thought processes—isn't confined to life-or-death situations. It also operates in the workplace, where it can have powerful unintended consequences.

Imagine your amygdala interprets an innocent comment from a colleague as a threat. It could trigger an instinctive "fight, flight, or freeze" response of anger, withdrawal, or denial. This can set off a downward spiral both internally (resentment or thoughts of revenge) and externally (passive-aggressive nodding to feign agreement or a heated row). But simply by being aware of this process, centered leaders can take stock, ground themselves, and choose the most constructive response. Instead of letting instinct take over, they can take ownership of the situation, understand it more fully, and seek a solution.

A survivor of the Auschwitz prisoner of war camp who went on to write *Man's Search for Meaning*, Victor Frankl, speaks of the power of exerting control over one's instinctive responses: "In between stimulus and response lies the freedom of choice." For leaders, this freedom manifests itself in a willingness to speak up and take ownership of their careers (and their lives) by facing fears, seizing opportunities, and making efforts to further their goals.

A powerful example of engaging comes from Jean Vanier, the Canadian founder of L'Arche. Taking its name from the French for "ark," it's an international organization that creates communities where people with and without mental disabilities can live together and support and learn from one another. Back in the early 1960s, Vanier's friendship with a French priest had led him to visit a number of institutions for mentally disabled people.

He was shocked by the conditions he found there: "a kind of warehouse of human misery" was how he put it.[34]

Convinced that the people incarcerated in these institutions had not only rights but gifts they could share with others, Vanier threw all his energies into what became a lifelong campaign to rethink the role of mentally disabled people in society. His first step was simple, but bold: he bought a house and invited two men to leave their institutions and share it with him. And so the first l'Arche community was born.

The idea and the community grew rapidly, and Vanier began to hold conferences and retreats around the world to share his experiences and develop a new model that was to transform the lives of thousands of people. L'Arche is now a federation of 137 communities spanning 40 countries. Vanier's engagement in overturning centuries of prejudice and ill treatment won him numerous awards, including the French Legion of Honor and the Companion of the Order of Canada. But the real winners are the residents of the l'Arche communities. A resident with no disabilities explains, "Since living here, I am convinced that spending time together is more important than what we do for people, or the skills we can teach them. Most of the folks [people with disabilities] aren't used to people choosing to be with them, and genuinely liking them. That's what we can really give."[35]

Another example of an engaging leader is Oprah Winfrey. Born into poverty in rural Mississippi, she has lived the archetypal "rags to riches" story. Her childhood home had no electricity or plumbing, she was often left to fend for herself, and she suffered physical and sexual abuse from an early age. These early experiences could easily have blighted her whole life. Instead, she found that she could channel them into her work, first as a radio anchor at the tender age of 19, and later on TV. In what at the time was a risky move, she engaged her audience by sharing her own experiences and fears directly with them.

After delivering a huge ratings boost within months of taking over the morning talk show *AM Chicago* in 1984, she went on to develop her reputation as "the queen of talk" over the course of a long TV career in which she created deep trust with audiences in the studio and at home by combining openness with "plainspoken curiosity, robust humor, and above all, empathy."[36] The phenomenal success of her multiple-award-winning *Oprah* show has made her one of the most influential people in the world according to the lists compiled by Forbes and *Time* magazine. She was even credited with helping Barack Obama in the 2008 presidential election by delivering him a million extra votes.[37]

Engaging is not just about being willing to take risks and pursue bold aspirations. It's also about doing more than is expected of you. Merck CEO Richard Clark led the creation of a joint venture with the Wellcome Trust to develop affordable vaccines for diseases that are rife in poorer countries. No one asked him to do it; he simply saw what had to be done and took the challenge upon himself. As he explains, "There is a critical need to develop new ways for scientific innovation to be translated effectively into new vaccines that can save lives and protect the health of people living in low-income countries. We believe that success in bringing forward these new vaccines can be best achieved through productive partnerships."[38] And so he went for it.

As these stories illustrate, engaging means being willing to step outside your comfort zone. That can feel awkward, stressful, unnerving, scary, even terrifying—"uncomfortable" is the least of it. But stepping outside your comfort zone can also be exhilarating, as anyone knows who has ever leaped out of a plane, taken a bungee jump off a bridge, or done any back-country skiing.

No matter how you feel, though, what actually happens when you step outside your comfort zone? In effect, what you're doing is entering a learning zone instead. As you learn, you get accustomed to situations that you used to find challenging; then you start to master them. In time, your comfort zone expands as you move from learning to mastery in one set of situations after another. And by stepping from your comfort zone into the learning zone on a regular basis, you also become comfortable with the *process* of doing so.

This process is right at the heart of continuous improvement, for organizations as well as individuals. It's about recognizing, in the words of Irish footballer Jim Goodwin, that "The impossible is often the untried." Continuous improvement won't happen unless leaders are prepared to spend a lot of their time trying to do things that were previously regarded as impossible.

ENERGIZING   Continuous improvement requires enthusiasm and commitment from a mass of people across the whole organization. This will be hard to sustain unless leaders systemically restore their own energy levels and create the conditions for others to do likewise.

Psychologist Mihály Csíkszentmihályi has observed that fully employing one's core capabilities to meet a goal or challenge creates a mental state of "flow," in which work becomes effortless and time seems to stand still.[39] Athletes describe this feeling as being "in the zone"; musicians call it "in the groove." Csíkszentmihályi studied thousands of subjects, from sculptors to factory workers, and asked them to record their feelings at intervals throughout the working day. When he correlated flow to performance, he found that individuals with frequent experiences of flow were more productive and derived greater satisfaction from their work. They also set themselves goals to increase their capabilities to meet greater challenges, thereby tapping into a seemingly limitless well of energy. In fact, their experience of flow was so pleasurable that they expressed a willingness to repeat flow-generating experiences even if they were not being paid to do so.

Flow sounds great, but how do we achieve it? According to Csíkszent-mihályi, it happens when we set goals that challenge us and require all our skills; when we give an effort our full attention and focus; and when we receive regular feedback from the environment so that we can fine-tune our efforts for the greatest possible impact. These conditions enable us to tap into all our energy sources in the moment.

But what if we do every one of these things and still fail? If that happens, and there are sure to be times when it does, our ability to pick ourselves up off the floor, restore our energies, and start again will be key. This is where the other four elements of centered leadership come together: reflecting on our purpose and strengths, maintaining a positive outlook, reaching out to our networks, and boldly moving on to the next challenge. The ability to recover gracefully from failure is at the heart of resilience—a leadership characteristic that is essential to leading continuous improvement.

To encourage flow, leaders can adopt specific practices that increase mindfulness. Anna Wise's book *The High-Performance Mind* explains how brainwave patterns affect our ability to perform.[40] She used an EEG (electro-encephalograph) machine to measure what happens in the brain when individuals move from a state of stress or distraction to a state of focus or flow. By building on these findings, researchers have developed techniques to help leaders achieve a degree of mastery in moving in and out of states of flow.

Simple tactics like energy management can also increase the amount of flow leaders experience in their work and personal life. Tony Schwartz and Jim Loehr, professional speakers, writers, and founders of the Energy Project, recommend that people should manage their energy rather than their time. Time is finite, so managing it is like dividing up a pie. But if you manage energy well, you generate more, and so the whole pie gets bigger.[41]

Our research shows that it's possible to adapt our routines at work and at home to boost our energy reserves and make the pie bigger. We can manage our personal stocks of cognitive, social, spiritual, physical, and emotional energy by identifying the situations that deplete or restore them. Which is which isn't always obvious, since the same activity can have different effects on different people. Take driving home at the end of the day. For some people, it can be calming and restorative—a buffer between work and home that provides a space to recover from the events of the day. For others, the same drive in the same car in the same traffic can be stressful and draining.

This puts a new spin on the concept of work/life balance. At work, we can encounter experiences that restore our energy as well as those that deplete it. Once we know which experiences have which effect, we can arrange our daily activities so as to keep our energy reserves topped up instead of emptying the tank.

Some enlightened companies have embraced this idea and actively encourage employees to top up their energy levels, whether by conventional or unconventional means. Staff at Google can devote as much as 20 percent of their time to working on whatever they choose, enabling them to take a break from their day job that both restores their energy and creates something of value. This proved a smart move for Google, too: it reckons that up to half of its new products have been hatched by staff pursuing their own pet projects. And not content with providing a gym to help employees keep fit, the company encourages them to walk between the scores of buildings spread across its extensive campus. Recognizing the importance of sleep in maintaining energy levels, Google allows staff to take breaks when they need it, and has even set up special "nap pods" at various locations across its site.[42] Nutrition is part of the energy equation, too, with 11 restaurants, numerous micro-kitchens for healthy snacks, and just a single vending machine, in which chips and cookies cost far more than the more nutritious alternatives available.

Other organizations are working along similar lines. ANZ sets aside relaxation rooms so that employees can recharge during the working day. It also allows employees to take up to four weeks of unpaid "lifestyle leave" on top of their normal annual entitlement to use as they see fit. In much the same way, Sony Europe offers "chill-out" rooms, recognizing that although its business is about technology, it depends on people.

In the end, though, it's up to us to take responsibility for energizing ourselves. That might mean something as simple as turning off our cell phones or setting aside a regular time in our day for reflection. Equally, it might mean something more elaborate. Consider the story of Jurek Gruhn, the president of Novo Nordisk US, a pharmaceutical company with particular expertise in diabetes care. When Gruhn was himself diagnosed with diabetes, he was forced to adopt a healthier lifestyle: "I eat breakfast now every day, I exercise much more, and I started rock climbing on a regular basis."[43] But he found that the energy payback made it all worthwhile: it wasn't just his health that improved, but his mental focus, emotional satisfaction, and spirit, too. He made changes in his working life as well. When unhealthy conflict came up, for instance, he tried to address it quickly and directly rather than let it fester below the surface, as he might have done before.

The Journey to Centered Leadership

Taken together, the five elements of centered leadership help people achieve their goals in work and life through a strong sense of purpose, belonging, lightness of being, resilience, and control. Centered leaders are well equipped to drive continuous improvement and to make the most of all the challenges and opportunities that come when you are doing something new every day. So how do you and others in your organization become more centered leaders?

In most cases, the journey to centered leadership takes a lifetime of experience. That said, it is possible to hasten your progress along the road. In fact, a transformation offers the ideal conditions: hectic activity, widespread uncertainty, and numerous opportunities for feedback.

As with any development effort, the best way for an organization to build centered leadership competencies will depend on its culture and context. However, most successful efforts share certain characteristics. They:

- **Have a direct link to performance improvement.** Centered leadership attributes are best developed in the context of a live business project that poses demands and offers opportunities that stretch the leader. This anchors learning in the real world and ensures it is retained.
- **Start from a quantifiable baseline.** The extent to which a leader embodies the five attributes of centered leadership can be established through a self-assessment coupled with 360-degree feedback. Gathering such information not only yields insights into strengths, gaps, and blind spots, but also sets a baseline against which to measure progress during the development journey.
- **Accommodate different learning styles.** People learn in different ways, so leadership development efforts need to employ a range of

cognitive, visual, and kinesthetic methods and media. Typical activities might include making videos, performing role plays, discussing real-life cases, telling stories, and taking part in simulations. People vary in their pace of learning, too, so at least part of the program must be self-directed.

- **Allow for self-discovery.** A directive approach is not the best way to reach bright, thoughtful people; they must *want* to change and grow. The secret to lasting leadership development is to instill a felt need to learn, and then offer content that enables participants to derive their own insights. To mangle a proverb, centered leadership programs are less about leading a horse to water than about making it aware that it's thirsty.

To see how the pieces of the jigsaw fit together, consider the case of a large chemical company that had devised a comprehensive process for building centered leaders. It selected 25 people who were high performers, good at leading people, eager to learn, and in positions of influence where leadership skills were most needed. Each of these 25 leaders then chose two senior sponsors and three junior people to coach. That multiplied the original 25 participants by five so that the program reached 125 people in all, creating a nucleus for change in the organization.

The learning journey for the 25 core participants revolved around eight days of forum-style training conducted in three sessions over six months.

The first forum focused on applying centered leadership principles to leading oneself. Participants learned to be accountable for their behavior in difficult situations, to regulate it, to manage their energy and attention so as to maintain their productivity, to develop a strong support network, to leave their comfort zone and commit to opportunities, and to use their personal vision to motivate themselves.

The second forum took the attributes of centered leadership and helped participants see how they could be used in leading and influencing others. The topics covered in this session included motivating others by tapping into their sense of meaning, turning difficult conversations into moments of learning, building relationships based on trust, and providing distinctive coaching and sponsorship.

The third forum applied centered leadership principles to leading organizational change. It looked at techniques for working with others to create organizational alignment, generating energy through storytelling, understanding system dynamics and where to intervene, creating an environment for learning and creativity, and keeping a balance between performance and health over time.

Before the forums began, participants gathered 360-degree feedback and did self-assessments. The process was repeated six months later. Between the forums, the participants undertook learning assignments to apply their newly acquired insights and skills in their work on their organization's transformation program. Reflection time was built into the field-work through regular individual coaching and small-group peer coaching sessions.

At the end of the journey the leaders had driven advances in performance and health in their parts of the organization, built strong and healthy networks, and become role models not just for "what to do" but also "how to be" in supporting continuous performance improvement.

Let's look at another case to see the specific gains that centered leadership can bring. When John Akehurst took over as CEO at Woodside Petroleum, it was evident that leadership was one among many areas in need of attention. The Woodside Country Club, as it had been dubbed, was in the bottom quartile globally for cost performance, and had a culture of complacency. To tackle these issues, Akehurst launched a transformation that included an extensive leadership program with days of experiential training on centered leadership principles. The program was not just for the senior team, but was cascaded through virtually all of Woodside's 2,000 employees.

By the end of the process, Woodside had such a strong institutional capability that it not only showed resilience to the subsequent series of layoffs and takeover attempts, but positively thrived. Employees' connection to meaning jumped from 50 percent to 80 percent, and their feeling of being inspired and energized from 60 percent to 85 percent. Moreover, as Akehurst explains, "The way we work together fundamentally changed. We used to spend a lot of time tending to people's egos and building fiefdoms. Through the performance leadership process we saw, there was a more creative, empowering, and encouraging way to lead that still allowed discipline and rigor to be pre-eminent. We also built the courage to go for it and make it happen."[44] In his seven years as CEO, Akehurst turned Woodside into a top-decile performer, creating AU$7 billion of new shareholder value on a base of AU$3 billion.

■ ■ ■

The "advance" stage differs from the other four stages in that it's never over. Your organization may have come to the end of its transformation, but there's no end to the task of continuously improving its performance and health.

That's not to say, though, that a continuously improving organization will have no need to go through a full-scale transformation ever again. Such is the pace of change that most organizations are likely to require step-change improvement programs from time to time in response to new customer needs, technological innovations, or shifts in the competitive landscape.[45]

But being a continuously improving organization represents a powerful competitive advantage. And if your organization can couple the experience that comes from a successful transformation with the capability to continuously improve everything it does, it will be virtually unstoppable, even in the most unpredictable of worlds. To get there, you'll need to put in place a robust continuous improvement infrastructure with knowledge sharing, improvement processes, learning methods, and dedicated expertise. And on top of that, you'll need to use your whole transformation as a platform to build centered leadership qualities that emanate from a core of self-mastery, and that drive continuous performance improvement in a way that energizes the organization, rather than exhausts it.

How does it feel to have worked through the five frames? Who better to ask than John McFarlane, who led the transformation that we described at the beginning of the chapter before retiring in 2007. As he sees it, the journey took ANZ "from a traditional banking culture into a modern, vibrant organization, creating a shared vision of an exciting organization that doesn't just create a one-time change, but gives us momentum into the future."

PART III

Putting It All Together

CHAPTER 8

The Senior Leader's Role

Does Change Have to Start at the Top?

B y this point, you should have a clear map of your journey to organizational excellence. This is a journey that will take you through the five
stages of aspire, assess, architect, act, and advance to improve both your
near-term performance and your long-term health. It's our firm belief that by
following this path, almost any organization can transform its performance
successfully and sustainably so that it can out-execute the competition consistently over time.

As we've seen again and again in the companies we feature in this book,
leadership and role modeling are central to the transformation journey.
Both of these should start right at the top of the organization. John Mackey
of Whole Foods Market explains why: "As the co-founder and CEO, I'm
the most visible person in the company . . . our team members are always
studying me . . . I'm always on stage."[1]

With that in mind, this chapter is devoted to the role of the senior leader
in spearheading a transformation. The senior leader means the CEO in a
corporation, the director of a government agency, the head of a nonprofit,
or whoever is in charge of an organization, no matter what their title may
be. Their role is fundamental: our 2010 survey shows that transformations
are 2.6 times more likely to succeed if they have strong involvement from
the top of the organization.[2]

Does that mean this chapter is for senior leaders only? Not at all. By
learning what the senior leader's role in a transformation should be, readers
at lower levels of an organization—and would-be leaders, too—can help
their own senior leader to fulfill it. If you're trying to change your organization, there's no doubt that the path will be easier and more direct if your
most senior leader is on your side, supporting you and playing a full role
in the change effort.

Reading this chapter gives you an insight into what you can expect of a senior leader who commits to this role. Through dozens of examples, you see what the most effective senior leaders do to lead from the top and channel the energies and passions of their organizations into remarkable feats of transformation and continuous improvement.

Don't forget that when you're trying to get your senior leader on board, you can draw on the influence model from Chapter 5. In doing so, you'll need to give some thought to their personal style and preferences. Whose opinions do they trust? What kind of transformation story will resonate with them? Do they understand and accept the role they need to play? Will they need to build new skills to play it? And are there any processes that would help to make all this happen?

It's also worth noting that the actions we commend to senior leaders, such as spotlighting successes and engaging others, are valuable steps for leaders at any level. But if the lead doesn't come from the top, efforts made further down the organization won't have the impact that they otherwise would.

What Only the Senior Leader Can Do

The senior leader's role is unique. The person at the top of the pyramid provides cues for everyone else in the organization as to what really matters around here.

A senior leader who's perceived as merely paying lip service to a transformation shouldn't be surprised when everyone else does the same. Fail to model the desired mindsets and behavior or opt out of "mission-critical" initiatives and you risk seeing the transformation lose focus and momentum. *Only the senior leader can ensure that the right people spend the right amount of time on driving the right changes.*

To bring home the importance of the senior leader's role, let's imagine it as a huge gear connected to progressively smaller ones. If the biggest gear does one click as it completes a rotation, the next gear down will click five or six times, and the gear below that 10 or 12 times. Go down a few more gears in the system, and the little gears are spinning very fast indeed.

What happens if the biggest gear changes its mind and decides to rotate in the opposite direction? The gear below screeches to a halt, and then starts moving in the opposite direction as well. Down the line, all the other gears start to shear. Sparks fly and the poor little gear at the bottom screeches so much that it shears right off and out of the system. Such is the power of the senior leader!

Yet surprisingly little has been written about the role of the senior leader in a transformation. Perhaps that's because there's no single recipe for success. The precise nature of the role will be influenced by the scale, urgency, and nature of the transformation, the organization's capabilities, and the senior leader's personal style. That said, our research and experience with scores of transformation efforts have enabled us to identify four key roles played by successful senior leaders:

- **Making the transformation meaningful.** The impact of the change story depends on the extent to which the senior leader makes it personal, openly engages others, and spotlights successes as they emerge.
- **Role modeling desired mindsets and behavior.** Successful senior leaders typically embark on a personal transformation journey of their own. Through their actions, they show what the new behavior looks like and encourage employees to adopt it in their own daily work.
- **Building a strong and committed top team.** To harness the transformative power of the top team, senior leaders must make tough decisions about who has the capability and motivation to make the journey.
- **Relentlessly pursuing impact.** Where significant customer impact or financial or symbolic value is at stake, there's no substitute for senior leaders rolling up their sleeves and getting personally involved.

In combination, these four roles help to ensure that the transformation effort wins what we call the "war for the middle." In most transformations we've seen, there's a small percentage of employees who are completely on board from the outset. At the other extreme, there's another small percentage who may never come on board, and are likely to leave the organization if the changes come to pass. But the majority are in the middle, trying to work out whether this is just a passing fad, whether real change can ever happen, and whether it's worth the energy to get on board and risk being let down again. For this very large group, seeing the senior leader playing these roles goes a long way in persuading them to believe, get on board, and invest in turning the transformation into a reality.

Making the Transformation Meaningful

Transformations call for extraordinary energy, as we've seen throughout this book. Leaders and employees are required to rethink and reshape the entire business while continuing to run it from day to day. A powerful transformation story helps employees to believe in the effort, but its impact will ultimately depend on the senior leader doing three things: making it personal, openly engaging others, and spotlighting successes as they emerge.

Make it Personal

Senior leaders who take the time to personalize the transformation story unlock much more energy than those who dutifully present the PowerPoint slides that their working team has prepared for them. But what does making it personal involve?

Senior leaders need to think carefully about such questions as "How does this relate to me?" and "Why does it matter to me personally?" Then they need to share the answers with others. Effective leaders often talk about pivotal experiences and formative influences in their own lives to underline their determination and demonstrate that obstacles can be overcome.

Indra Nooyi, the CEO of PepsiCo, is open about the struggles she had after setting off from India with a scholarship and not much else: "I had the immigrant feeling arriving in the U.S. . . . . I had to do an extra-good job; if it didn't work out, where was I going to go?"[3] She uses the story as a rallying cry to get her colleagues to work harder in the battle of the brands in the hope of one day getting to the very top.

Andy Grove, a former CEO of Intel, the world's largest maker of semiconductor chips, conveys the importance of courage and decisiveness by describing his escape from Hungary during the Russian occupation and his determination to make a new life in the United States. John Chambers, CEO of Cisco, describes growing up with a learning disability to illustrate "how we can overcome anything that comes our way, and why it is so important to treat others as you would want to be treated."[4] David Roberts alludes to lessons from his hero Monty Roberts (the real-life horse whisperer) when he talks about the transformation he led as CEO of Personal Financial Services at Barclays Bank.

David Novak, the CEO of Yum! Brands, which owns franchises including KFC, Pizza Hut, and Taco Bell, neatly summarizes how a personal approach helps employees feel connected to the collective effort: "They see their CEO and it makes a big company small." He points out that when employees get knowledge directly from their senior leader, they "care more about the company and [they're] more committed."[5]

Openly Engage Others

Once the senior leader has crafted a clear transformation story, success comes from seizing every opportunity to talk about it with employees, explain what it means, draw out its relevance to different parts of the business, and prompt others to find a personal meaning of their own.

Leaders of successful transformations invest huge personal effort in taking their story out into the organization. While he was the CEO at IBM, Lou Gerstner flew more than a million miles to meet thousands of customers, employees, and business partners.[6] He famously had a sign in his office that declared "A desk is a dangerous place from which to view the world" to act as a constant reminder of the importance of engaging with people inside and outside the organization.[7]

As Intuit CEO Steve Bennett explains, "A CEO can't make a series of changes by sending out e-mails. Change management has to happen face to face. It's a big commitment of time."[8] Bennett saw this approach pay off in his turnaround of Intuit from an underperforming tech start-up into a producer with double-digit revenues and four times the earnings it had when he took the helm.

When Corrado Passera became CEO of Banca Intesa, he faced an urgent need to stem the decline in its performance and health. So he traveled the length and breadth of Italy to start spreading the transformation story to the bank's 60,000 employees: "It is a long process, but you have to put your face in front of the people if you want them to follow you."[9]

Sometimes leaders need to work especially hard to engage challenging stakeholder groups. Om Prakash Bhatt, chairman of State Bank of India, invested a considerable amount of his time with trade unions: "I spent four days with 30 leaders from across the country . . . [even though] some of my best advisers at the bank warned that the leaders weren't trustworthy and could be disruptive . . . what hooked them was not only the quality of the discussions and the revelations but that the chairman was willing to spend so much time with them, eating and drinking, even singing and dancing."[10]

Another powerful technique for senior leaders to adopt is to turn "telling" into "asking." This is a great way to reinforce desired mindsets and create a deeper sense of personal ownership among employees. Instead of cascading a story down through the organization, leaders adopt two-way communications such as town halls, electronic dialogues, and meetings.

Even chance conversations can be put to good use. At Emerson Electric, CEO David Farr makes a point of asking virtually everyone he encounters the same four questions: "How do you make a difference?" (to find out whether people are aligned on the company's direction); "What improvement ideas are you working on?" (to emphasize continuous improvement); "When did you last get coaching from your boss?" (to probe people development); and "Who is the enemy?" (to make sure people name a competitor and not some other department). This sends a clear message that these issues matter and that employees need to have good answers—if not right at that moment, then certainly when they are asked next time.

Once the story is out there, the senior leader's role becomes one of constant reinforcement. As Alan G. Lafley, former CEO of P&G, notes, "Excruciating repetition and clarity are important—employees have so many things going on in the operation of their daily business that they don't always take the time to stop, think, and internalize."[11]

Paolo Scaroni, who has led three Italian public companies through major change as CEO of Techint, Enel, and Eni, explains that he likes to "find three or four strategic concepts that sum up the direction in which the company should be moving, build up an organization that believes in these concepts, and then repeat, repeat, and repeat them throughout the organization."[12]

Spotlight Success

As the transformation progresses, an engaging way to reinforce the story is to spotlight where success is being achieved. This helps crystallize what the transformation means and gives people confidence that it really is happening.

Infosys chairman N. R. Narayana Murthy describes how high-performing teams are invited to make presentations to employees across the company "to show other people that we value such behavior."[13] Harry M. Jansen Kraemer Jr., former chairman and CEO of health-care company Baxter International, forwarded his entire 55,000-strong workforce an e-mail from a woman thanking them for creating a product that had extended her father's life by 15 years. He told his employees, "This is what we do."

Daniel R. DiMicco, CEO of Nucor, one of the largest steel producers in the United States, tells a story about a shipping department supervisor to illustrate the importance of taking the initiative. The supervisor asked for US$2,000 to study sister plants in other regions, and duly returned with ideas to save more than US$150,000 a year in his area alone. At Brazilian bank Itaú Unibanco, the chairman and top team take part in an awards night to acknowledge and celebrate people's efforts to bring innovation to the organization. The event is followed up with extensive communications throughout the bank, sending a strong message that "We want more of this."

When the senior leader shines a spotlight on success, it helps turn any feelings of fatigue, resistance, or blame into creativity, passion, and a drive to succeed. We encourage leaders to live by Tom Peters' adage, "Celebrate what you'd like to see more of."

As a final thought, bear in mind that "success" doesn't necessarily mean getting things right. Failure—for the right reasons—can be equally worth celebrating when it provides valuable lessons for your organization. That's what happens at Google, as CEO Eric Schmidt explains: "We celebrate our failures. This is a company where it's absolutely okay to try something that's very hard, have it not be successful, and take the learning from that."[14]

Role Modeling Desired Mindsets and Behavior

No matter how much employees *want* to believe in the transformation story, they won't unless the senior leader's actions back it up. "Every move you make, everything you say, is visible to all. Therefore the best approach is to lead by example," advises Joseph M. Tucci, CEO of EMC.[15]

The senior leader acts as the chief role model for the whole organization. Fulfilling this role involves undergoing personal transformation and taking symbolic actions.

Undergo Personal Transformation

Earlier in the book we discussed people's tendency to think they are better at certain things than they really are. Some people believe that this self-serving bias becomes more pronounced at the top of an organization. Kevin Roberts, CEO of global advertising agency Saatchi and Saatchi, notes that "The further up the company you go the stupider you become . . . you start believing your own stuff."[16]

In their capacity as chief role model, senior leaders should heed Gandhi's advice that "For things to change first I must change." By this we mean that senior leaders need to model not just the desired end state of the transformation, but also the *act* of transformation itself. When someone at the top of an organization has the humility to admit they still have things to learn, that's the hallmark of a great role model. So is having the courage to stick at the challenge of adopting a new way to behave.

John Akehurst, a former CEO of Woodside Petroleum, reflects that "It took a lot of effort for me to recognize that I, as the chief executive, am entirely responsible for the culture of the organization. . . . I had an amazing insight into how dysfunctional my behavior was, what an impact it had on other people, how much baggage we were all carrying around."[17]

When N. R. Narayana Murthy decided to relinquish his authority as CEO to take on the novel role of "chief mentor" at Infosys in 2002, he had to reinvent himself: "You have to sacrifice yourself first for a big cause before you can ask others to do the same. . . . A good leader knows how to retreat into the background gracefully while encouraging his successor to become more and more successful in the job."[18]

This type of transformation doesn't have to involve a lot of fanfare. When "Neutron Jack" Welch traded in the tough-guy image he'd acquired during the cost-cutting era at GE and adopted a "hard-headed, soft-hearted" persona instead, he didn't make a big deal about it. All the same, it signified a huge cultural change for both him and his organization.

As we've already seen, a senior leader's transformation journey involves a series of steps. The leader should seek 360-degree feedback on how their behavior ties in with the objectives of the broader program; have their diary analyzed to reveal how much time they actually spend on transformation priorities; commit to a shortlist of personal objectives; and get professional coaching on how to achieve them. Many senior leaders report that this experience is especially powerful when all the members of an executive team pursue personal transformation journeys at the same time. That way, individual objectives can be discussed and reinforced in a challenging yet supportive environment.

Take Symbolic Actions

For a leader, the quickest way to send shockwaves through an organization, as we noted in Chapter 5, is to perform one or two thoughtfully conceived symbolic acts that signal that things will be different from now on. The greatest impact comes when the leader performing these acts is the head of the whole organization.

When John Wilder, CEO of the Texas energy utility TXU, gave a large bonus to a woman who had taken leadership of a key business initiative, "It helped employees understand that rewards will be based on contributions, and that 'pay for performance' could actually be put into practice."[19] Daniel DiMicco of Nucor underscored his "focus on the front line" by flying commercial, forgoing an executive parking place, and making a fresh pot of coffee in the office if he happened to take the last cup.

Personal compensation is one area where simple steps by senior leaders can send powerful messages to everyone else in the organization. When times are hard, some leaders choose to draw a nominal salary and take their compensation in the form of stock options instead to show their commitment to creating value in the long term. John Mackey, CEO of Whole Foods Market, has gone a step further. He is so committed to his company's mission that he's decided not to take compensation of any kind: "I have reached a place in my life where I no longer want to work for money, but simply for the joy of the work itself and to better answer the call to service that I feel so clearly in my own heart."

Going to work at the front line can be another powerful symbolic act. To show the value he placed on creating a friendly and welcoming atmosphere for customers and colleagues, former Southwest Airlines CEO Herb Kelleher spent his holidays serving peanuts with flight attendants, loading baggage, and assisting ground crews. Michael Dell reinforces the need to stay focused on the customer by spending one day a month in Dell's call center working alongside the staff who deal with customer queries.

We'd like to end with a warning: important though it is to take actions that support your organization's goals, it's just as important to avoid behaving in a way that contradicts or undermines them. One packaged goods company was undergoing a transformation to capture the value of collaboration. When problems that cut across businesses were brought to his attention, the hockey-loving CEO would dismiss them with "I don't care how you do it. Crash 'em against the boards if you have to—just get it done." The result: things *didn't* get done, employees were dismayed at the mixed messages, resistance to change mounted, and cynicism prevailed.

Building a Strong and Committed Team

The senior leader's team should be a valuable asset in leading the transformation. Sharing a meaningful story and role modeling the desired mindsets and behavior will increase the odds of getting the team on board. But it's vital to devote time and effort to building the team as well.

Understand, Then Act Quickly

Successful senior leaders take the time to assess the capabilities of the individual members of their team and then act swiftly on their findings. Some seek third-party input to create an objective basis on which to make their assessments. Many senior leaders find it helpful to map team members by their skill and will or use a matrix of performance and leadership behaviors like the one illustrated in Exhibit 5.5 in Chapter 5.

Methods such as forced rankings or forced distributions (allocating a certain percentage of employees into various performance categories by using a bell curve, quartiles, or other linear approach) are often used to assess leaders' motivation and capability to lead transformation. Such mechanisms help to establish a clear picture of who is genuinely on board and who isn't. Though seldom discussed openly because of the anxiety they can generate, these tools can nevertheless be useful aids for senior leaders in targeting their efforts to build a strong and committed team.

Once a senior leader is equipped with all the relevant facts, it's not hard to know what to do with team members who are low in both skill and will—those who deliver poor results and exhibit unhelpful behavior. But what about individuals who are "high skill, low will"—those who deliver strong results but behave in unhelpful ways? The answer may lie in coaching and mentoring, redefining roles, and adjusting incentives.

In the end, though, the people on your team are the measure of how serious you are about having a healthy organization. Jack Welch was in no doubt: "If you get results without living our values, I'm coming for you." Corrado Passera concurs: "If necessary, you have to get rid of those individuals—even the talented ones—who quarrel and cannot work together."[20]

But how do senior leaders know *when* to act? The following questions offer a litmus test. Do team members know exactly what they need to do as individuals to make the transformation happen? Is it clear what will happen if they don't get on board? Have they been given a chance to build the skills they need? Is the senior leader modeling the desired mindsets and behavior?

If the answer to all these questions is yes, then decisive action is justified. As Steve Luczo, the CEO of Seagate, the world's largest manufacturer of hard drives, reflects, "We said, we will work as a team. So we needed to find out who was on the bus and who was not and to do it fast. I got rid of two top people in the first three to four months."[21]

When leaders make tough decisions like these, it shows that they mean business. The good news is that surprising though it may seem, this often encourages other team members to get on board. When a senior leader responds swiftly and decisively to employees' behavior and results, it has an immediate impact on the rest of the organization. High performers become more motivated, low performers opt out, and the majority in the middle get jolted out of their complacency, with many people choosing to raise their game.

Invest in Team Time

Even with the right team in place, it takes time for a group of smart, ambitious, and independent-minded individuals to align on a direction. If you are the senior leader, it falls to you to determine how much of your team's time is spent on the transformation effort, and how effective it will be.

In general, the first order of business for a team is for members to agree on a few basics. What should their collective role be—in other words, what can *only* the team achieve, as opposed to its individual members? How often should the team meet, and where? Which transformation-related issues should it discuss, and which should it avoid? What behavior should it expect of itself, and what behavior should it refuse to tolerate?

These agreements are often summarized in a team charter for leading the transformation. This can be checked from time to time to confirm that the team is on the right track. Corrado Passera brought his team together periodically to "share almost everything," "be clear to everyone who is doing what," and "keep the transformation initiatives, budgets, and financial targets knitted together."[22]

Consider Sir David Nicholson's approach when he took over at the NHS in 2006, charged with leading one of the most sweeping reforms in its 60-year history. He could have started out of the gates with a frenzied focus on setting targets and developing initiatives; instead he chose to invest the bulk of his time in aligning his top team and the wider organization. Over the course of a year, the top team invested half of their scheduled time together in working on their cohesiveness and reflecting profoundly on their mindsets and how they would need to change so that the NHS could deliver on its reforms. Nicholson recalls, "It would have been easy for me to push forward with agendas, plans, and targets; we were used to this way of working in the NHS. Doing so might have resulted in our delivering some modest successes, but it would not have fundamentally changed us as an organization to deliver bigger, better, and bolder results in the long term."[23]

As a rule of thumb, 80 percent of the time the team spends together should be devoted to dialogue, and just 20 percent to presentations. Effective dialogue requires a well-structured agenda. Binding decisions shouldn't be made until the team has spent ample time on three separate activities: personal reflection to ensure that members form an independent point of view from the beginning; discussion in pairs or small groups to refine thinking and explore deeper assumptions; and whole-team discussion. To keep people focused, little tolerance should be shown for deep dives into minutiae (not seeing the forest for the trees) or lack of engagement (non-committal head-nodding).

Having everyone attend in person rather than via conference calls makes team time far more productive. Former Disney CEO Michael Eisner ruefully notes that "The worst decisions I ever made were on conference calls. It is critical for successful alignment to get your team together and discuss eyeball to eyeball."[24]

For all its challenges, building your team in this way is immensely rewarding. When Steve Luczo made teamwork at the top the number-one priority in his turnaround of Seagate, it had the desired effect. As his colleague, former CFO Charles Pope, noted, "People in the company now see us as a team. We get feedback that we are on the same wavelength. We are synched now. We respect one another. We've built the ability to align goals."[25]

Relentlessly Pursuing Impact

A former managing director of Time Life, C. D. Jackson, memorably observed that great ideas need landing gear as well as wings. Kicking off a transformation is one thing, but sticking with it through all the hard slog of execution is what really matters. There's no substitute for channeling your personal energy into ensuring that your organization's transformation effort delivers impact. "I was an outrageous champion of everything we did," Jack Welch said of his involvement in numerous GE transformation initiatives including Six Sigma, the Workout program, reinventing Crotonville, and the A-Class leadership initiative.[26]

Roll Up Your Sleeves

Any initiative with significant customer, financial, or symbolic value must have the senior leader's personal involvement if it's to achieve maximum impact. This should ensure that critical project decisions are made quickly, but without sacrificing the value of collective debate. It also helps sow the seeds for a culture of candor and decisiveness.

For some senior leaders, the need to roll up their sleeves may require them to rethink their priorities. Larry Bossidy, former chairman and CEO of AlliedSignal and former chairman of Honeywell, notes that "Many people regard execution as detail work that's beneath the dignity of a business leader. That's wrong . . . it's a leader's most important job."[27]

Bernard Arnault of LVMH has built the company he chairs from a modest family-owned business into a US$22 billion luxury goods conglomerate. But becoming one of the world's wealthiest men didn't make him lose touch with what goes on in his organization. He personally reviews fashion collections for star brands such as Dior and Louis Vuitton to ensure that every item does justice to the heritage of the brand. "They say God is in the detail," says Dior CEO Sidney Toledano; "here, the boss is in the detail."[28]

Sam Palmisano kicked off IBM's effort to build trust into its culture by launching what he called "the US$100 million bet on trust." Twenty-two thousand managers were allocated $5,000 each per year that they could spend—with no questions asked—to generate business, develop client relationships, or respond to an urgent need from a colleague. According to Palmisano, "I personally made sure the program made the point—we will live by our values."[29]

Another eminently hands-on leader is "merchant prince" Mickey Drexler, who acquired his nickname by turning around major retailers such as Gap and Ann Taylor. As chairman and CEO of J. Crew, he took the company from losses of US$40 million in 2002 to its sale for US$3 billion in 2010. On one notable occasion, a casual remark from a call-center operator that bridesmaids buy their dresses at J. Crew prompted him to launch what became a highly profitable line of formal clothing.[30] He had a public address system installed at his company's headquarters and speaks to staff as often as a dozen times a day. He visits stores five times a week and has been known to get agitated about color assortments and even buttons. Such deep involvement allows Drexler to pick up new trends well before the competition does. "You have to go, you have to see, you have to feel," he explains.[31]

Leaders who roll up their sleeves are willing to come down from the executive suite and help resolve thorny operational issues, too. Peter Gossas, head of Sandvik Materials Technology, observes that "If there's a problem, it can be helpful if I come to the work floor, step up on a crate so that everyone can see me, and have a discussion with a shift unit that may be negative to change." Speaking from a lifetime's experience in the steel industry, he adds, "It's hard for me to walk into a melt shop and not begin discussing ways to solve operational problems."[32]

Hold Leaders Accountable

Successful senior leaders aren't slow to step up to transformation challenges or operational problems. But neither do they lose sight of their responsibilities as top managers: chairing reviews to assess progress against plans, celebrating successes, identifying root causes, helping to solve problems, and holding other leaders to account for keeping the transformation on track. Holding leaders accountable involves looking at both activities (are people doing what they said they would?) and impact (is it going to create the value we expected?).

In reviews, a central role for the senior leader is to ensure that decisions are firmly rooted in facts. When Kevin Sharer kicked off the transformation of Amgen, he made it clear that where review meetings were concerned, "The days of winging it are over."[33] When Bill Gates was CEO of Microsoft, he kept close tabs on the progress of more than 100 improvement initiatives at any given time.

Staying on top of a transformation program isn't easy. As Larry Bossidy comments, "This immense personal commitment is time consuming and fraught with emotional wear and tear in giving feedback, conducting dialogues, and exposing your judgment to others."[34] The senior leader must also ensure that the organization strikes the right balance between performance and health, and doesn't allow one to overshadow the other. Daniel Vasella, CEO of Novartis, warns that "Once you become dominated by the pressure of making the quarter, even unwittingly . . . you'll begin to sacrifice things that are vital for your company over the long term."[35]

■ ■ ■

Generalizations are notoriously dangerous, but if we were to try to put our finger on the single most important aspect of the senior leader's role in a transformation, it would be shifting the culture of the organization. Leader after leader tells us that's so.

Take just one example. Sheikh Mohammed bin Essa Al-Khalifa, chief executive of Bahrain's Economic Development Board, was charged with leading a complete transformation of his country's century-old education system. What was his biggest challenge? "I always worried that we were going to have to spend millions to fix the educational system. But it turned out the solution wasn't the money. It was the soft things—which are usually harder."[36]

Indeed, managing the soft things is anything but an easy option, as we hope we've established by now. It calls for just as much effort and rigor as managing the hard stuff, and invariably makes more work for busy people to do. But it's worth it. Indeed, it can make all the difference between a successful transformation and an unsuccessful one.

As we saw in Chapter 1, when change programs fail, it's more often than not down to unproductive management behavior, unhelpful employee attitudes, or both. These factors are to blame in more than 70 percent of unsuccessful transformations. Companies that know these odds and understand how to turn unhelpful behavior and negative mindsets into helpful and positive ones will stand a much better chance of making their transformation a success.

This brings us back to the senior leader. Theirs is the pivotal role in making change happen because they set the tone for everyone else in the organization. What they do and how they act can have more influence on the behavior and attitudes of the people they lead than any other intervention in a transformation program. Theirs is an enormous responsibility, but when carried out well, it can create enormous satisfaction, as well as enormous impact.

CHAPTER 9

The Five Frames in Action

How Do You Make a Great Organization Even Better?

We've now shared with you what we see as the essential ingredients for building and sustaining an organization that will thrive in both the short and the long term. The key is to put equal emphasis on, and apply equal rigor to, both the performance and the health aspects of your organization. To do that, you follow a proven five-stage process, the 5As (aspire, assess, architect, act, and advance). Within each stage, you apply the relevant frame from the five frames of performance (namely strategic objectives, capability platform, portfolio of initiatives, delivery model, and continuous improvement infrastructure) and health (namely health essentials, discovery process, influence model, change engine, and centered leadership).

But what does this look like in practice? You've already seen part of the answer in the case studies of Coca-Cola, Grupo Nacional Provincial, Bombardier Aerospace, P&G, Telefónica, and ANZ that introduce Chapter 1 and the five chapters in Part II. Each case concentrates on the aspect of transformation covered in that chapter. Throughout the book, we've also drawn on many other examples from leaders and organizations across the world to bring the points we make to life. What you haven't yet seen, though, is a complete account of a transformation from beginning to end—one that illustrates how all the parts come together in a full-blown transformation program.

That's what this chapter is about. Here we've chosen to profile Wells Fargo. Why? First and foremost, it's an instructive example of the five frames in action. But unlike many of the other transformations we've looked at, it shows how the approach can be applied at an organization that's already thriving, but wants to do even better. The five frames approach is not just for organizations facing tough times, or needing a turnaround; it can also help you move from good to great, or make a great organization better still.

The Story Begins

When John Stumpf became CEO of Wells Fargo & Company, times were good. He'd taken the reins gradually between August 2005 and June 2007 as he progressed from leadership of the company's community bank operations to president and chief operating officer, and then CEO. Not only was the leadership transition seamless, but Stumpf was inheriting a well-oiled performance machine. From 2000 to 2005, the company's total assets and operating revenues had both grown at a rate of 11 percent, and net income at 14 percent. This kind of performance positioned Wells Fargo as one of the leading supra-regional banks in the United States, and indeed as one of the leading banks globally.

Such an environment was undoubtedly a blessing, but it presented a real leadership challenge, too. Performance had been so strong that assets needed to grow at 9 percent a year simply to meet expectations. Stumpf sensed that the tailwinds favoring the industry wouldn't last forever, and that the bank's business models might not serve it so well if conditions changed. Continuing as before didn't seem an option. Nor did tinkering with the organization for the sake of it. All the parts of the business were performing so well that it wasn't obvious where change was needed. Even if it had been, how could more than 150,000 employees be motivated to change without a burning platform?

Another challenge for Stumpf was that he was taking over from a long-serving CEO who had become something of a legend in the banking industry. Dick Kovacevich had worked for Norwest Bank since 1986, after moving from Citicorp to become chief operating officer and head of the retail banking group. He rose to chief executive in 1993 and oversaw impressive growth through acquisitions, culminating in the 1998 merger with Wells Fargo. At that point, he was given the position of CEO and president of the newly formed company.

Always outspoken, Kovacevich was confident, decisive, and quick to step in when necessary. He was also a strong believer in accountability and empowerment, qualities that had been hardwired into the company's culture by the creation of 84 business units. P&Ls were pushed down to the lowest level possible, and the ethos was "run it like you own it." Managers were given the tools they needed and expected to run their business in a self-reliant way.

So Stumpf had to work out how to lead the organization in *his* way. Which of his predecessor's leadership attributes should he emulate, and which should he change? And given Kovacevich's larger-than-life persona and powerful legacy, how could Stumpf keep the organization on his side in areas where he and the prevailing culture seemed to differ?

Setting the Right Aspirations

As it happened, Stumpf had been reflecting on these challenges for some time. On becoming president—a clear signal he had been chosen to succeed Kovacevich—Stumpf had commissioned a small team to pull together the facts on Wells Fargo's performance and health. The analysis confirmed his instinct that the world outside was changing in ways that no bank, however successful, could afford to ignore. The industry was facing a tightening regulatory environment, the economics of the business were getting tougher as credit quality declined, Wells' traditional approach of growing through acquisition was being hampered by a lack of suitable targets, and the yield curve had inverted. (This is a relatively rare situation in which long-term debt instruments have a lower yield than short-term instruments of the same credit quality, suggesting that recession is on the way.)

A look at customer trends also gave Stumpf food for thought. Increasingly savvy customers were demanding that their banks offer them a more integrated experience across multiple product categories. More broadly, consumers were starting to care more about the companies they were buying from and wanted to know what they stood for and whether they always delivered on their promises. When Wells did deep digs into its own data, it found that customer loyalty scores, though not in themselves a cause for alarm, weren't up to the industry-leading levels it achieved on many other dimensions, and nor were customer attrition rates in key businesses. In the meantime, analysts appeared to expect the bank to meet or exceed its historic growth rate even though conditions in the outside world were changing.

On the health side, the analysis confirmed that Wells Fargo was a strong, execution-oriented organization. Employees, known as team members, took their cue from the bank's vision to "help our customers succeed financially." The top team helped keep alive Wells' clear set of values through constant repetition and role modeling. The recognition that "People are our competitive advantage" was translated into abundant opportunities for talented people to develop and grow within the organization. The conviction that "Our strategy is execution" was evident in the relentless effort to do better every day. Morale was high, too: the ratio of engaged to disengaged team members (or the "happy to grumpy" ratio, as Stumpf called it) was 4:1, far above the national average of 1.9:1.[1]

Faced with these facts, Stumpf brought his top team together in a two-day off-site session to grapple with the data and debate what Wells Fargo's aspirations should be for the next era. The session was structured to give all team members an opportunity to provide input so that everyone felt a sense of ownership for the ideas and decisions that emerged. Over the course of the discussion, the team started to develop a powerful aspiration that they summed up in the phrase "One Wells Fargo." They were starting to realize that a huge amount of value lay in "mining the seams" of the organization: working together more effectively across lines of business in order to break down silo thinking and give customers a better experience that fulfilled more of their financial needs.

As they started to envision the impact these ideas might have, the team worked on developing a medium-term aspiration. Although they understood that a more difficult environment was in store, they decided that their goal would be to maintain Wells Fargo's track record of double-digit compound annual growth in earnings per share and revenue. To this end, they doubled down on the bank's long-term cross-sell aspiration of "going for gr8" (eight products per customer) with the medium-term goal of adding at least one product on average to its already industry-leading cross-sell rates. The team also set performance targets for customer loyalty and attrition in all key businesses.

On the health side, thinking about One Wells Fargo helped the team see how the bank's focus on execution played out in practice. Performance was being maximized within each line of business, but not necessarily across the organization as a whole. Management practices relating to customer focus, strategic clarity, and collaborating to share ideas and information were all strong *within* lines of businesses, but they needed to be distinctive *across* them as well. If One Wells Fargo was the strategy, then organizational changes would clearly be needed to make it a reality. In terms of archetypes, the bank needed to keep the discipline associated with its "execution edge" archetype while migrating toward a "market focus" archetype to ensure that it would be able to achieve its performance aspirations.

When the bank's top 300 leaders met at their annual Connections Conference, they confirmed and refined these aspirations and gave their input into the next stages of the transformation.

Assessing Readiness for Change

Now that the organization had set the broad outlines of its medium-term performance and health aspirations, it formed several teams to make them concrete by identifying potential barriers and planning what needed to be done to make change happen. One team was dedicated to understanding what capabilities were strategically important, another focused on issues related to mindsets, and others dug more deeply into potential opportunities. Each team was headed by a pair of leaders from different business units, a device to ensure that collaboration across silos was not just the goal but part of the actual *process* of change. It also gave leaders the opportunity to role model the changes they wanted to see.

The team working on *capabilities* analyzed vast amounts of information across lines of business in order to determine what really mattered in creating a distinctive One Wells Fargo experience for customers. The team correlated data from industry and proprietary customer-loyalty databases with expressed customer preferences and actual purchases, and linked the patterns to measures such as share of wallet, tenure, and profitability. The results gave them a clear view of the technical, management, and behavioral systems that they would need to address to reach their aspirations. Thematically, these capabilities related to the extent to which customers perceived that "you are easy to do business with," "you understand me," "you provide me value," "you make me feel valued and appreciated," and "you give me helpful advice."

The team working on *mindsets* conducted a series of interviews and focus groups to gain insight into attitudes that might help or hinder Wells in realizing its performance and health aspirations. The first mindset they identified was perhaps the most obvious: "Run it like you own it." This created a sense of accountability and empowerment that needed to be preserved. However, in keeping with the theme of One Wells Fargo, "run it like you own it" needed to be expanded so that it didn't apply to a business unit or group, but to the whole bank. Interactions across lines of business that had customers in common were the exception, but they needed to become the rule so that decisions could be optimized for the customer across the whole organization. A new mindset was needed: that a 95 percent answer for a business is right if it's the 100 percent answer for the customer and the enterprise.

The second mindset to be uncovered was "We know our business best"—a mindset rooted in the success of the company's vision and values over many years. Wells often had banks and other companies at its door asking "How can we learn from you?" There was a risk it might become more insular than was healthy. Confidence would still be needed, but it should be manifest in a mindset of "The customer knows best, and we can learn from others how best to serve the customer."

Stumpf immediately started to reflect this target mindset in his speeches. He peppered them with references to companies such as Starbucks, Apple, and Target. When he talked to his staff, he would ask, "How can we tailor our products and services to our customers' needs as well as Starbucks tailors its coffee to its customers? What can we do to make our products and services as intuitive and easy to use as the iPod? When it's snowing, people from Target's cosmetics aisle lend a hand in its snow-shovel aisle—how can we be as agile in working across our businesses to respond to customers' needs?"

The third mindset uncovered by the team was "Our strategy is execution." Once again, Wells needed to preserve the virtues of this mindset, but it also needed to carve out space to pursue longer-term thinking. It had a tendency to eschew large-scale, multiyear cross-business projects in favor of incremental near-term efforts. It wasn't that things needed to slow down; rather, the bank needed to extend its customary rigor to complex efforts that didn't necessarily fit into the annual planning cycle. The mindset needed was not that execution was the strategy, but that excellent execution against all strategies was key.

The mindset team also reinforced the importance of keeping the mindset that "People are our competitive advantage" and using the broad vision of fulfilling customers' financial needs as a compass for all decision making.

Architecting What Needed to Be Done

As the teams assessed Wells Fargo's readiness for change, they also gathered and analyzed ideas for what to change and how to do it. Some six months after his initial session with the senior team, and four months after the top 300 session, Stumpf reassembled his senior team for another two-day off-site working session to grapple with the working teams' recommendations.

The senior group jointly put together a balanced portfolio of initiatives for Wells to pursue. All were company-wide efforts that needed to be driven by the collective advocacy of the senior team if they were to happen at the right speed and achieve the right impact. In addition, they were all carefully chosen to ensure that the five drivers of customer loyalty were being fully addressed.

The first set of initiatives was geared to making the bank "easier to do business with." They included efforts to reduce wait times, prevent problems, resolve them more quickly, settle claims, digitize documents, simplify customer correspondence, and streamline product pricing. The second set of initiatives was aimed at helping customers feel "you know me." They included efforts to enable customers to interact with Wells in their preferred language and efforts to share customer knowledge across the organization to improve the customer experience and upgrade credit decisions. In a similar way, the theme of "you provide me value" translated into efforts to contact customers when their situation changed to offer them products that better suited their new needs. "You make me feel valued" prompted efforts to use a customer's overall relationship with the company as a basis for setting prices. Finally, "you give me advice" drove efforts to provide employees with better tools to support financial planning.

On the health side, the bank decided on a raft of actions to instill its desired mindsets through role modeling, communications, formal reinforcement, and skill building. The One Wells Fargo language was to be embodied in all the company's communications across its magazine, intranet, speeches, and other channels. The iconic "Vision and Values" booklet—written by Kovacevich for Norwest in 1993—underwent the most significant change in its history with the addition of a new section on One Wells Fargo. The bank decided to put new loyalty metrics in place and upgrade its IT systems to give frontline team members better customer information. To build skills and capabilities, it decided to increase the focus on talent rotation across lines of business and pursue a more uniform leadership model. New "field and forum" leadership development programs would emphasize collaboration and customer focus.

These initiatives aside, most of the interventions directed at mindsets were engineered into the way performance initiatives were organized and implemented. By having senior managers continue to co-lead initiatives, staffing teams with the most promising leaders from any business or function, creating a central team to coordinate activity (something of a novelty in Wells' highly decentralized culture), and undertaking a number of other efforts, the bank ensured that its performance initiatives would also help to achieve the desired shifts in its health.

Once the senior team was aligned on the way forward, it was time for the top 300 leaders to roll up their sleeves. During a multiday off-site meeting, they helped refine the portfolio of initiatives and the actions to influence mindsets, and worked out what these would mean for them as individuals. The session was itself designed to model the power of working together as

One Wells Fargo, with multiple breakouts and table discussions to ensure that everyone would benefit from the group's ingenuity and diversity.

Taking Action

The program was structured into a 1,500-day plan, counted in days rather than years to reflect the bias for action. The message was that every day mattered in achieving the company's medium-term aspirations. The structure of the program was clear: at the highest level, the goal was to work as One Wells Fargo for the customer. That meant creating an experience where customers felt that "you are easy to do business with," "you understand me," "you provide me value," "you make me feel valued and appreciated," and "you give me helpful advice." All communications made it clear that achieving this goal would require equal emphasis on implementing the portfolio of initiatives and instilling the needed mindsets, or what Stumpf referred to as the "spirit and way of thinking" of One Wells Fargo.

This program of activity was broken down into three 500-day phases, each with its own portfolio of "quick win," "big rock," and "test and learn" initiatives. Quick wins were relatively easy "no regrets" efforts such as digitizing documents and making communications more customer friendly. These were done fast to generate momentum, and were mostly rolled out in "big bang" fashion. Big rocks were large, complex efforts: one such initiative was aimed at improving the prevention and resolution of customer problems. These efforts were generally scaled up using a geometric approach. Test-and-learn initiatives were higher-risk efforts such as simplifying pricing and moving to a relationship-based approach. These were piloted to gather information and assess their impact. Once proven, they were scaled up in a linear fashion so that implementation could be adjusted as more data became available.

Wells established clear accountability and oversight for the program. The full executive team held a regular review of overall progress against metrics and milestones, while different subsets of the group acted as steering committees for individual initiatives. Dedicated funding was set aside for these efforts, and business-unit targets and budgets were adjusted to reflect expected cross-company "gives and gets." The initiative teams were staffed with talented leaders from a range of functions. Delivery against initiative objectives was built into individual performance expectations and reviews.

To support this ownership model, the bank set up a program-management team with a full-time staff of six members who reported to a senior leader. The team's role included measuring results and impact, facilitating coordination and information sharing across initiatives, providing targeted problem-solving support to initiative teams, prompting the generation of more ideas, and making recommendations for adjusting the program over time. The team conducted regular monitoring at four levels: financial impact (measured by total return to shareholders, assets, income, revenues, and so on); key performance indicators (such as customer loyalty, share of wallet, and customer attrition); health (via a pulse check with key questions on collaborating for the customer, plus the Gallup Q12 employee engagement survey); and initiative and program milestones (such as on time, on budget).

An internal communications program helped unleash energy to spread the One Wells Fargo spirit. It included the in-house *Connections* magazine, an interactive employee intranet, and news bulletins for leaders. In addition, a group of 25 senior change leaders was charged with helping to keep motivation and engagement high throughout the change program. The group met monthly to discuss progress, celebrate successes, and share ideas across business units.

The broader group of 300 leaders who had participated in shaping the program was convened annually. To encourage efforts at the grassroots level, several cross-business councils were formed around topics of shared interest such as marketing, customer segments, and regions. Finally, all team members were strongly encouraged to bring the One Wells Fargo mindset into their daily work. Any requests for support in doing so were quickly granted.

Advancing through Continuous Improvement

The idea of One Wells Fargo had been born in an off-site meeting in December 2005, and the change program had been formally launched eight months later in August 2006. By the end of the first 500 working days, in mid-2008, the effort was paying dividends.

Thanks to the equal emphasis on the portfolio of performance initiatives and the health-oriented spirit and way of thinking—on top of continuing efforts within lines of business to out-execute the competition—Wells' cross-sell was up by 18 percent to an extraordinary 5.2 products per customer. Customer loyalty measures in the community bank, where the bulk of the initial efforts were targeted, had jumped from 34 percent to 45 percent, and customer attrition had dropped from roughly 20 percent to less than

10 percent. The growth in earnings per share over the period was 17 percent compared with a peer average of minus 3 percent, total returns to share-holders grew by 5.5 percent compared with 2.6 percent, and net revenue grew by 31 percent compared with 11 percent.

On the health side, the number of team members who felt that their way of working helped make things easy for customers had increased by 23 per-cent, and those feeling that collaboration across businesses was benefiting customers had increased by 16 percent. Moreover, the ratio of engaged to disengaged employees in the community bank had leaped from an already high 4:1 to a truly distinctive 7:1.

Toward the end of the first 500 days, the world outside began to change in ways that no one could have predicted. Deteriorating credit quality and the inversion of the yield curve meant that institutions such as Northern Rock and Countrywide Financial were no longer able to obtain financing through the credit markets. The fire-sale of Bear Stearns to JP Morgan Chase under fears it would collapse foreshadowed the turmoil to come. By October 2008, major financial institutions such as Lehman Brothers, AIG, and Washington Mutual had failed, been acquired under duress, or been taken into government ownership. A global financial crisis was under way—the worst the world had seen since the Great Depression of the 1930s.

The work that Wells Fargo had done to improve its performance and health had left it in a position of strength. The bank had also refrained from participating in most of the industry practices that were implicated in the crisis. These included adjustable-rate mortgages (ARMs) that transferred part of the interest-rate risk from the lender to the borrower according to criteria that were often difficult for customers to understand; the aggressive use of mortgage-backed securities (MBS); and credit default swaps (CDS), a form of credit insurance.

In mid-October 2008, U.S. Secretary of the Treasury Henry Paulson called the leaders of the nation's biggest financial institutions together to inform them that the government would be recapitalizing the banking sys-tem by taking ownership of significant shares in each institution. Wells Fargo was able to insist that the investment was not necessary, given its strong internal capital-generating capabilities and its avoidance of most of the mortgage-related woes of its rivals. In the end, however, Paulson made it clear he wasn't asking—to which Wells Fargo notably conceded with "We are Americans first, bankers second."

During this period, Wells Fargo beat out the global giant Citigroup to acquire Wachovia Bank, a purchase that brought with it a complementary footprint and capability set. Wells Fargo was dominant in the west and midwest of the United States, whereas Wachovia was strongest on the east coast and in the south. Wachovia was known for its customer service, whereas Wells Fargo was known for its cross-sell capability. The merger was approved on the night of October 12, 2008, and the deal closed shortly afterward on December 31. With the addition of Wachovia, Wells Fargo became one of the 20 largest companies in the United States by revenues, entering the Fortune 20.

The merger ranks as the biggest in the history of U.S. financial services and created the twelfth-largest company in the country. With almost 280,000 employees, Wells employs one in every 500 working adults in the United States. On the customer side, a third of all U.S. households hold accounts at the bank, as do one in 10 small businesses. Wells has a branch or ATM within two miles of half of all U.S. households and businesses, and processes one in six checks written in the United States. Its daily online transactions total 9.75 million, more than the combined transactions of e-Bay and Amazon at their peak.

In the two years following the merger, the company posted record profits every quarter. It also cleaned up the loan portfolio it inherited from Wachovia, including helping more than 3 million customers stay in their homes and forgiving over US$3.6 billion in mortgage principle. These numbers testify to the skillfulness with which the early stages of the integration were handled. Customers focus didn't miss a beat either: in the 2009 American Company Satisfaction Index, Wells came top among large retail banks. In addition, it played an important role in helping the U.S. economy get back on its feet by lending more than US$150 billion to businesses to help stimulate the economy. Wells also came second in the list of most generous givers of philanthropic dollars in 2010 according to *BusinessWeek*.

The One Wells Fargo program first conceived when Stumpf became president of the company was quickly integrated into the all-consuming merger effort. The program infrastructure was put to good use to help leaders understand and manage the impact the merger was having on customers. Instead of launching the second wave of program initiatives as originally planned, the relevant team leaders were diverted to work on merger initiatives, where they were able to make good use of their well-exercised muscles for working across the company on behalf of the customer. The committees charged with supporting collaboration across businesses were expanded to become powerful problem-solving forums for the integration. And the "write your own lottery ticket" approach was adopted once again in a series of integration summits that brought together hundreds of working teams across the company to ensure that a One Wells Fargo view was taken throughout the creation and execution of the integration plan.

■ ■ ■

Wells' merger with Wachovia has made the rallying cry of One Wells Fargo all the more important. The work on integrating the two companies continues as we write, and is expected to take until the end of 2012. What then? The organization is already gearing up for the next round of One Wells Fargo performance and health initiatives that will equip it to stay ahead of the competition long into the future. For now, though, the bank's experience over the period of 2005–2008 stands as a vivid illustration of how to make change happen at scale in an organization.

When asked to look back and identify the key ingredient in the effort, John Stumpf—now chairman, CEO, and president—nominates "getting the right balance between the initiatives we were driving from the top of the house with creating the right spirit, ways of thinking, and ways of working throughout the organization." In the end, what mattered was "our 150,000 team members making the right One Wells Fargo decisions day in and day out." Ever true to his company heritage, however, Stumpf adds, "And having a time-tested set of vision and values to build upon and a great team to make it happen didn't hurt either!"

That brings us back to our central theme. The "vision and values" and "great team" that Stumpf credits as key factors in Wells' success are hallmarks of an organization that places as much weight on sustaining its health as on delivering performance and financial results. Getting that "and" into performance and health is what gives organizations ultimate competitive advantage. Not only does it enable them to make a successful transformation, it enables them to stay on top from then on.

CHAPTER 10

Making It Happen
Do You Have What It Takes?

I n the 1999 film *The Matrix*, the protagonist, Neo, is offered a choice of two pills: one red, one blue. If he takes the red pill, it will show him that he's living in an illusion. He'll discover the painful truth that reality is far more complex and makes far more demands on him than he'd ever imagined. But if he chooses the blue pill, he'll go back to his old life, in blissful ignorance of the illusion. After a moment's thought, he takes the red pill—a choice that marks the beginning of an epic personal journey. In a series of heroic acts, Neo finally frees the human race from a prison: one it had created for itself through its dependence on intelligent machines that would ultimately turn against it.

We suspect that many leaders—perhaps you?—will be faced with a similar choice after reading this book. If you choose the red pill, you're committing yourself to adopting the approach to organizational excellence that we've outlined here, an approach that is equally balanced between performance and health. The catch is that if you take this path, it will be more challenging than others you could follow, and make more demands of you as a leader. And despite the science that we've brought to bear, it's still a path that leads you into unknown territory—a leap of faith, if you will.

The alternative is the blue pill. Put the book down or hand it to a friend or colleague and go about managing and leading in the same way you've always done. Chances are it's served you reasonably well in the past, it keeps you within your comfort zone, and it fits in with what the people around you have come to expect.

This chapter is for those of you who choose the red pill. It's for those who feel, as we do, that it's simply not good enough that only a third of excellent organizations stay excellent over the long term. It's for those who agree with Einstein that "Insanity is doing the same thing and expecting a different result" and recognize that to achieve a different result, they need to strike a better balance between human and mechanistic approaches to leading an organization. And it's for those who see that this path will not only make them more successful, but also bring benefits for their team, their organization, and ultimately society as a whole.

Here you'll find answers to the four questions we get asked most often by those who choose the red pill. They are all variations on the theme of "help me get started": what to do if you can't get your senior leader on board, what the program of work looks like for putting the five frames into practice, when to move from one stage of your transformation to the next, and how to catch up on weaknesses or gaps when your transformation is already in mid-flight. We close by recapping a set of underlying principles to keep in mind as you embark on your journey.

What If I Can't Get My Senior Leader on Board?

During the many Change Leaders Forums we've held over the past few years, we've heard this question more often than any other. People say, "I know this is important, and I understand that to build an excellent organization you have to put equal emphasis on performance and heath, but my senior leader doesn't get it or doesn't agree, so what can I do?" In response, we offer three pieces of advice.

First, a question for you: Have you done everything in your power to help your senior leader get on board? As we indicated in Chapter 8, this means applying the thinking behind the influence model. Have you discussed a performance- and health-based approach with them directly? Have you understood what they really care about—the sources of meaning that motivate them—and have you drawn on these passions in telling a compelling story? Have you identified who your leader looks to for advice, and got these individuals on your side? Have you put your leader in contact with other senior leaders or advisers who've gone through performance and health transformations of their own, and can share their battle-hardened wisdom and experience? Have you helped your leader get up to speed on what a transformation would look like by talking about this book or giving them a copy to read?

We're struck by the number of people who assume that their leader won't be comfortable with the idea of placing as much emphasis on health as on performance. When tested, this assumption frequently proves untrue. More often than not, it comes down to a misperception: it's not that leaders actually reject the idea of working on health, but rather that they're unaware of the existence of a scientific approach that's both practical and reliable.

If using the influence model as we've suggested isn't enough to get your leader on board, our second piece of advice is to find a way to prove the power of the approach on a small scale. Talking about a successful transformation is like describing what an apple tastes like. You can explain that it's sweet, sharp, fresh, juicy, and so on, but if the person you're talking to has never eaten an apple, they won't "get" what it tastes like until they take their first bite. So try to find a small-scale pilot in your organization that doesn't need full support to be successful, either because an appetite for change already exists (or can be developed quickly), or because your leader is willing to lend support on an experimental basis. If you can get agreement to do this "taste test" in a targeted area, your leader can experience the approach and the impact firsthand instead of just hearing about them. That should be enough to prove the benefits of making an apple a day part of the management menu, so to speak.

Our third piece of advice is this: if none of the above pans out, go ahead anyway. Do all the things you can do to maximize the likelihood of success on both the performance and health fronts, regardless of whether your senior leader is fully committed to playing their role. Don't give up. All the evidence we've found shows that even if you can't adopt all our recommendations, every aspect of health that you pursue gives you a better chance of becoming and staying successful. It's a bit like your own health: even if your favorite meal is burgers and chips, going to the gym three times a week still pays dividends. So although you'd undoubtedly do better to have your senior leader on board, you're not automatically doomed to failure if you don't; it's just that achieving success will be more difficult.

In everything we've said here, we've assumed that not having your senior leader on board simply means that they're unlikely to play the role we described in Chapter 8. That's one thing. But if for some reason your senior leader is actively opposed to your performance and health efforts, that's something else entirely. If you're still in this situation even after following the steps above, you'd be wise to consider investing your time and energy in another organization where your efforts are more likely to bear fruit. In other words, when you can't change your leader, it's time to change your leader.

What Does It Look Like to Put the Five Frames into Practice?

In Part II of this book we presented the five frames of performance and health as an approach to help you maintain the right balance between these

Exhibit 10.1

Scheme of Work in a Performance and Health Transformation

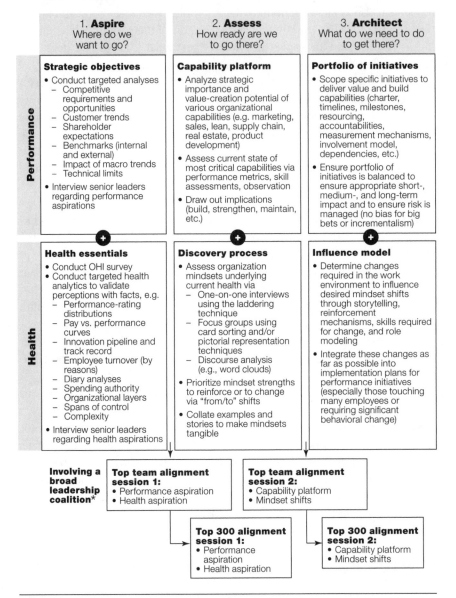

1. **Aspire** Where do we want to go?	2. **Assess** How ready are we to go there?	3. **Architect** What do we need to do to get there?

Performance

Strategic objectives
- Conduct targeted analyses
  - Competitive requirements and opportunities
  - Customer trends
  - Shareholder expectations
  - Benchmarks (internal and external)
  - Impact of macro trends
  - Technical limits
- Interview senior leaders regarding performance aspirations

Capability platform
- Analyze strategic importance and value-creation potential of various organizational capabilities (e.g. marketing, sales, lean, supply chain, real estate, product development)
- Assess current state of most critical capabilities via performance metrics, skill assessments, observation
- Draw out implications (build, strengthen, maintain, etc.)

Portfolio of initiatives
- Scope specific initiatives to deliver value and build capabilities (charter, timelines, milestones, resourcing, accountabilities, measurement mechanisms, involvement model, dependencies, etc.)
- Ensure portfolio of initiatives is balanced to ensure appropriate short-, medium-, and long-term impact and to ensure risk is managed (no bias for big bets or incrementalism)

Health

Health essentials
- Conduct OHI survey
- Conduct targeted health analytics to validate perceptions with facts, e.g.
  - Performance-rating distributions
  - Pay vs. performance curves
  - Innovation pipeline and track record
  - Employee turnover (by reasons)
  - Diary analyses
  - Spending authority
  - Organizational layers
  - Spans of control
  - Complexity
- Interview senior leaders regarding health aspirations

Discovery process
- Assess organization mindsets underlying current health via
  - One-on-one interviews using the laddering technique
  - Focus groups using card sorting and/or pictorial representation techniques
  - Discourse analysis (e.g., word clouds)
- Prioritize mindset strengths to reinforce or to change via "from/to" shifts
- Collate examples and stories to make mindsets tangible

Influence model
- Determine changes required in the work environment to influence desired mindset shifts through storytelling, reinforcement mechanisms, skills required for change, and role modeling
- Integrate these changes as far as possible into implementation plans for performance initiatives (especially those touching many employees or requiring significant behavioral change)

Involving a broad leadership coalition*

Top team alignment session 1:
- Performance aspiration
- Health aspiration

Top team alignment session 2:
- Capability platform
- Mindset shifts

Top 300 alignment session 1:
- Performance aspiration
- Health aspiration

Top 300 alignment session 2:
- Capability platform
- Mindset shifts

*Each session typically covers the content from the previous frame and then brainstorms to provide input into the next frame, and is conducted in a "write your own lottery ticket" fashion

Exhibit 10.1 *continued*
Scheme of Work in a Performance and Health Transformation

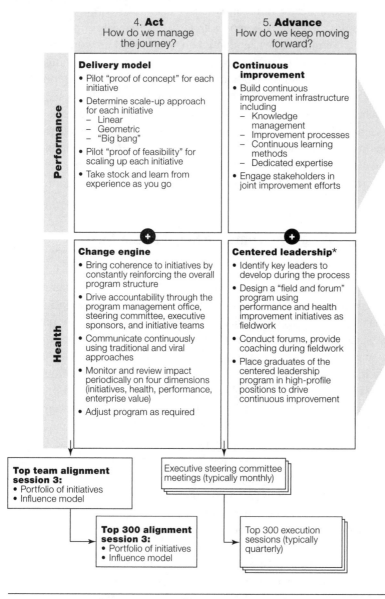

---

*Note that frame 5 marks the end of the centered leadership development process, which typically begins in the "aspire" frame

two dimensions as you progress through the five stages in a transformation. Leaders have told us that it's useful to have a plan of how to organize the work involved, and so we've drawn up a simple map of the overall transformation journey as illustrated in Exhibit 10.1.

The exhibit pulls together all the discrete pieces of work that make up a performance and health transformation. What needs to be done in the first stage, "aspire"? The work begins with targeted analyses of performance and health and culminates in a session where senior leaders work creatively together to set aspirations. In the second stage, "assess"? Further investigation of capabilities and an in-depth analysis of mindsets using the tools and approaches we've described. And so on through each remaining stage.

The scheme illustrated in the exhibit is a generalized example based on our experience of many transformations. As we've said many times now, every company's journey will be unique, tailored to its particular combination of internal and external factors. But the scheme can be used as a convenient point of departure as you think through what's right for your organization.

When Should We Move from One Stage to the Next?

The five frames of performance and health can be applied to many different organizational challenges and opportunities, as the examples in this book demonstrate. But whatever your reason for embarking on a transformation, you'll need to fulfill certain criteria before you progress from one stage to the next. In the text box opposite, we present two tests for each stage—the first for performance, the second for health—that you can apply to check if you're ready to make the move. Once you've passed all of these tests, you'll have completed the formal transformation program, and your organization will be characterized by continuous improvement in performance and health.

But do bear in mind, as we've noted before, that change doesn't happen in such a linear stage-by-stage fashion in real life. What you learn during one stage often prompts you to revisit decisions you've made in an earlier one. And as we saw in Chapter 7, the journey to centered leadership is one that needs to start at the first stage and continue through all the rest. (For the sake of simplicity, we've made it the last item in our checklist as the destination to aim for.) Even if you double back to revisit earlier decisions, it's important not to jump ahead from one stage to the next until your organization is ready. Ensuring that you can answer the questions in the list in the affirmative is a good way of knowing when that moment has come.

The 10 Tests of Transformational Change

If you can answer yes to both questions on a specific stage in the transformation, your organization is ready to move to the next stage.

Aspire

1. Do we have a compelling medium-term vision for change that includes specific performance targets, and does a critical mass of leaders feel deep ownership of it?
2. Do we have a shared language, robust baseline, and clear aspirations for the health of our organization, and does a critical mass of leaders feel deep ownership of these things too?

Assess

3. Do we know what capabilities are strategically important for delivering our change vision, and do we have a solid assessment of the state of these capabilities in our organization today?
4. Do we have a clear insight into the mindsets that underlie current limiting and liberating behaviors, as well as the mindsets that are needed to make our health aspirations a reality?

Architect

5. Have we defined a concrete set of performance improvement initiatives that will deliver our change vision, and are they balanced in terms of timing and risk?
6. Do we have a robust plan for influencing healthy mindsets that leverages storytelling, reinforcement mechanisms, skill building, and role modeling, and have we integrated these efforts into our performance initiatives?

Act

7. Have we tailored the delivery model for each initiative in our portfolio to take account of scale, capacity, urgency, difficulty, and customization needs?
8. Have we generated energy for change by providing a coherent structure for the program, creating formal and informal ownership, and building in regular evaluation to identify where adjustments are needed?

Advance

9. Have we put in place the structure, processes, systems, and people to drive continuous improvement in both performance and health?
10. Throughout the transformation, have we methodically developed a group of committed leaders who have the qualities to drive continuous improvement from now on?

How Can We Catch Up in Areas We've Neglected?

As management consultants, we often receive calls from leaders whose change programs have somehow got stuck. On inspection, we typically find that the reason they can't move on is that they haven't paid sufficient attention to some aspect of health or performance at an earlier stage of the transformation. The question then becomes how to get the program back on track. Can the organization make up for what it has neglected? Does it need to start all over again? Is it better off staying on the horse it's already riding? Or should it change horses midway through the race?

We find that the point of failure most often comes in the fourth stage of the transformation, "act," when organizations find that plans don't get implemented as quickly as expected or achieve the desired impact. The usual reason is a lack of discipline and rigor in tackling the health frames in the first three stages of the transformation. Where this is the case, most of the work done on the performance side is likely to stand, and the way forward is to invest time and resources in making good the missing health elements. In practical terms, this means completing the OHI, developing a health aspiration based on a chosen archetype, digging into the mindsets that matter, and using the influence model to bring about any needed mindset shifts, taking care to build these actions into the implementation of the portfolio of performance initiatives.

More generally, the answer is to go back to wherever failure first occurred in the journey and backfill from there. A company that didn't set clear medium-term "tough but doable" performance aspirations based on a combination of facts and intuition would do well to go back to the first performance frame ("strategic objectives") and start again, even if it has already gone a long way on its transformation journey. The same goes for a company that didn't set clear and measurable aspirations for its health, except that in this case it will need to revisit the first health frame ("health essentials"). A company that's suffering from waning commitment and low energy levels but has laid a solid foundation in the first three stages may simply need to fine-tune the "change engine" frame in the "act" stage. And so on.

Most often it's health rather than performance factors that have been neglected. If that's the case, we'd emphasize that the right time to make a start—as with personal health—is always *right now*. Every day you push forward on performance without tending to your health takes away from your longevity.

Of course, if your organization is already so unhealthy that it's fighting for its life, the first order of business will be to stem the bleeding. Broader health concerns can be put on hold. But most organizations aren't in this state, or not yet. Our aspiration for you is that your organization never finds itself in a critical condition. Following our balanced approach to performance and health will stop that happening, but it will also do much more. Tending to health regularly will make your organization fighting fit and put it in the best possible position to succeed at everything it aspires to achieve.

Principles Underlying Our Approach

As we come to the end, we'd like to reiterate three of the principles that sit behind everything you've read. They are right at the heart of our findings, and we'd encourage you to keep them in mind so that you stay grounded in the fundamentals of performance and health as you embark on and progress through your own journey.

The first principle is that *performance and health matter as much as one another—and can be measured and managed with equal rigor.* As we said earlier, the most important word in performance and health is "and." In all the decisions you make and actions you take as a leader, we encourage you to address both dimensions at once whenever you can. But bearing in mind that it's the health aspects that are most often neglected, we suggest you put extra emphasis on that side of the equation.

For most leaders, doing what we recommend will mean stepping outside their comfort zone. But as we saw in our exploration of centered leadership, when we leave our comfort zone, we enter a learning zone. If we keep pushing ourselves to go beyond our usual limits, our comfort zone will eventually expand, and we'll have more power to make change happen.

The second principle is that *performance and health are both things you should be managing today.* Just as performance requires a quarter-by-quarter, month-by-month, day-by-day focus from leaders, so does health. Sometimes people equate health with the long term (something to manage tomorrow) and performance with the short term (something to manage today). This thinking couldn't be more flawed. Our research shows that the way you manage your health today is responsible for at least 50 percent of your ability to continue to perform in the future. And we'd add a word of warning: the higher an organization is riding in its performance, the more likely it is to be complacent about its health. Leaders of today's high-performing organizations would be well advised to watch out for this tendency, and deal with it quickly should it arise.

The third principle is that *nothing changes unless behavior does*. In the end, improving an organization's performance and health comes down to getting people to do things in a different way. That requires us to understand why we behave the way we do, and to be aware of the things that can stop us achieving the impact we're striving for. We need to accept the predictable inherent biases that make us human, no matter how irrational they may seem in the cold light of logic. The approaches and tools we use should always be viewed through the lens of "How does this help us to understand and influence the behaviors we need to achieve our aspirations?"

Our research and experience indicate that by putting these three principles into practice through the five frames approach, your organization will be well on its way to sustaining high performance and leadership no matter what its industry or field may be.

The real power of the five frames approach lies in its ability to transform human systems. In this book, we've sometimes used the words "transformation" and "change" to mean the same thing. In reality, though, they refer to very different processes. In nature, when a caterpillar becomes a butterfly, or a tadpole a frog, it goes through a transformation, not a change. The caterpillar doesn't just become a bigger, fatter caterpillar; it becomes something else entirely. And when something has gone through a transformation, it can't go back to what it was before. A butterfly can't revert to being a caterpillar. It has been fundamentally altered, taking on a new form that gives it more freedom and a better chance to survive and thrive in its environment.

And in a transformation, it isn't just the systems that win, but also the individuals within them. David Whyte once wrote that "Work, paradoxically, does not ask enough of us, yet exhausts the narrow part of us we bring to the door."[1] The five frames approach addresses this paradox by tapping into our highest aspirations and deepest motivations at work. When we put the approach into practice, it unleashes tremendous energy for change across huge groups of people. Having witnessed the impact on many occasions, we can confidently say that leaders who use the five frames to pursue organizational excellence will find that the work is among the most—if not *the* most—fulfilling of their careers.

■ ■ ■

In the end, whether the approach we've explored in this book makes its way into the mainstream of management thinking will be up to you, our readers. Certainly we're convinced—and we hope that by this point you are, too—that the evidence is too compelling to dismiss, and that the potential impact on customers, shareholders, employees, communities, and society at large is too great to ignore. But will *you* put it into practice? We're back to the "red pill or blue pill" choice.

We often hear leaders talk about what they'd *like* to do, what they *want* to do, and what they'll *try* to do. Our experience with such leaders is that little actually gets done. Why? It's because the language they use betrays inner doubt. At the first sign of resistance or challenge they back down, reverting to the approaches they are comfortable with.

On the other hand, leaders who use what's sometimes called the language of mastery—those who talk about what they *will* do and what they *can be counted on* to accomplish—produce very different results. The inner commitment and conviction that shine through their choice of words mean that when they adopt a new approach, they'll stay the course. They'll follow things through and expect to be judged by what they achieve.

So where are you in relation to performance and health? Would you like to, do you want to, will you try to? Or will you, can you be counted on to? In the spirit of a good Hollywood ending, we turn to another cinematic classic to offer you encouragement. To quote *Star Wars* Jedi Master Yoda, "Do or do not. There is no 'try.'"

Notes

Introduction

1. Personal interview.
2. Ovum.
3. John Tiefel, "Chaos By Design: An Interview with the CEO of Zain," *Voices on Transformation* 3, McKinsey & Company, 2009.
4. Based on the application of the McKinsey corporate performance analysis tool developed by Richard Foster and Sarah Caplan and used extensively in the research for their book *Creative Destruction: Why Companies that Are Built to Last Underperform the Market—And How to Successfully Transform Them* (New York: Doubleday/Currency, 2001).
5. Personal interview.
6. Frederico Oliveira, "Transforming a High-Performing Company: An Interview with Roberto Setubal," *McKinsey Quarterly*, April 2009.
7. "I Can't Get No . . . Job Satisfaction, That Is: America's Unhappy Workers," Conference Board Research Report #1459-09-RR, January 2010.
8. U.S. Bureau of Labor Statistics, using data on nonfarm businesses.
9. Stefan Stern, "Share the Power," in "Managing Employees through the Recovery," *Financial Times,* March 22, 2010, Special Report.
10. François Bouvard, Thomas Dohrmann, and Nick Lovegrove, "The Case for Government Reform Now," *McKinsey Quarterly*, June 2009.
11. Based on analysis in Stuart Cranier and Des Dearlove, "Excellence Revisited," *Business Strategy Review*, March 2002, updated to 2006.

Chapter 1   The Big Idea

1. Dean Foust, "Gone Flat," *BusinessWeek*, December 20, 2004.
2. Adrienne Fox, "Refreshing a Beverage Company's Culture," *HR Magazine*, November 1, 2007.
3. Ibid.

4. Interview by Gautam Kumra and Jim Wendler, "The Creative Art of Influence: Making Change Personal," *Voices of Transformation* 1, McKinsey & Company, 2005.

5. "What Successful Transformations Share," *McKinsey Quarterly* survey, January 2010.

6. Larry Bossidy, *Execution: The Discipline of Getting Things Done* (New York: Crown Business, 2002).

7. Personal interview.

8. William C. Taylor, *Practically Radical* (New York: William Morrow, 2011).

9. Mel Cowan, "Pixar Co-Founder Mulls Meaning of Success," USC News Bulletin, University of Southern California, December 10, 2009.

10. C. W. Nevius, "Pixar Tells Story Behind *Toy Story*," *San Francisco Chronicle*, August 23, 2005.

11. Ed Catmull, "How Pixar Fosters Collective Creativity," *Harvard Business Review*, September 2008.

12. Bernard Simon and Telis Demos, "GM Listing Marks Successful Turnround," *Financial Times*, November 18, 2010.

13. Ibid.

14. See www.financialstability.gov/docs/AIFP/Chrysler-Viability-Assessment .pdf

15. David Brooks, "The Quagmire Ahead," *New York Times*, June 1, 2009.

16. Wendy Zellner and Stephanie Anderson Forest, "The Fall of Enron," *BusinessWeek*, December 17, 2001.

17. Vicky Ward, *The Devil's Casino* (Hoboken, NJ: John Wiley & Sons, 2010).

18. "Gulf of Mexico Oil Leak 'Worst US Environment Disaster,'" BBC News, May 30, 2010 at www.bbc.co.uk/news/10194335

19. Ed Crooks, Sylvia Pfiefer, and Sheila McNulty, "Energy: A Sea Change Needed," *Financial Times*, October 6, 2010.

20. Sarah Boseley, "Mid Staffordshire NHS Trust Left Patients Humiliated and in Pain," *Guardian*, February 24, 2010.

21. Foundation Trusts are hospitals in the NHS that are regulated by the government, but have their own board and CEO. They enjoy relative freedom to define their agenda and manage budgets, and as a result are keen to maintain their Foundation Trust status.

22. Katherine Murphy, Director of the Patients Association, in "Outrage Greets Mid Staffordshire Hospital Report," *Guardian*, March 17, 2009.

23. *Independent Inquiry into Care Provided by Mid Staffordshire NHS Foundation Trust January 2005–March 2009*, vol. I, Stationery Office, London, February 24, 2010.

24. "What Successful Transformations Share," *McKinsey Quarterly* survey, January 2010.

25. Ian Davis, "How to Escape the Short-Term Trap," *McKinsey Quarterly,* April 2005.

26. "What Successful Transformations Share," *McKinsey Quarterly* survey, January 2010.

27. Analysis based on Michael Beer and Nitin Nohria, editors, *Breaking the Code of Change* (Boston: Harvard Business School Press, 2000); Kim S. Cameron and Robert E. Quinn, *Diagnosing and Changing Organizational Culture: Based on the Competing Values Framework* (Reading, MA: Addison-Wesley, 1999); Bruce Caldwell, "Missteps, Miscues: Business Re-Engineering Failures Have Cost Corporations Billions and Spending Is Still on the Rise," *InformationWeek*, June 20, 1994; "State of Re-Engineering Report (North America and Europe)," *CSC Index*, 1994; Tracy Goss, Richard Tanner Pascale, and Anthony G. Athos, "The Reinvention Roller Coaster: Risking the Present for a Powerful Future," *Harvard Business Review*, November 1, 1993; John P. Kotter and James L. Heskett, *Corporate Culture and Performance* (New York: Free Press, 1992).

28. In Stratford Sherman, "How Tomorrow's Leaders Are Learning Their Stuff," *Fortune*, November 27, 1995.

29. Louis Lavelle, "Eight Isn't Enough," *BusinessWeek*, February 28, 2005.

Chapter 2   The Science

1. With hindsight, we now know that their views were often influenced by their company's choice of archetype—a subject we explore in Chapter 3.

2. In terms of geographic reach, 35 percent of respondents are in North America, 29 percent in Europe, 26 percent in China, India, and other developed economies in Asia, and the rest in other regions. Half of the panel comes from privately held companies, 39 percent from publicly held companies, and the rest from government and nonprofit organizations.

3. For more information, see "Organizing for Successful Change Management: A McKinsey Global Survey," July 2006; "Creating Organizational Transformations: McKinsey Global Survey Results," August 2008; and "What Successful Transformations Share: McKinsey Global Survey Results," March 2010, all at www.mckinseyquarterly.com

4. The technical requirement for journals was a top 50 impact factor or immediacy score as calculated in the 2007 Journal Citation Reports—Social Science Data for Business Journals.

5. C. K. Bart and M. C. Baetz, "The Relationship between Mission Statement and Firm Performance: An Exploratory Study," *Journal of Management Studies* 35, no. 6 (1998).

6. J. C. Collins and J. I. Porras, *Built to Last: Successful Habits of Visionary Companies* (New York: Random House, 2005).

7. B. Schneider, M. G. Ehrhart, D. M. Mayer, J. Saltz, and K. Niles-Jolly, "Understanding Organization–Customer Links in Service Settings," *Academy of Management Journal* 48, no. 6 (2005): 1017–1032.

8. S. Lieberson and J. F. O'Conner, "Leadership and Organizational Performance: A Study of Large Corporations," *American Sociological Review* 37, no. 2 (1972): 117–30.

9. A. B. Thomas, "Does Leadership Make a Difference to Organizational Performance?" *Administrative Science Quarterly* 33, no. 3 (1988): 388–400.

10. J. P. Kotter and J. L. Heskett, *Corporate Culture and Performance* (New York: Free Press, 1992).

11. G. G. Gordon and N. DiTomaso, "Predicting Corporate Performance from Organizational Culture," *Journal of Management Studies* 29, no. 6 (1992): 783–798.

12. S. H. Wagner, C. P. Parker, and N. D. Christiansen, "Employees that Think and Act Like Owners: Effects of Ownership Beliefs and Behaviors on Organizational Effectiveness," *Personnel Psychology*, no. 56 (2003): 847–871.

13. J. B. Avey, B. J. Avolio, C. D. Crossley, and F. Luthans, "Psychological Ownership: Theoretical Extensions, Measurement, and Relation to Work Outcomes," *Journal of Organizational Behavior* 30 (2009): 173–191.

14. S. Davis and T. Albright, "An Investigation of the Effect of Balanced Scorecard Implementation on Financial Performance," *Management Accounting Research* no. 15 (2004): 135–153.

15. J. Gittell, "Coordinating Mechanisms in Care Provider Groups: Relational Coordination as a Mediator and Input Uncertainty as a Moderator of Performance Effects," *Management Science* 48, no. 11 (2002): 1408–1426.

16. A. M. McGahan and M. E. Porter, "How Much Does Industry Matter, Really?" *Strategic Management Journal* 8, no. 4 (1997): 15–30.

17. J. Stuckey, *Perspectives on Strategy,* McKinsey Staff Paper, 2005, available on request from McKinsey & Company.

18. R. Takeuchi, "Intellectual Human and Social Capital as Mediators of HR System and Outcomes: Different Mediating Mechanisms," presented at the annual meeting of the Academy of Management, August 2005.

19. J. Krueger and E. Killham, "Feeling Good Matters," *Gallup Management Journal,* December 8, 2005.

20. D. A. Harrison, D. A. Newman, and P. L. Roth, "How Important Are Job Attitudes? Meta-Analytic Comparisons of Integrative Behavioral Outcomes Time Sequences," *Academy of Management Journal* 49, no. 2 (2006): 305–325.

21. L. J. Harrison-Walker, "The Measurement of Word-of-Mouth Communication and an Investigation of Service Quality and Customer Commitment as Potential Antecedents," *Journal of Service Research* 4, no. 1 (2001): 60–75.

22. C. Cano, F. Carrillat, and F. Jaramillo, "A Meta-Analysis of the Relationship between Market Orientation and Business Performance: Evidence from Five Continents," *International Journal of Research in Marketing,* no. 21 (2004): 179–200.

23. S. Zahra and J. Covin, "The Financial Implications of Fit between Competitive Strategy and Innovation Types and Sources," *Journal of High Technology Management Research,* no. 5 (1994): 183–211.

24. A. Paladino, "Investigating the Drivers of Innovation and New Product Success: A Comparison of Strategic Orientations," *Journal of Product Innovation Management,* no. 24 (2007): 534–553.

Chapter 3 Aspire

1. Personal interview.

2. "Creating Organizational Transformations," *McKinsey Quarterly* survey, July 2008.

3. "Tesco Chief Sir Terry Leahy to Retire," BBC News, June 8, 2010, at www.bbc.co.uk/news/10262193; Marcus Leroux, "Sir Terry Leahy Checks Out at Tesco After 14 Years," *The Times,* June 9, 2010.

4. At a press conference in July 1993.

5. Rajat Gupta and Jim Wendler, "Leading Change: An Interview with the CEO of P&G," *McKinsey Quarterly,* July 2005.

6. Gautam Kumra, "Leading Change: An Interview with the Managing Director of Tata Motors," *McKinsey Quarterly,* January 2007.

7. In an annual survey conducted by Brand Finance and *Economic Times.*

8. "Jack Welch Reinvents General Electric, Again," *The Economist*, March 30, 1991. Some details of GE's story are also taken from Noel M. Tichy

and Stratford Sherman, *Control Your Destiny or Someone Else Will* (New York: HarperCollins, 2005), and www.fundinguniverse.com/company-histories/General-Electric-Company-Company-History.html

9. "What Successful Transformations Share," *McKinsey Quarterly* survey, January 2010.
10. At a McKinsey leadership retreat for senior executives in February 2010.
11. Personal interview.
12. Claudia Croft, "Natalie Massenet: The Woman behind Net-a-Porter," *Sunday Times*, March 8, 2009.
13. Quoted in Eva Wiseman, "One-Click Wonder: The rise of Net-a-Porter," *Observer*, July 11, 2010.
14. Addy Dugdale, "Crib Sheet: Natalie Massenet, Founder of Net-a-Porter," *Fast Company*, April 2, 2010.
15. Kate Walsh, "Net-a-Porter Delivers a Dozen Millionaires," *Sunday Times*, April 4, 2010.
16. Debate between Daniel Kahneman and Gary Klein, "Strategic Decisions: When Can You Trust Your Gut?" *McKinsey Quarterly,* March 2010.
17. "What Successful Transformations Share," *McKinsey Quarterly* survey, January 2010.
18. "'Goals Gone Wild': How Goal Setting Can Lead to Disaster," Knowledge@Wharton, February 18, 2009.
19. Fred Kapner, "Pushing the Envelope," *Financial Times,* March 1, 2002.
20. John Roberts, *The Modern Firm* (Oxford: Oxford University Press, 2004).
21. Archetypes were identified by performing a comprehensive cluster analysis of the OHI database.
22. Adam Morgan, *The Pirate Inside* (Hoboken, NJ: John Wiley & Sons, 2004).
23. Speaking at P&G's annual meeting for shareholders in October 2004.
24. Peter Burrows, "Welcome to Planet Apple," *BusinessWeek,* June 28, 2007.
25. Ibid.
26. A. G. Lafley and Ram Charan, *The Game-Changer: How You Can Drive Revenue and Profit Growth with Innovation* (New York: Crown Business, 2008).
27. Gary Parkinson, "How the Goldman Sachs Diaspora Spread Its Influence Across the Globe," *Independent*, December 20, 2005.
28. Susanne Craig, "How Goldman Sachs Makes (and Unmakes) Its Partners," *New York Times*, September 12, 2010.

29. See "Creating Organizational Transformations," *McKinsey Quarterly* survey, July 2008.

30. Example taken from Alex Bellos, *Here's Looking at Euclid: A Surprising Excursion through the Astonishing World of Math* (New York: Free Press, 2010).

31. For more on Coca-Cola's transformation under Isdell, see the beginning of Chapter 1.

32. Gautam Kumra, "Leading Change: An Interview with the Managing Director of Tata Motors," *McKinsey Quarterly,* January 2007.

33. Alex Dichter, Fredrik Lind, and Seelan Singham, "Turning Around a Struggling Airline: An Interview with the CEO of Malaysian Airlines," *McKinsey Quarterly,* November 2008.

34. Quoted in Bronwyn Fryer and Thomas A. Stewart, "Cisco Sees the Future: An Interview with John Chambers," *Harvard Business Review,* November 2008.

Chapter 4   Assess

1. Quotes in this section come from Bruce Simpson, "'Flying People, Not Places': The CEO of Bombardier on Building a World-Class Culture," *Voices on Transformation* 4, McKinsey & Company, 2010.

2. Joint survey between Global Reputation Pulse and *Canadian Business*, 2010.

3. "What Successful Transformations Share," *McKinsey Quarterly* survey, January 2010. Subsequent references to surveys in this chapter refer to this source.

4. Daniel Gross, *Forbes Greatest Business Stories of All Time* (New York: John Wiley & Sons, 1997).

5. Erin E. Arvedlund, "McDonald's Commands a Real Estate Empire," *New York Times*, March 17, 2005.

6. This story comes from Alan Deutschman, "Change or Die," *Fast Company*, May 1, 2005.

7. Roger Bannister, *The Four-Minute Mile* (Guilford, CT: Lyons Press, 1981).

8. Louis Gerstner, *Who Says Elephants Can't Dance?* (New York: Harper-Collins, 2002).

9. See, for instance, Chris Argyris, *Knowledge for Action: Guide to Overcoming Barriers to Organizational Change* (New York: Jossey-Bass, 1993).

10. Quoted on Tim Gallwey's website www.theinnergame.com

11. The quote and example come from Alan Deutschman, "Change or Die," *Fast Company*, May 1, 2005.

12. Quoted in Joe Keohane, "How Facts Backfire: Researchers Discover a Surprising Threat to Democracy: Our Brains," *Boston Globe*, July 11, 2010.

13. Example borrowed from Jerry Wind, Colin Crook, and Robert Gunther, *The Power of Impossible Thinking: Transform the Business of Your Life and the Life of Your Business* (Upper Saddle River, NJ: Wharton School, 2004).

14. For more details on this approach, see Bernard J. Mohr and Jane Magruder Watkins, *The Essentials of Appreciative Inquiry* (Waltham, MA: Pegasus Communications, 2002), which is also the source of the bowling teams example.

15. Example taken from Terry Burnham and Jay Phelan, *Mean Genes* (New York: Perseus, 2000).

16. Quoted in David L. Cooperrider, Diana Whitney, and Jacqueline M. Stavros, *The Appreciative Inquiry Handbook: For Leaders of Change* (San Francisco, CA: Berrett-Koehlerz, 2008).

17. Bruce Simpson, "'Flying People, Not Places': The CEO of Bombardier on Building a World-Class Culture," *Voices on Transformation* 4, McKinsey & Company, 2010.

Chapter 5   Architect

1. The story of P&G's turnaround and quotes from A. G. Lafley are taken from Rajat Gupta and Jim Wendler, "Leading change: An interview with the CEO of P&G," *McKinsey Quarterly*, July 2005. Some details are drawn from A. G. Lafley and Ram Charan, *The Game-Changer: How You Can Drive Revenue and Profit Growth with Innovation* (New York: Crown Business, 2008).

2. "What Successful Transformations Share," *McKinsey Quarterly* survey, January 2010. Subsequent references to survey data in this chapter refer to this source.

3. For more on EMC's turnaround, see Felix Brück and Jack Welch, "Leading Change: An Interview with the CEO of EMC," *McKinsey Quarterly,* August 2005.

4. For more on Tata's turnaround, see Gautam Kumra, "Leading Change: An Interview with the Managing Director of Tata Motors," *McKinsey Quarterly,* January 2007.

5. See   www.ted.com/talks/dan_ariely_asks_are_we_in_control_of_our_ own_decisions.html

6. Giancarlo Ghislanzoni and Julie Shearn, "Leading Change: An Interview with the CEO of Banca Intesa," *McKinsey Quarterly,* August 2005.

7. See, for instance, Danah Zohar, *Spiritual Intelligence* (London: Blooms-bury, 1999); Don Beck and Christopher Cowen, *Spiral Dynamics* (Oxford: Blackwell, 1996); and Richard Barrett, *Liberating the Corporate Soul* (Oxford: Butterworth-Heinemann, 1998).

8. John Mackey, "Creating a High-Trust Organization," posted on huffing tonpost.com on March 14, 2010.

9. Cited by Chip Heath and Dan Heath, "The Curse of Knowledge," *Harvard Business Review,* December 2006.

10. Robert H. Miles, "Beyond the Age of Dilbert: Accelerating Corporate Transformations by Rapidly Engaging All Employees," *Organizational Dynamics* 29, issue 4, Spring 2001.

11. Lawrence M. Fisher, "Symantec's Strategy-Based Transformation," *Strategy+Business*, issue 30, Spring 2003.

12. Sam Allis, "In Small Steps, He Takes a Giant Leap," *Boston Globe*, September 3, 2009.

13. Robert Kegan and Lisa Laskow Lahey, *How the Way We Talk Can Change the Way We Work: Seven Languages for Transformation* (New York: Wiley Jossey-Bass, 2003).

14. Personal interview.

15. Quoted in Robert Howard, "The CEO as Organizational Architect: An Interview with Xerox's Paul Allaire," *Harvard Business Review,* September 1992.

16. Upton Sinclair, *I, Candidate for Governor, and How I Got Licked* (New York: Farrar & Rinehart, 1935).

17. Felix Brück and Jack Welch, "Leading Change: An Interview with the CEO of EMC," *McKinsey Quarterly,* August 2005.

18. Quoted in James Dunn, interview with Jack Welch, *Leadership Victoria*, spring 2003.

19. Example borrowed from Terry Burnham and Jay Phelan, *Mean Genes: From Sex to Money to Food—Taming Our Primal Instincts* (New York: Penguin, 2001).

20. Example borrowed from Dan Ariely, *Predictable Irrationality: The Hidden Forces that Shape Our Decisions* (New York: HarperCollins, 2008).

21. Example borrowed from Stephen Dubner and Stephen Levitt, *Freakonomics: A Rogue Economist Explores the Hidden Side of Everything* (New York: Doubleday, 2005).

22. Sam Walton, *Sam Walton: Made in America* (New York: Bantam, 1993).

23. Lisa Cameron, "Raising the Stakes in the Ultimate Game: Experimental Evidence from Indonesia," *Economic Inquiry* 37, no. 1, 1999, and E. Hoffman, K. McCabe, et al., "On Expectations and the Monetary Stakes in Ultimate Games," *International Journal of Game Theory,* no. 25, 1996.

24. Victor H. Vroom and Kenneth R. MacCrimmon, "Toward a Stochastic Model of Managerial Careers," *Administrative Science Quarterly,* June 1968.

25. IBM research; John Whitmore, *Coaching for Performance: Growing People, Performance and Purpose* (London: Nicholas Brealey, 3rd edition, 2002).

26. Described in J. M. Darley and C. D. Batson, "From Jerusalem to Jericho: A Study of Situational and Dispositional Variables in Helping Behavior," *Journal of Personality and Social Psychology* 27, no. 1, 1973.

27. J. Cone and M. Woodard, "Action Learning Helps PepsiCo's Sales Leaders Develop Business Acumen and Innovation Skills," *Global Business and Organizational Excellence*, May/June 2007.

28. In Johan Ahlberg and Tomas Nauclér, "Leading Change: An Interview with Sandvik's Peter Gossas," *McKinsey Quarterly,* January 2007.

29. See, for instance, Daniel Goleman, *Emotional Intelligence: Why it Can Matter More than IQ* (London: Bloomsbury, 1996).

30. Reported in Rupert Neate, "Vodafone's 'Depressingly Thin' Talent Pool under Fire from Analyst," *Daily Telegraph,* November 26, 2009.

31. James Delahunty, "Apple Boosting Chip Design Capabilities," April 29, 2009, at www.afterdawn.com/news/article.cfm/2009/04/30/apple_boosting_chip_design_capabilities

32. Kenneth Labich, "Is Herb Kelleher America's Best CEO?" *Fortune,* May 2, 1994.

33. Quoted in Jon Ashworth, "Time to Move on for Chief Who Is Best 'Being Me,'" *The Times,* June 21, 2004.

34. Kurt Lewin, *Principles of Topological Psychology* (New York: McGraw-Hill, 1936).

35. Karl Lorenz, *King Solomon's Ring* (New York: Crowell, 1952).

36. Mark D. Alicke and Olesya Govorun, "The Better-Than-Average Effect," in Mark D. Alicke, David A. Dunning, and Joachim I. Krueger, editors, *The Self in Social Judgment: Studies in Self and Identity* (New York: Psychology Press, 2005).

37. Ola Svenson, "Are We All Less Risky and More Skillful than Our Fellow Drivers?" *Acta Psychologica,* vol. 47, no. 2, February 1981.

38. Vera Hoorens and Peter Harris, "Distortions in Reports of Health Behaviors: The Time Span Effect and Illusory Superiority," *Psychology and Health,* vol. 13, no. 3, 1998.

39. Michael Bergdahl, *What I Learned from Sam Walton: How to Compete and Thrive in a Walmart World* (Hoboken, NJ: John Wiley & Sons, 2004).

40. Interview by Gautam Kumra and Jim Wendler, "The Creative Art of Influence: Making Change Personal," *Voices on Transformation* 1, McKinsey & Company, 2005.

41. Richard Tanner Pascale and Jerry Sternin, "Your Company's Secret Change Agents," *Harvard Business Review,* May 2005.

42. Personal interview.

43. Rajat Gupta and Jim Wendler, "Leading Change: An Interview with the CEO of P&G," *McKinsey Quarterly*, July 2005.

Chapter 6 Act

1. Quotes in this section come from Josep Isern and Julie Shearn, "Leading Change: An Interview with the Executive Chairman of Telefónica de España," *McKinsey Quarterly,* August 2005.

2. Quoted in Peter de Wit, "Scaling Up a Transformation: An Interview with Eureko's Jeroen van Breda Vriesman," *Voices on Transformation* 4, McKinsey & Company, 2010.

3. "Organizing for Successful Change Management," *McKinsey Quarterly* survey, June 2006.

4. "What Successful Transformations Share," *McKinsey Quarterly* survey, January 2010. Subsequent references to research or surveys in this chapter refer to this source.

5. Personal interview.

6. We look at the CEO's personal role in leading the transformation later, in Chapter 8.

7. Giancarlo Ghislanzoni and Julie Shearn, "Leading Change: An Interview with the CEO of Banca Intesa," *McKinsey Quarterly,* August 2005.

8. John Vidal, "She Has Changed the National Perspective about Plastic Bags in a Few Months. She Should Be Prime Minister," *Guardian,* November 23, 2007.

9. "How Obama Used Social Networking Sites to Win," INSEAD Knowledge, July 10, 2009.

10. Quoted in Carolyn Aiken and Scott Keller, "The CEO's Role in Leading Transformation," *McKinsey Quarterly*, February 2007.

11. Josep Isern and Julie Shearn, "Leading Change: An Interview with the Executive Chairman of Telefónica de España," *McKinsey Quarterly*, August 2005.

Chapter 7 Advance

1. Mark Westfield, "Lame Duck Bank Is Flying," *The Australian*, April 27, 2001.

2. Quoted in Ron Krueger, "A Cultural Transformation Journey," NSW Business Chamber, at www.nswbusinesschamber.com.au/?content=/channels/Building_and_sustaining_business/Sustainability/Sustainable_business/culturaltransformationjourney.xml

3. Quoted in ANZ's 2002 annual report.

4. See "What Successful Transformations Share," *McKinsey Quarterly* survey, January 2010. Subsequent references to research or surveys in this chapter refer to this source unless otherwise indicated.

5. Bill Gates, *The Road Ahead* (New York: Viking, 1995).

6. "Taking a Lean Approach to Warehouse Management Logistics," *Vision*, 2–1, 2005.

7. Debate between Daniel Kahneman and Gary Klein, "Strategic Decisions: When Can You Trust Your Gut?" *McKinsey Quarterly*, March 2010.

8. Examples drawn from Susanne Hauschild, Thomas Licht, and Wolfram Stein, "Creating a Knowledge Culture," *McKinsey Quarterly*, February 2001.

9. Joseph A. De Feo and William W. Barnard, *Juran Institute's Six Sigma Breakthrough and Beyond: Quality Performance Breakthrough Methods* (New York: McGraw-Hill, 2004).

10. Peter de Wit, "Scaling Up a Transformation: An Interview with Eureko's Jeroen van Breda Vriesman," *Voices on Transformation* 4, McKinsey & Company, 2010.

11. "Developing the Global Leader of Tomorrow" survey, 2008, Ashridge Business School.

12. *McKinsey Quarterly* survey of 1,147 executives in financial services, July–October 2009. See Joanna Barsh and Aaron De Smet, "Centered Leadership through the Crisis: McKinsey Survey Results," *McKinsey Quarterly*, October 2009.

13. Joanna Barsh, Josephine Mogelof, and Caroline Webb, "How Centered Leaders Achieve Extraordinary Results," *McKinsey Quarterly*, October 2010.

14. See, for instance, Danah Zohar, *Spiritual Intelligence* (London: Bloomsbury, 1999); Don Beck and Christopher Cowen, *Spiral Dynamics* (Oxford: Blackwell, 1996); and Richard Barrett, *Liberating the Corporate Soul* (Oxford: Butterworth-Heinemann, 1998).

15. See, for instance, Abraham Maslow, "A Theory of Human Motivation," *Psychological Review* 50, no. 4, 1943.

16. Kennon M. Sheldon and Sonja Lyubomirsky, "Achieving Sustainable Gains in Happiness: Change Your Actions, Not Your Circumstances," *Journal of Happiness Studies* 7, no. 1, 2006.

17. See, for instance, William C. Compton, *An Introduction to Positive Psychology* (Stamford, CO: Thomson Wadsworth, 2005); Tal Ben-Shahar, *Happier: Learn the Secrets to Daily Joy and Lasting Fulfillment* (New York: McGraw-Hill, 2007); and Martin E. P. Seligman, *Authentic Happiness: Using the New Positive Psychology to Realize Your Psychology for Lasting Fulfillment* (New York: Free Press, 2004).

18. Gary Hamel, "Moon Shots for Management," *Harvard Business Review*, February 2009.

19. Personal interview.

20. Martin Seligman, *Learned Optimism: How to Change Your Mind and Your Life* (New York: Vintage, 2006).

21. Quoted in Jim Collins, *Good to Great: Why Some Companies Make the Leap . . . and Others Don't* (New York: Random House, 2001).

22. Quoted in Joanna Barsh and Susie Cranston, *How Remarkable Women Lead: The Breakthrough for Work and Life* (New York: Random House, 2009).

23. In a commencement address at Stanford University in 2005.

24. Ronald A. Heifetz and Marty Linsky, *Leadership on the Line* (Cambridge, MA: Harvard Business School Press, 2002).

25. See, for instance, Roy F. Baumeister, "Is There Anything Good about Men?" address to the American Psychological Association, 2007; Shelley E. Taylor, *The Tending Instinct: Women, Men, and the Biology of Our Relationships* (New York: Holt, 2003).

26. Jack Welch, *Jack: Straight from the Gut* (New York: Warner Books, 2001).

27. Personal interview.

28. Jonathan Haidt, *The Happiness Hypothesis: Finding Modern Truth in Ancient Wisdom* (New York: Basic Books, 2006).

29. Quoted in Charles C. Manz, Frank Shipper, and Greg L. Stewart, "Everyone a Team Leader: Shared Influence at W. L. Gore & Associates," *Organizational Dynamics* 38, no. 3, 2009.

30. Bronwyn Fryer and Thomas A. Stewart, "Cisco Sees the Future: An Interview with John Chambers," *Harvard Business Review,* November 2008.

31. Joanna Barsh, Josephine Mogelof, and Caroline Webb, "How Centered Leaders Achieve Extraordinary Results," *McKinsey Quarterly*, October 2010.

32. See, for instance, J. B. Rotter, *Social Learning and Clinical Psychology* (New York: Prentice-Hall, 1954), and "Generalized expectancies of internal versus external control of reinforcements," *Psychological Monographs* 80, 1966.

33. W. H. Murray, *The Scottish Himalayan Expedition* (London: Dent,1951).

34. Jean Vanier, *Becoming Human* (Mahwah, NJ: Paulist Press, 1998).

35. Pamela J. Cushing, "Shaping the Moral Imagination of Caregivers: Disability, Difference and Inequalityin l'Arche," unpublished PhD thesis, McMaster University, Canada, 2003.

36. Richard Zoglin, "Oprah Winfrey: Lady with a Calling," *Time*, August 8, 1988.

37. Steven D. Levitt, "So Much for One Person, One Vote," *New York Times*, August 6, 2008.

38. Quoted in "Wellcome Trust and Merck Launch First of its Kind Joint Venture to Develop Vaccines for Low-Income Countries," Hilleman Laboratories press release, September 17, 2009.

39. See, for instance, Mihály Csíkszentmihályi, *Flow: The Psychology of Optimal Experience* (New York: Harper & Row, 1990).

40. Anna Wise, *The High-Performance Mind* (New York: Jeremy P. Tarcher/Putnam, 1997).

41. Tony Schwartz and Catherine McCarthy, "Manage Your Energy, Not Your Time," *Harvard Business Review*, October 2007.

42. Tony Schwartz, Jean Gomes, and Catherine McCarthy, *The Way We're Working Isn't Working: The Four Forgotten Needs that Energize Great Performance* (New York: Free Press, 2010).

43. Example from Joanna Barsh, Josephine Mogelof, and Caroline Webb, "How Centered Leaders Achieve Extraordinary Results," *McKinsey Quarterly*, October 2010.

44. Personal communication.

45. Heike Bruch and Jochen I. Menges, "The Acceleration Trap," *Harvard Business Review,* April 2010.

Chapter 8   The Senior Leader's Role

1. John Mackey, "Creating a High-Trust Organization," posted on huffing tonpost.com on March 14, 2010.
2. "What Successful Transformations Share," *McKinsey Quarterly* survey, January 2010. Subsequent references to research or surveys in this chapter refer to this source.
3. "Women at the Top: Indra Nooyi," *Financial Times* supplement, November 16, 2010, at http://womenatthetop.ft.com/articles/women-top/ca66b59e-ed92-11df-9085-00144feab49a
4. Bronwyn Fryer and Thomas A. Stewart, "Cisco Sees the Future: An Interview with John Chambers," *Harvard Business Review,* November 2008.
5. Jia Lynn Yang, "A Recipe for Consistency," *Fortune,* October 29, 2007.
6. Lou Gerstner, *Who Says Elephants Can't Dance? Inside IBM's Historic Turnaround* (New York: HarperCollins, 2002).
7. Rupert Cornwell, "The Iconoclast at IBM," *Independent,* August 1, 1993.
8. William A. Sahlman and Alison Berkley Wagonfeld, "Intuit's New CEO: Steve Bennett," Harvard Business School case, May 24, 2004.
9. Giancarlo Ghislanzoni and Julie Shearn, "Leading Change: An Interview with the CEO of Banca Intesa," *McKinsey Quarterly,* August 2005.
10. Roger Malone, "Remaking a Government-Owned Giant: An Interview with the Chairman of the State Bank of India," *McKinsey Quarterly,* April 2009.
11. Quoted in Carolyn Aiken and Scott Keller, "The CEO's Role in Leading Transformation," *McKinsey Quarterly,* February 2007.
12. Giancarlo Ghislanzoni, "Leading Change: An Interview with the CEO of Eni," *McKinsey Quarterly,* August 2006.
13. Quoted in Carolyn Aiken and Scott Keller, "The CEO's Role in Leading Transformation," *McKinsey Quarterly,* February 2007.
14. Speaking at a Techonomy conference, August 4, 2010.
15. Felix Brück and Jack Welch, "Leading Change: An Interview with the CEO of EMC," *McKinsey Quarterly,* August 2005.
16. Quoted in "Expert Business Advice: Want Great Business Ideas? Leave Your Office!" press release, August 4, 2004, at pressbox.co.uk.
17. Personal interview.

18. Quoted in Carolyn Aiken and Scott Keller, "The CEO's Role in Leading Transformation," *McKinsey Quarterly*, February 2007.

19. Warren L. Strickland, "Leading Change: An Interview with TXU's CEO," *McKinsey Quarterly*, February 2007.

20. Giancarlo Ghislanzoni and Julie Shearn, "Leading Change: An Interview with the CEO of Banca Intesa," *McKinsey Quarterly*, August 2005.

21. Quoted in Rosabeth Moss Kanter, Douglas Raymond, and Lyn Baranowski, "Driving Change at Seagate," Harvard Business School case, September 30, 2003.

22. Quoted in Carolyn Aiken and Scott Keller, "The CEO's Role in Leading Transformation," *McKinsey Quarterly*, February 2007.

23. Personal interview.

24. Quoted in Suzy Wetlaufer, "Common Sense and Conflict: An Interview with Disney's Michael Eisner," *Harvard Business Review*, January 2000.

25. Quoted in Rosabeth Moss Kanter, Douglas Raymond, and Lyn Baranowski, "Driving Change at Seagate," Harvard Business School case, September 30, 2003.

26. Jack Welch, *Jack: Straight from the Gut* (New York: Warner Books, 2001).

27. Larry Bossidy, *Execution: The Discipline of Getting Things Done* (New York: Crown Business, 2002).

28. Alessandra Galloni, "Being Bernard Arnault," *Wall Street Journal*, March 5, 2009.

29. Paul Hemp, Samuel J. Palmisano, and Thomas A. Stewart, "Leading Change When Business Is Good," *Harvard Business Review*, December 2004.

30. Jason Tanaka Blaney, "A Whole New Crew," *Time*, March 15, 2007.

31. Nick Paumgarten, "The Merchant," *New Yorker*, September 20, 2010.

32. Johan Ahlberg and Tomas Nauclér, "Leading Change: An Interview with Sandvik's Peter Gossas," *McKinsey Quarterly*, January 2007.

33. Carolyn Aiken and Scott Keller, "The Irrational Side of Change Management," *McKinsey Quarterly*, April 2009.

34. Larry Bossidy, *Execution: The Discipline of Getting Things Done* (New York: Crown Business, 2002).

35. Personal interview.

36. Josselyn Simpson, "Transforming a Nation's Education System: An Interview with the Chief Executive of Bahrain's Economic Development Board," *Voices on Transformation* 4, McKinsey & Company, 2010.

Chapter 9   The Five Frames in Action

1. As measured by the Gallup Q12 employee engagement survey.

Chapter 10   Making It Happen

1. David Whyte, *The Heart Aroused: Poetry and the Preservation of the Soul in Corporate America* (New York: Doubleday Currency, 1996).

Recommended Reading

Ariely, Dan. *Predictably Irrational: The Hidden Forces that Shape Our Decisions*. New York: HarperCollins, 2009.

Barsh, Joanna, and Susie Cranston. *How Remarkable Women Lead: The Breakthrough Model for Work and Life*. New York: Crown Business, 2009.

Beer, Michael, and Nitin Nohria. *Breaking the Code of Change*. Boston: Harvard Business School Press, 2000.

Boyatzis, Richard, and Annie McKee. *Resonant Leadership: Renewing Yourself and Connecting through Mindfulness, Hope, and Compassion*. Boston: Harvard Business School Press, 2005.

Collins, James C., and Jerry I. Porras. *Built to Last*. New York: HarperCollins, 1994.

Fifty Lessons Limited. *Managing Change: Lessons Learned—Straight Talk from the World's Top Business Leaders*. Boston: Harvard Business School Press, 2007.

Gallwey, Timothy W. *The Inner Game of Work: Overcoming Mental Obstacles for Maximum Performance*. London: Texere, 2003.

Goleman, Daniel. *Emotional Intelligence: Why It Can Matter More than IQ*. London: Bloomsbury, 1996.

Hamel, Gary. *The Future of Management*. Boston: Harvard Business School Press, 2007.

Harvard Business Review on Change: The Definitive Resource for Professionals. Boston: Harvard Business School Press, 1998.

Heath, Chip, and Dan Heath. *Switch: How to Change Things When Change Is Hard*. New York: Random House, 2010.

Kegan, Robert, and Lisa Laskow Lahey. *How the Way We Talk Can Change the Way We Work: Seven Languages for Transformation*. New York: Jossey-Bass, 2003.

Kofman, Fred. *Conscious Business: How to Build Value through Values*. Louisville, CO: Sounds True, 2007.

Kotter, John P. *Leading Change*. Boston: Harvard Business School Press, 1996.

Mourkogiannis, N. *Purpose: The Starting Point of Great Companies*. Basingstoke, Hants.: Palgrave Macmillan, 2008.

Peale, Norman Vincent. *The Power of Positive Thinking*. London: Vermilion, 1990.

Peters, Thomas J., and Robert H. Waterman Jr. *In Search of Excellence*. New York: Harper & Row, 1982.

Pettigrew, Andrew, and Richard Whipp. *Managing Change for Competitive Success*. Oxford: Blackwell, 1993.

Schein, Edgar H. *Organizational Culture and Leadership*. New York: Jossey-Bass, 2004.

Senge, Peter M. *The Fifth Discipline: The Art and Practice of the Learning Organization*. New York: Random House, 1993.

Ulrich, David, and Wendy Ulrich. *The Why of Work: How Great Leaders Build Abundant Organizations that Win*. New York: McGraw-Hill, 2010.

Acknowledgments

M ake a difference. Most humans seem wired to want to do this in the world. Our hope is that this book will make a difference by enabling leaders to create and sustain truly excellent organizations—organizations where people's full potential is cultivated and unleashed. Although we don't yet know how much of a difference *Beyond Performance* will make, there are a number of people who have already made a difference by helping to shape the thinking and the development of the book you now hold in your hands.

The lineage of thinking on organizational excellence can be traced back to 1982, when McKinsey & Company's Tom Peters and Robert Waterman wrote *In Search of Excellence*, one of the best-selling and most influential management books of all time. We owe them our thanks for the groundbreaking work on which we are building. In many ways, *Beyond Performance* represents the accumulated wisdom of McKinsey, its clients, and its friends on the topic of organizational excellence over the intervening three decades. With that in mind, we would also like to acknowledge the contributions of all those—far too many to name here—who will see traces of their work somewhere in these pages.

Although we haven't been so bold as to entitle our book *Excellence Found*, we believe it does have a number of new truths and better methods to offer. Credit for many of these goes to a host of people who are passionate about helping individuals and institutions achieve their full potential, and who have taken time over the years to talk with us, work with us, and share their insights. It is our privilege to be able to pass on what we have learned from them.

Among those we'd like to mention by name are 30 senior leaders from around the world who graciously gave us their time, wisdom, and stories:

- John Akehurst, former CEO of Woodside Petroleum, who in seven years transformed it into a top-decile performer, creating AU$7 billion of new shareholder value on a base of AU$3 billion.

- Don Argus, retired chairman of BHP Billiton, who oversaw the merger that created the world's largest diversified resources company, with a market capitalization of US$190 billion in 2010.
- Alejandro Baillères, CEO of Grupo Nacional Provincial, who restored Mexico's largest insurance company to its former glory in the transformation that we featured in Chapter 3.
- Saad Al-Barrak, former CEO of Zain, who led the transformation of the Kuwait-based telco into a regional presence serving 56 million people in the Middle East and Africa.
- Om Prakash Bhatt, chairman of State Bank of India, who transformed the former monolith into a Fortune Global 500 company.
- Pierre Beaudoin, president and CEO of Bombardier, who led its aerospace division through the most tumultuous times the airline industry has ever known, as we saw in Chapter 4.
- Sir William Castell, chairman of the Wellcome Trust, who led the UK's largest charity to expand its vision to challenges such as climate change and population control.
- Fulvio Conti, CEO of Enel, who masterminded the transformation of the monopolistic Italian energy player into an international force.
- Adam Crozier, CEO of ITV, who led one of the biggest corporate turnarounds in the UK in his former role as CEO of Royal Mail.
- Tom Glocer, CEO of Reuters and subsequently Thomson Reuters, who led his company to become a world leader in information services, with more than US$12 billion in revenue.
- John Hammergren, chairman, president, and CEO of McKesson, who led the company as it doubled its revenues to US$108.7 billion and rose to fourteenth place in the Fortune 500.
- Idris Jala, former CEO and managing director of Malaysian Airlines, who led the state-controlled carrier from the brink of bankruptcy to record-breaking profits in less than two years.
- Ravi Kant, vice chairman and former managing director of Tata Motors, who helped it transform from a leading commercial vehicles manufacturer to India's largest carmaker, with a strong international presence.
- Leo Kiely, CEO of MillerCoors, who guided the company's growth through a succession of mergers and acquisitions that produced the third-largest brewer in the United States.
- Alan G. Lafley, retired CEO of P&G, who led a transformation that doubled the company's sales, quadrupled its profits, and increased its market value by more than US$100 billion, as we saw in Chapter 5.

- Julio Linares, managing director and COO of Telefónica de España, who led its transformation from a loss-making domestic incumbent telco into a global player delivering double-digit revenue growth, as we saw in Chapter 6.
- N. R. Narayana Murthy, chairman and chief mentor of Infosys Technologies, who helped build a company started with US$250 in seed capital into a leader in consulting and information technology.
- Richard Parsons, who as chairman and CEO turned around Time Warner, and subsequently became chairman of Citigroup.
- Corrado Passera, managing director and CEO of Banca Intesa, where he led a major turnaround, and former managing director at Poste Italiane, where he led the restructuring that produced the company's first operating profit in 50 years.
- Alessandro Profumo, former CEO of UniCredit, who led the bank through a series of well-orchestrated mergers that saw its market capitalization increase from €1.5 billion (US$2.2 billion) to €37 billion (US$53.4 billion).
- Michael Sabia, president and CEO of the Caisse de dépôt et placement du Québec, and former CEO of Bell Canada, the country's largest phone company, where he led a turnaround.
- Paolo Scaroni, CEO of multinational oil and gas company Eni, who previously led corporate turnarounds at Enel, Italy's leading electric utility, and U.K. glassmaker Pilkington.
- Roberto Setubal, CEO and vice chairman of Itaú Unibanco, who led the merger of Itaú and Unibanco to form one of the world's top 20 banks by market capitalization.
- John Stumpf, CEO of Wells Fargo, who engineered the purchase of Wachovia that secured a coast-to-coast presence across the United States and created the country's fourth-largest bank by asset size, and led the transformation we featured in Chapter 9.
- Jim Sutcliffe, former CEO of Old Mutual, who expanded the insurer's international operations in Asia, Europe, the United States, and South America before becoming chair of the U.K.'s Board for Actuarial Standards.
- Joseph M. Tucci, chairman, president, and CEO of EMC, who rebuilt the company after its share value fell by 90 percent in nine months at the end of the dot-com boom, and has delivered double-digit annual earnings growth since 2005.
- John Varley, former group CEO of Barclays Bank, who grew it into the world's tenth-largest banking and financial services group, and the twenty-first largest company overall.

- Daniel Vasella, chairman and former CEO of Novartis, who led the successful merger between Ciba-Geigy and Sandoz, and holds the record as the longest-serving CEO in the pharmaceutical industry.
- Willie Walsh, CEO of British Airways, who within three years led the near-bankrupt Aer Lingus to become a profitable low-cost carrier, before leading a transformation at his current company.
- C. John Wilder, former chairman and CEO at TXU, who oversaw its financial and operational turnaround before leading it in one of the largest leveraged buyouts in the world.

All of their stories are full of human drama, high-stakes decision making, battles won and lost, and wisdom gained. In writing this book, we have done our best to do justice to the extraordinary work of leaders such as these.

Our experiences with senior executives helped inform our view of what works and what doesn't work; to understand *why*, we looked to academia. Why does getting a wide group of people involved in developing a strategic direction seem to yield much better results than just telling employees what to do? Why do leaders who follow their natural instincts to solve a problem themselves often sabotage their ability to make change stick? How is it that hard-working, well-meaning, and capable people can find themselves working together in ways that prevent everyone performing to their best ability? It was in the process of exploring questions like these that we were greatly assisted by academic colleagues who brought to our work their experience, insights, and robust ability to challenge. They are:

- Heike Bruch, Professor of Strategic Leadership and Director of the Institute for Leadership and Human Resources Management, Universität St Gallen
- Douglas T. Hall, Morton H. and Charlotte Friedman Professor of Management, Boston University School of Management
- Andrew Pettigrew OBE, Professor of Strategy and Organization, Saïd Business School, University of Oxford
- Michael Tushman, Paul R. Lawrence MBA Class of 1942 Professor of Business Administration, Harvard Business School

We didn't stop at senior executives and academics, though. Whether this book makes a difference will largely be determined by whether our prescriptions are reliable—whether they yield the same results in different environments. This is where we pay tribute to the many change leaders who have helped us test and refine our methods: typically people one or two levels below the senior leader who are responsible for activating change in their organization. For several years we have brought together groups of people playing this role in a series of two-day peer-learning events known as the Change Leaders Forum. We have held forums in locations including the United States, the United Kingdom, France, Dubai, and South Africa. There is now a community of more than 1,000 alumni who have acted as a source of inspiration, a sounding board, and a test bed for the insights in this book. As they have often been the first to field-test new ideas and approaches, they have had to endure the inevitable "Uh oh" moments that happen whenever thinking is pushed beyond the boundaries. They've done it so you don't have to. We can't thank them enough.

We also want to thank our colleagues at McKinsey who worked side-by-side with us to develop the thinking and prove the approaches that we describe here. First, on the big idea of organizational health, we want to thank Aaron De Smet, Bill Schaninger, and Mark Loch for their pioneering work. Without these three people and the others who support them, the organizational health index (OHI) and its database would never have existed, and neither would this book. Their contribution was not limited to the data whose breadth and depth provides us with such a distinctive research base; we also derived a huge benefit from their extraordinary ability to draw practical insights from this rich source.

Next up, there's Josep Isern, Mary Meaney, Giancarlo Ghislanzoni, and Felix Brück, who have all played important roles in the evolution of our thinking on how organizations can achieve transformational change. This group laid the foundation for how to think in an integrated way about the performance and health aspects of a transformation program.

Then there's Michael Rennie, Carolyn Aiken, and Tom Saar, who have brought real innovation to the practice of influencing shifts in mindsets and behavior. In a context where managing the "hard stuff" is seen as table stakes, they have gone above and beyond the call of duty to bring insight, rigor, and discipline to managing the "soft stuff."

Further, we thank our colleague Lowell Bryan—the accomplished author of books such as *Race for the World*, *Market Unbound*, and *Mobilizing Minds*—from whom we've taken the concept of strategy as a portfolio of initiatives. Finally, we thank Joanna Barsh and Susie Cranston (joint authors of *How Remarkable Women Lead*), Johanne Lavoie, and Caroline Webb for their cutting-edge research into what it means to be a centered leader.

We also thank our colleagues who have spearheaded the design and delivery of the Change Leaders Forums around the world, and in particular Simon Blackburn, Arne Gast, Judy Malan, and Kausik Rajgopal.

Special thanks also go to colleagues who have led the charge on our behalf when it comes to the on-the-ground research and project management of this effort. Alice Breeden toiled tirelessly in the initial stages of the development of the "five frames" research and synthesis. Seham Husain helped us go the last mile so that what you hold in your hands reflects our latest and best thinking. Throughout the writing process we've worked closely with Jill Willder, our editor, who has made this book eminently more readable and understandable than it otherwise would have been. We also thank Josselyn Simpson, who made the publishing process as pain-free as possible and in so doing put her editorial stamp on the content. Similarly, we are grateful to Bill Falloon, executive editor at John Wiley & Sons, whose feedback has been invaluable.

And when it comes to making a difference, we also owe a deep debt to our families for their patience, sacrifices, and support for us in the writing process, in our careers, and in our lives in general. When writing this book, we didn't ask how many working days we had before the next deadline, but rather how many weekends. A heartfelt "thank you" goes from Colin to his wife Sharon and their children Cameron and Jodie, and from Scott to his wife Fiona and their three boys Lachlan, Jackson, and Camden.

Finally, we want to thank you, our readers, for your interest in this book. It reflects our thinking at a particular point in time, and we will continue to refine it as new truths and better methods reveal themselves. In this spirit, we welcome any feedback you are willing to share. You can reach us at scott.keller@mckinsey.com and colin.price@mckinsey.com.

About the Authors

Scott Keller is a director in McKinsey's Southern California office, and leads its transformational change practice in the Americas. He has also lived and worked in Australia, where he co-founded the firm's Performance Leadership Institute, and in Latin America. His work focuses on helping senior leaders to conceive and manage large-scale transformation programs.

He has written a book for colleagues and clients, *The Performance Culture Imperative* (with Carolyn Aiken and Michael Rennie), as well as several articles on organizational behavior, including "The Irrational Side of Change Management" and "The CEO's Role in Leading Transformation."

Outside McKinsey, Scott is a co-founder of the multiple-award-winning Digital Divide Data, a social enterprise that utilizes a sustainable IT service model to benefit some of the world's most disadvantaged people. He was previously a manufacturing manager with P&G and a photovoltaic engineer for the U.S. Department of Energy. He holds an MBA and a BS in mechanical engineering from the University of Notre Dame, Indiana.

Scott lives in Seal Beach, California, where he and his family witness the power of transformation daily as they help one of their children who has special needs to reach his full potential.

Colin Price leads McKinsey's organization practice worldwide. Based in London, he has also lived and worked in New York. He has advised many of the world's largest corporations, several national governments and heads of state, and a number of charitable institutes. His interests encompass leadership and mergers as well as organizational health.

Colin has written six books, including *Mergers: Leadership, Performance, and Corporate Health* with his colleague David Fubini and Maurizio Zollo of INSEAD, and *Vertical Takeoff* with Sir Richard Evans, former chairman of British Aerospace.

Colin believes the business and academic worlds have much to learn from each other. Outside McKinsey, he is an associate fellow at Saïd Business School, University of Oxford, and a visiting professor at Bath University, in his home town. He holds degrees in economics, industrial relations and psychology, and organizational behavior.

Colin has two children and is married to Sharon, a coach and psychotherapist, which always keeps things interesting!

Index